Give Peace
a Stance

Give Peace
a Stance

Phasing Harmony into Our Lives

by
Hanoch Teller

New York City Publishing Company

$$12 \ ^{11} \ _{10} \ ^{9} \ _{8} \ ^{7} \ _{6} \ ^{5} \ _{4} \ ^{3}$$

Library of Congress Cataloging-in-Publication Data

Teller, Hanoch.
    Give peace a stance : stories and advice on promoting and maintaining peace / by Hanoch Teller.
        p.   cm.
    ISBN 1-881939-00-6
    1. Jewish way of life—Anecdotes. 2. Jews—Anecdotes.
3. Interpersonal relations—Religious aspects—Judaism—Anecdotes. I. Title.
BM723.T42 1992
296.3'87873—dc20   92-27956

Distributed by:
FELDHEIM PUBLISHERS   J. LEHMANN
200 Airport Executive Park   Hebrew Booksellers
Spring Valley, NY 10977   20 Cambridge Terrace
                               Gateshead
                               Tyne & Wear

In tribute to our former Soviet brethren
whose seventy-year-long thirst for their heritage
can at last be quenched, and
whose role in the Ingathering of the Exiles
will surely herald the arrival of
the Prince of Peace.

May they drink deeply
from the wellsprings of Torah,
and join the ranks of Torah scholars
who promote peace in the world.

YOSEF AND EDIE DAVIS
AND FAMILY
CHICAGO, ILLINOIS

In Memory of
Abraham Weinreb *z"l*

ר׳ אברהם בן הרב חיים יצחק ז״ל

A true disciple of Aaron Hacohen, whose ways and
manners were the epitome of peace.

In Memory of
Jacob Weiden *z"l*

ר׳ יעקב בן ר׳ יוסף הלוי ז״ל

A precious jewel in the crown of his community,
whose every action bespoke the ways of peace.

ת.נ.צ.ב.ה.

THE DAVIS FAMILY

Also by Hanoch Teller

Once Upon a Soul
Soul Survivors
'Souled!'
The Steipler Gaon
Sunset
Courtrooms of the Mind
Above the Bottom Line
Pichifkes
The Bostoner
Bridges of Steel, Ladders of Gold
"Hey, Taxi!"
The Best of Storylines

О ТОМ, ЧТО НА ДУШЕ

APPROBATION FROM HAGAON HARAV MEYER HERSHKOWITZ Shlita

ב"ה

Bais Binyomin
Talmudic Research Center

DEDICATED TO THE MEMORY OF
BENJAMIN PRUZANSKY ז"ל

ישיבת בית בנימין

ע"ש ר' בנימין יהודה הלוי פרוזנסקי ז"ל

Rabbi Simcha Schustal
Rabbi Meyer Hershkowitz
Roshei Hayeshiva

Rabbi Dovid Hersh Mayer
Rabbi Tzvi Pruzansky
Menahalei Hayeshiva

מכתב ברכה

לכבוד ידידי היקר והנעלה הרב חנוך יונתן טלר שליט"א

מאד שמחתי לשמוע שמע"כ מתכונן להוציא לאור עולם בשפה האנגלית עוד חיבור חדש. ליקוט סיפורים בענין גודל מדת השלום. אשר אין ערוך לנחיצות והתועלת לחיבור כזה. ידוע מעלת השלום שאי אפשר להיות לאדם שום ברכה רק ע"י השלום ורשאח"ל לא מצא הקב"ה כלי מחזיק ברכה אלא השלום. — והנה מתן תורה, שהוא נשמת כל מציאותו של הכלל ישראל, לא זכינו לו רק ע"י "ויחן שם ישראל נגד ההר" — כאיש אחד בלב אחד - אבל שאר כל החניות בתרעומות ובמחלוקת. בפרש"י בשם המכילתא. ובפרק השלום סוף מסכת דרך ארץ זוטא. אמר הקב"ה הואיל ושנאו ישראל את המחלוקת ואהבו את השלום, הרי השעה שאתן להם את התורה. ועוד שם ה' עוז לעמו יתן ה' יברך את עמו בשלום. דבכדי שיתקיים המתנה ה' נצטרך לברכה דשלום.

אמנם רבים הם הנסיונות בזה וצריך שיהא להאדם אהבה לשלום ושנאה למחלוקת. ולכן שינה הכתוב בלשונו אצל השלום מבשאר מצות וכתב "בקש שלום ורדפהו" וכמבואר בחז"ל שם דאין צריך לשלום רק ע"י שבורחים מן המחלוקת ורודפין אחר השלום. וזהו ע"י שיהא מוכן לוותר ולהיות מעביר על מדותיו. ובגמרא דרבי ישמעאל שם. דוויתר הקב"ה על שמו שנכתב בקדושה, שימחה על המים כדי להטיל שלום בין איש לאשתו.

ועד כדי כך גדול השלום ושנאת המחלוקת אשר גם אצל רשעים של דור הפלגה אשר גם הם הי' חמור ועונש מעל דור המבול, מ"מ כיון שנהגו אהבה ורעות ביניהם, הועיל זה בעדם, שלא יאבדו מעוה"ז כמו דור המבול. בפרש"י שם.

והנה כבר זכה הרב המחבר לזכות את הרבים בחיבוריו הקודמים, שהסכימו עליהם גדולי ומאורי ישראל שליט"א, בראותם רב התועלת שבהם, שהסיפורים מושכים לב הקוראים ומעוררים אותם לשפר מעשיהם ודרכיהם. ה' יהי' בעזרו גם בחיבור הנוכחי, שיצליח ויעשה רושם גדול על הקוראים ויצא מזה חיזוק בענין רדיפת השלום. ויברכהו הקב"ה שיזכה להמשיך עוד בפעולותיו לטובת הרבים. ויה"ר שנזכה לביאת גואל צדק בב"א.

ידידו ומוקירו, המברכו בכט"ס

מאיר הערשקאוויץ — י"ג תמוז, תשנ"ב

APPROBATION FROM HAGAON HARAV
SHAMSHON BRODSKY Shlita

בס"ד

Beth Hamedrash Rabeinu Yaakov Moshe

1221 Avenue "S"
Brooklyn, N.Y. 11229

Rav Shamshon Brodksy
Rabbi

APPROBATION FROM HAGAON HARAV
MOSHE HEINEMANN Shlita

RABBI MOSHE HEINEMANN
401 Yeshiva Lane
Baltimore, MD. 21208
Tel. (301) 484-9079

משה היינעמאן
אב״ד ק״ק אגודת ישראל
באלטימאר
טל. 764-7778 (301)

בס״ד

ראה ראיתי עליס לתריפה תעפמו של ידידי הרב חנוך יונתן טולר שליט״א, המפורסם
בכוחו הגדול של סוף מעשה במחשבה תחלה, אודות ענין השלו׳ שהוא שמו של הקב״ה
וסיוס המשנה וברכת כהניס, ובלתי השלו׳ אין שאר הברכות כלוס.

אין לנ איך משיגיס השלו׳ בין בדיבור ובין במעשה, לכן עלינו לשבח המחבר — הנ״ל
שמפרסם ענין השלו׳ בין המוני העם בין כין לקטניס ובין לגדוליס בין לפשוטיס ובין לחשוביס
ואעפ שהכל מבינים בשכלם חשיבות השלו׳, מ״מ מי שמעשיו מרוביס מחכמתו חכמתו
מתקיימת.

יה״ר שאלו הסיפורים יחזקו את ענין השלו׳ בלכות בית ישראל ונטה כולנו שכם אחד
לעבוד את ד׳ ביחד.

וע״ז בעה״ח לכבוד הרב המחבר שליט״א ולכבוד חשיבות ענין השלו׳ דרביעי בשבת
לסדר תדרש שלוס ועובתם כל ימיך אחד עשר יום לחדש אלול שנת תשנ״ג כ'פ'ק'
ועה בחה״ר — ברוך גר כ״ליה כ'משפחת היינעמאן החונ'ּ מתא באלטּעירא—

Contents

Thanks

It is a personal honor, and a tribute to the importance of this book's message, that this volume is graced by Rabbi Zev Leff's masterful Foreword. His insightful comments stress the centrality and worthiness of the subject, and hopefully elevate the contents from the realm of entertainment to that of inspiration.

The seeds of this book were sown close to three decades ago by my parents, who instilled in me this guiding principle. Yeshiva education has nurtured it, fostering and fortifying what our Sages have designated *Gadol Hashalom* — "Great is peace," a treasure exceeding all others. And one rainy winter evening, on a Brooklyn-bound D train, Mr. Stanley Hershfang urged me to propagate this sacred precept in book form.

For over seven years and through a dozen titles, MARSI TABAK has been my collaborator and mentor, repeatedly saving me from myself, and my readers from ponderous prose.

Another partner in this particular endeavor was the highly-talented Chaim Meyerson, who deserves much praise for his outstanding contribution. Leibel

Estrin was a key member of the supporting cast.

New York City Publishing Company, my publisher, and Feldheim Publishers Inc., my distributor, are a delight to work with. I thank every member of their devoted staffs, especially the indefatigable typesetter Hannah Hartman. I am indebted as well to Rabbi Sholom Klass, whose *Tales of our Geonim* provided background material for the story, "Peace at any Price." Mr. and Mrs. Joel Moldovsky's legal expertise is reflected in "Nothing but the Truth."

I cannot begin to enumerate the other individuals who have furthered this project in some way by providing support and encouragement. My friends sustain me; it is as simple as that. Similarly, I am grateful to my lecture audiences, who are so receptive to the messages my books and their author attempt to convey.

While on the road for lecture tours, a host of individuals make these excursions — which are not pleasure trips — extremely pleasurable. In the interest of brevity (and as a speaker I am well aware of this value!), I feel compelled to merely acknowledge the *sweetest* people in the world, the Paskesz family in Brooklyn. Honorable *mentschen* goes to Zev, Debbi *and* Nomi Davis, and to Saul and Sherry Zimmerman. I have also benefited greatly from my recent acquaintance with Oscar and Aviva Rosenberg. To Reb Simcha Katz: This book is a tribute to you.

My wife — in addition to providing cookies, nosh and other nourishment during exhausting and famishing writing sessions — is a beacon of peace and fortress of tranquility.

My paeans of praise and thanksgiving go, above all, to the Almighty, Whose Name is Peace.

Author's Note

At the risk of engaging in self-plagiarism, I reiterate what was said in the Acknowledgments and Disclaimer section of *"Hey, Taxi!"*:

It would appear that some readers are the victims of an incurable, if not altogether harmless, malaise of knowing better than the author who his characters "really" are. Since nothing can discourage them from this obsession, it would be pointless for me to try to assure them that the names and settings are entirely fictitious and the products of my own imagination. Nevertheless, I do assert, and warn these incorrigible readers, that a search for resemblances between my characters and actual persons, living or dead, is carried out at the considerable risk of perpetuating and aggravating their own affliction.

I have taken great care to disguise the protagonists of my stories; the subject mandates it.

Argument and strife are ugly topics to describe; it cannot be done without conveying some of the animosity — and sheer absurdity — common in most fights. To describe a scene of marital strife, for example, as though the couple were having an amicable discussion, would be an insult to a thinking person's intelligence. I have therefore, as always, attempted to relate the whole story, including its disagreeable aspects, for I have faith in the common sense of my readers. Possibly, the argument-prone among them will, upon seeing in black on white the ludicrousness of such bickering, realize how their own contentiousness affects others.

The most incredible story in this volume (which comprises Book Two) remarkably is the one that I have recounted the most faithfully. The Rambam teaches that it is a mitzvah to mock idol-worship. The astonishing number of Jews caught up in the madness herein portrayed, however, is no laughing matter. Nonetheless, I suspect that the Rambam's instruction has been adequately fulfilled. My motivation in publishing the saga, aside from the touching theme of *shalom bayis* so evident as the story unfolds, was to alert readers to the insidious dangers posed by this widespread cult. If Book Two adds even in the smallest measure to a better understanding of the problem, it will have been worth producing.

Shalom — peace, harmony, unity — is indeed a lofty and worthy ideal; however, peace is *not* the "ultimate" value. There are times when the Torah dictates that we take a stand which appears, *prima facie*, antithetical to peace. The pursuit of *shalom* is a mitzvah, and accordingly — as with all halachic matters — your local Rabbinic authority should be consulted for guidance.

❀

There is a humbling aspect to writing about moralistic subjects. During this book's gestation period, I found myself avoiding an honest examination of my characters' inner thoughts and feelings. Why? Because my personal psychological apparatus had me believe that I was somehow different from (which is to say, better) than the people about whom I was writing. To really look at them meant to acknowldege that I was *not* different, and that as a human being with human foibles, what happened to them could just as well happen to me.

I pray that I will be spared their dilemmas. But if I am confronted with the trials of maintaining harmony or averting strife, I hope that I will have their fortitude to meet such challenges and indeed give peace a stance.

I have tried to be fair to the actors in my stories, but to the extent that fairness is constrained by truth, I hope I have erred on the side of the latter.

ויהי רצון שנזכה כולנו להתענג על רוב שלום (תהלים ל"ז , י"א)

Hanoch Teller
Elul 5752
September 1992
Jerusalem תו"י

Foreword
by Rabbi Zev Leff

Rabbi Shimon ben Chalafta said: "The Holy One, Blessed be He, found no vessel with which to convey blessing to the Jewish People more suitable than *shalom*" (*Uktzin* 3:12).

"Great is *shalom*" — the Torah was given only to establish *shalom*, as the Rambam teaches: "Its (the Torah's) ways are the ways of pleasantness, and all of its pathways are *shalom*" (*Hilchos Chanukah*). Similarly, we find that the benefit of the study of Torah is also to bring *shalom* to the world. As our Sages relate, Torah scholars increase *shalom* in the world (*Berachos* 64a). *Shalom* is so important that when there is a suspicion of infidelity between husband and wife, God directs that His holy Name be erased in order to restore *shalom*.

The Rabbis teach that for the sake of *shalom*, one may at times alter the truth or communicate half-truths. This license they derive from the fact that God himself altered a statement made by our Mother Sarah that might have caused tension between her and our Father Avraham.

What, in fact, is the true meaning of the concept of *shalom*, that it should merit such prominent and overriding importance?

Shalom does not mean the absence of differences and argument; nor does it describe a state of blissful serenity and passivity. The true definition of *shalom* is not "peace," but rather "harmony and perfection." *Shalom* need not be passive at all; it can in fact be dynamically active. Even conflicting and opposing forces can create *shalom*.

The concept of *shalom* is rooted in the fact that God created a world that — on all levels — depends on the harmonious coordination of all of its many diverse components in order to achieve perfection. Hence, God's very name is *Shalom*, because he is the ultimate unifier of all of Creation. All of the diverse forces of nature must coalesce to engender a properly functioning universe; all the diverse occupations of human beings must operate in unified harmony to provide the services needed to effect a properly functioning society.

Similarly, our ability to fulfill the 613 mitzvos encumbent upon us from Sinai is only possible when all components of the Jewish People — men and women; Kohanim, Levi'im, and Yisraelim — harmoniously function as one entity, each performing the role uniquely applicable to him or her. It was necessary that we receive the Torah at Sinai as one person with one heart, for as diverse individuals, no one has all 613 mitzvos applicable to him.

This harmonious cooperative effort does not negate the existence of dynamic argument, debate, and difference of opinion. Quite to the contrary, *machlokes l'shem shamayim* — debate and dispute for the sake of Heaven (such as the disputes of Hillel and Shammai) — are the contestants of real *shalom*, for they lead to the ultimate Truth. For debate and dispute to be "for the sake of Heaven," both parties must have only one purpose at heart: to seek the Truth. In this manner, they do not argue *against* each other to achieve personal vindication and triumph, but rather *with* each other, for the purpose of arriving at the ideally correct solution.

Such harmonious cooperative efforts must pervade all strata of man's relationships, from the personal relationship between one's body and soul, to the relationships between one's self and one's spouse and family, one's neighbors, and one's nation, as well as relationships between nations. The overall guide that directs how this harmony can and should be achieved is the Torah.

Hence, the Torah and those who toil in it bring perfection to the world. When the harmony is disrupted, God's presence is diminished. He therefore directs that His holy Name be erased, so that the stark reality of diminished Godliness will be manifest as long as disharmony and divisiveness remain in the home.

It is *shalom*, therefore, that represents the true, substantive eternal reality of a perfect world, and therefore it takes precedence over what may appear to be factual phenomena. When those facts, in this temporal world, are the source of divisiveness and strife, they must yield to the real Truth, which is eternally real, which contributes to the perfection of the world. Hence, *shalom* is the essential Truth and in this life, all blessing is conveyed through the harmonious function of a perfect world, functioning with *shalom*.

The Torah admonishes us not to be like Korach *v'cha'adaso*. The rebellion of Korach is the embodiment of *machlokes lo l'shem Shamayim*, divisive dispute. The Torah reveals that the root of that rebellion lies in the phrase *"vayikach Korach"* — Korach took himself off to one side. He removed himself from the collective, harmonious efforts of the community, to function as an isolated individual.

There are three major factors that cause this separation from the communal effort and isolation from humanity: "Jealousy, insatiable desire, and vainglory remove one from the world." These three traits cause one to remove himself from the unified world effort and disrupt *shalom*.

One who is afflicted with jealousy fails to appreciate his own role and self-worth and focuses obsessively on wanting to be someone else. This suppresses his ability to contribute his unique part towards the perfection of society.

One who is stricken with insatiable desire wishes only to satisfy himself, with complete disregard for others. As King Solomon put it: "For lust, one desires to be alone." In addition, the more materialistic one is, the less in touch he is with the spiritual unity that underlies all of the very diverse and separate material components of this universe.

And finally, one obsessed with personal glory will not want to share that glory with others and hence will shy away from a collective effort.

In opposition to this, the Rabbis relate that one who dreams of a river, a bird or a pot should anticipate *shalom* in his life. Perhaps the significance of these three items is their negation of the three roots of divisiveness.

The river represents the awesome power of running water, which is beneficial and productive as long as it does not overflow its boundaries and become a distructive flow. This symbol counteracts jealousy, encouraging one to recognize his bounds and limitations.

The symbol of the bird — light, flexible, and yielding — counteracts the haughty, vain person who takes himself too seriously and is therefore weighted down with *kavod* [*kavod*, honor, is derived from the Hebrew word *kaved*, which means heavy]. He becomes inflexible, stubborn and unyielding.

Lastly, the symbol of the pot represents the

medium that allows fire and water to coexist and perform the function of cooking. The pot, which unites these conflicting forces and enables them to work in harmony, itself receives nothing for its efforts but rather is burned and blackened. This symbol counteracts the avaricious individual who always bases his involvement on behalf of others on: "What's in it for me?"

Rabbi Hanoch Teller has once again tackled a very difficult subject and, as usual, has done it in a superb fashion. His anecdotes and stories will leave one inspired, intellectually and emotionally. Rabbi Teller personally is a true disciple of Aharon, one who loves *shalom*, pursues *shalom*, loves people and brings them closer to Torah.

We can now add one more item to those that portend *shalom* in a dream: One who sees *Give Peace a Stance* in a dream — and most certainly one who reads it and contemplates its message — can most assuredly expect an intensification of *shalom* in his life.

Hashem will give strength to His people when Hashem will bless His people with peace.

ד׳ עוז לעמו יתן ד׳ יברך את עמו בשלום

Rabbi Zev Leff
Moshav Matityahu

Peace Seekers

Plantagonists

SHRAGA AHARONOFF was fond of saying that the way an undeserving fellow like himself could become a dynastic heir and revered spiritual leader was as easy as $a+b=c$: a (Aharonoff) plus b (Basya ["Bashinku"] Terchmer, his wife and eldest daughter of the late Reb Yonkel Luzer of Czardishov), equals c (the Czardishover Rebbe). That is, when Bashinku's father went to his final reward, leaving behind no sons to inherit the position of Rebbe, the mantle of leadership fell on Shraga's rather narrow shoulders.

An obscure yet surprisingly (and blessedly) populous chassidic court that had immigrated to America en masse in 1923, the Czardishovers were not renowned

for any significant religious or communal achievement;
nor had any Czardishover ever made a serious contribution to the body of Torah literature or scholarly
writings. However, these chassidim prided themselves
on their piety and the myriad acts of lovingkindness
they routinely performed, most too minor to mention.
(Actually, the Czardishovers were far too *modest* to
mention them.)

Shraga would be the first to admit that he was
singularly unqualified for the role of Rebbe. He lacked
leadership qualities, regal bearing, and intellectual
acuity. His features were nondescript, he told jokes
badly, and his voice had an annoying tendency to get
squeaky like a bar mitzvah boy's whenever he became
emotional. This had caused him considerable embarrassment on several occasions since he'd taken the
Czardishover helm, as despite his lackluster demeanor
he was frequently called upon to deliver a *vertl*, and at
the very moment that his brief but painstakingly prepared dissertation would reach its zenith, his voice
would crack and croak and the point of the *vertl* would
be utterly lost.

No one was more aware than Shraga of his lack of
achievement in life. Circumstances had propelled him
to a position of some influence, yet in his two years as
Rebbe he felt he had failed to make his mark on the
community in general or on the Czardishovers in particular. Shraga wanted, more than anything, to rise
above his mediocrity and accomplish something mean-
ingful, not for his own sake, but for the sake of his
chassidim. And this was the very thought that filled his
mind as he walked home one Thursday night from his
Chumash shiur.

Even the weekly *shiur*, Shraga thought ruefully, was not the result of his initiative but one of the obligations he'd assumed upon becoming Rebbe. It was the *shiur* his father-in-law had given for forty years, and he had inherited it along with the title.

After delivering his first *shiur*, Shraga adopted the custom of taking a long nocturnal constitutional, during which he would review in his mind the entire lesson he had just taught, looking for flaws and ways to correct them. This custom of pondering and perambulating after the *shiur* soon turned into a veritable ritual. Every week he would follow the same route, which led him to a Jewish neighborhood on the other side of town.

Midway through his peregrination, at the point where he would usually turn and head for home, was a cul-de-sac lined with identical bow-fronted terraced houses, each one narrow and neat and on street level. For all the similarity of architecture and landscaping, however, one home stood out: all of its lights blazed and some kind of PA system was in operation. Closer inspection would reveal that the noise emanating from that house and filling the cul-de-sac was aided by neither amplifier nor loudspeaker.

"Noise" is actually too mild a term to describe the sonic experience that blasted from that house. The volume of the ruckus plucked the nerves in Shraga's head, the lyrics of the cacophonous diatribes rent his soul.

This clearly was no disagreement over the meaning of a *Tosefta* or a perplexing *Rambam*. It was an argument between husband and wife about to terminate the little that was left of their beleaguered marriage.

Apparently the dispute did not end after one round, for week after week Shraga heard the same screams and shouts, the decibel level high enough to shatter windows and the vocalizations accompanied by what sounded like violence of the nonverbal variety.

Shraga had no way of knowing if the couple fought every day, every night, or only on Thursday nights just as he was passing by. Regardless, he was certain that his stumbling upon this dispute was not mere happenstance. There had to be a reason it had been placed in his path.

Ever present in the young Rebbe's mind was the realization that now that he was a communal leader and no longer just an anonymous yeshiva student, he had a responsibility to the community at large. And although technically this couple resided outside his "jurisdiction," they were still a part of the town's Jewish community. By extension, then, they fell within his purview.

Furthermore, Shraga reasoned, as a Jew he was forbidden to stand idly by when confronted with such obvious strife. Did Rabbinic literature not teach that the Biblical injunction, "You may not stand by your brother's blood," refers to far more than only manslaughter?

Another thought occurred to him as well: Even though many marital disputes cannot be resolved, some of them — perhaps just a tiny minority — are over matters so trivial that a little cosmetic counseling would suffice to save the marriage. If he could, even in a small way, help rescue a foundering marriage, he would feel more worthy of his title.

The famous tale of the Maggid of Koznitz's *"Shalom Bayis Kugel"* came to Shraga's mind. It told of a couple on the verge of uncoupling because the husband's true love was... kugel. The man looked forward to Shabbos all week long just to eat kugel. Descended from a long line of kugel aficionados, he wanted to carry on his family's time-honored tradition of having the kugel as the first dish served at the Shabbos meal.

His wife, however, followed a different tradition. In her family the kugel was always served toward the end of the meal. She was well aware of her husband's obsessive love of kugel, but how could she violate a sacrosanct custom?

The woman's intransigence on such a pivotal issue, contended the kugelmaniac, constituted grounds for divorce.

As both parties were adamant to uphold their traditions, the two of them, resigned to the ignominious fate of having entered into an incompatible relationship, visited the holy Maggid of Koznitz. Once they had sought the sagacious counsel of a spiritual giant such as he, their consciences would be clear: they would know they had gone through all the motions before formally severing their marital bonds. The wise Maggid would of course agree immediately that the case was a hopeless one, resolvable only by divorce.

But lo and behold, the sainted Maggid of Koznitz devised a scheme to save the marriage, and without imposing excessive compromise on either aggrieved party. His suggestion? A *Shalom Bayis Kugel*!

From that day onward, *two* kugels would be served on Shabbos. As far as the woman was concerned, the

Shalom Bayis Kugel was the one served at the beginning of the meal, and the *real* kugel was served, as her tradition ordained, at the end. To the husband, the opposite was the case, and it was the *real* kugel that was served first, with the *Shalom Bayis Kugel* for dessert.

It was hard for Shraga to imagine that the argument that he, and everyone else in a one-mile radius, had overheard was about kugel... but then again, he told himself, you never know unless you inquire. The young Rabbi had an idea, and come next Thursday night — armed and ready — he would pay the couple a visit. That is, if they were still fighting. That is, if they were still *married*.

A shoe came crashing through the front window, and Shraga added: "That is, if they're still *alive!*"

A week passed, and Shraga Aharonoff's resolve also seemed to be passing; he hardly felt equal to the task. It was one thing to arbitrate a dispute or try to settle a quarrel that landed in one's lap (and he had little enough experience at that); to intrude on a private household in which a belligerent shouting match was in progress, where two adults were having post-adolescent tantrums, was quite another thing altogether.

But there was no denying the element of communal responsibility. Shraga was, after all, a Rebbe, and his intercession in this matter might just do the trick. How could he pass up the opportunity to try and make peace between man and wife (and possibly make his mark in the bargain)?

As Shraga approached the house, these two voices vied in his head for dominance, briefly drowning out the voices of the Golden Gloves contenders. It would be a pity to walk away now, he told himself, when he had made such elaborate plans... Shraga looked down at his prop, his own little *Shalom Bayis Kugel* of sorts, and drew the inspiration he needed.

The young Rebbe raised his fist to knock on the door, but he couldn't find an interval between screams when his knock would be heard. Minutes ticked by and there was no respite in sight. Knuckles poised, he waited in freeze-frame until his arm ached, then switched arms and waited some more.

Ten minutes elapsed and Mr. and Mrs. Shapiro, as Shraga read their family name on the mailbox, were still at it. It was getting late. Shraga knew that if he did not make his move right now, he probably never would.

Closing his eyes and holding his breath, the Czardishover Rebbe rapped tentatively on the door. He shuddered at what he might find on the other side and feared the worst. Images of pools of blood, torn clothing and splintered furniture flashed before his eyes. Nonetheless, he continued his incessant knocking, pounding on the door harder and harder until the screaming abruptly came to a halt. Shraga's ears were assaulted by the roar of absolute silence. Seconds later the sound of furniture being shifted and straightened came from behind the door, followed by a male voice demanding, "Who's that?"

"Eh... Aharonoff, Shraga Aharonoff," he replied, just barely managing to conceal his telltale nervous squeak, "uh... Rabbi Shraga Aharonoff."

The door opened a crack and Shraga beheld a middle-aged man, red-in-the-face but still in one piece. The man's chest heaved and his breath came in rasps, as if from recent exertion. His shirttails were half in, half out, his glasses were askew and his hair unkempt. "Beat it!" he snarled, and prepared to slam the door.

"Don't you dare slam that door, Marvin!" came a shrill voice from over his shoulder. The door opened wider and the other half of the couple appeared, a woman likewise disheveled, with two bright crimson spots high on her pale cheeks.

Mrs. Shapiro cleared her throat and asked, "Can we help you?"

No sooner had she posed the question than her husband interrupted with, "We gave already. Now beat it!"

Shraga hadn't anticipated a warm welcome, but even so, things were not exactly going according to plan. Still, he did have a foot in the door.

"I'm not a charity solicitor," Shraga proclaimed, in an exaggeratedly affable tone to put everyone, including himself, at ease. "I happened to be in the neighborhood, just passing by you might say, when I heard this commotion going on." The young Rebbe looked up to see how he was doing.

Mr. Shapiro's face purpled with rage. "Who the devil are you?" Shraga's unwilling host exploded. He looked and sounded like a man rocketing towards a coronary.

"My name is Shraga Aharonoff, and I live about two miles east of here," Shraga said, stalling for time and inching his way into the foyer. "I'm the Rabbi at the *shtibel* on Riverside Street. It's actually not my shul, but I took over when my father-in-law — who was the real Rabbi there — passed away."

"I know the place," Mrs. Shapiro chimed in, nodding her head. Shraga released an anxious sigh of relief at the first hint of dialogue. "They're chassidim there," she explained to her husband, "which means he's a Rebbe."

Marvin responded with a raised eyebrow and a cynical twist of the lips that implied, "Him?!"

"I guess that's so," Shraga admitted somewhat abashedly, his voice croaking out of control.

The Shapiros stared at him for long moments. "So, what can we do for you?" Mrs. Shapiro asked impatiently. They looked eager to get back to the business of fighting.

"Eh, well, I was kind of wondering what I could do for *you*. You see, I hate to intrude on others, but as there seems to be some disagreement here, I was hoping that maybe I could be of help..."

"Forget it, kid," Mr. Shapiro growled, dismissing Shraga's suggestion with a flick of his hand. "This is no 'disagreement'; this is a fight which is coming to its bitter end. You're too late." He turned his back on Shraga and headed towards the arena. "Get rid of your Rebbe, Myra," he ordered. "We got some unfinished business here."

"Pardon me, Mr. Shapiro? I don't know if it's really too late, as you said. I mean, there's a way of telling if it's really too late."

"Look here, Rebbe, or Rabbi, or whatever you call yourself," Myra said in a tight whisper, "this is a private affair and you have no right to barge in here and tell us..."

"Heaven forfend!" Shraga quickly squeaked. "I only thought that maybe you were unaware of the existence of something that might bring an end to your strife, one way or another."

This momentarily piqued Myra's curiosity, but the gong for ROUND 2 was about to sound. Shraga knew his time was running out and soon he'd be back outside on the Welcome mat.

"I'm not going to give you a Torah lecture," the young Rebbe assured her. "Just spare me another moment to show you what I have here."

Myra threw her husband a questioning glance and Marvin shrugged elaborately, rolled his eyes, and then grimaced, making it abundantly clear what he thought Aharonoff's chances were.

Shraga took this as a "yes" and produced his little prop. "I brought this plant with me..." Until now he had been trying to conceal it, an exercise akin to keeping a boa constrictor in a paper bag. "You know how some plants keep insects away, and others have medicinal powers? Well, this one has proven effective time and again at determining the state of marital relationships."

"Uh-huh," the Shapiros grunted in unison.

"Yes! It's true! All you have to do is put it outside — I see that you have a little garden in front — and if it lives, then that's a sign that the marriage will thrive."

"Gimme a break," Marvin groaned, rolling his eyes again. Myra seemed only slightly less skeptical.

"I'm telling you," Shraga continued with a confidence he didn't know he possessed, "this plant — it's called a Peace Lily — is very sensitive to the auras human beings emit. If it senses that your auras are incompatible, it shrivels up and dies." To his own amazement, that entire speech came out in a properly modulated voice, despite its high baloney content.

"Myra, the man is a lunatic! He claims he's a Rebbe, pretends he's a marriage counselor, and lectures about botany. I don't believe it. Right here in my own home, in my own living room, a crackpot walks in at quarter to eleven at night and tells me how a plant is going to save my life! What next?"

The insult was a compliment to Shraga. Maybe, he hoped, his intrusion would get Shapiro to start speaking to his wife again, as the man's antagonism would be aimed at him and away from the Mrs.

"We don't need a plant to tell us we're incompatible, Rabbi," Myra said. "Anyone on the block could probably tell you that. What's your angle?"

"Angle? I'm not angling for anything," Shraga replied. "I'm sorry I bothered you. I'll leave you to your fighting now." He turned as if to go, but Myra's curiosity got the better of her and she moved to bar his way.

"What did you mean about knowing whether or not it's too late for us?" she asked.

"It's really quite simple. If the plant dies, that will mean that the marriage is hopeless and you should split up instead of continuing to argue and tear each other to pieces. You'll both be better off. But if the plant flourishes, it's a sign that your marriage is fundamentally sound and worth saving. Then you can patch up your differences, quit fighting, and get on with living together happily."

The room became quiet as the Shapiros digested the mumbo-jumbo Shraga had just fed them. Although Marvin pretended to be deeply absorbed in removing a gravy stain from his shirt, Shraga sensed that the man's sudden interest in sartorial matters was merely a cover for his introspection.

"So does this mean you're willing to give it a try?" he squeaked hopefully.

"Listen, Rabbi," Marvin said in almost normal decibel range. "I'm a fabric cutter by profession, been one for thirty years. I don't know from any ear, nose and throat stuff, but I can tell you you definitely gotta get your hearing checked. I consider planting that performing parsley, or sweet pea, or whatever it's called, about as productive as planting a yo-yo."

"C'mon, Marvin," Myra cajoled, "it's a pretty plant and besides, what have we got to lose?"

"THERE YOU GO CONTRADICTING ME AGAIN! — Oh, I'm sorry, Planty." Marvin caught himself in mid-bellow and feigned an affectionate pat on a lily leaf. "I didn't mean to give off a bad aura." Sarcasm oozed from every syllable.

All of a sudden everyone's eyes riveted on the lily to see if it had indeed sustained any damage. For long moments six eyes examined it from every angle and perspective.

"I think we'd better plant it right away," Shraga suggested with conviction.

"I can't believe this is happening," Marvin muttered

under his breath as he followed his wife and the Rabbi outside. Myra opened up the garage to get a spade, while Marvin parked himself in the middle of the driveway. It was clear that he was going to maintain spectator status during the entire operation.

Shraga selected a point of incision in the garden which met with Myra's approval. He then turned to Marvin to honor him with the groundbreaking for the *Shalom Bayis Plant*, but Shapiro stopped him cold with a flat don't-push-your-luck look. Shraga did some fancy footwork and altered the vector of his gaze to inspect the night sky and locate the Big Dipper.

Remembering his manners, the young Rabbi relieved Myra of spade duty and did the honors himself. He made quick work of the task, then stood up, clapped the dirt from his hands and pronounced, "We did it." Myra grinned appreciatively, while Marvin exhibited all the symptoms of incipient nausea. But the fight had gone out of him and Shraga suspected that he was only keeping up appearances. After all, the man had an image to maintain.

Taking his cue, Shraga commented as he departed, "Just take care of your plant and we'll be able to monitor... er, the status of things."

"Thank you so much, Rabbi Aharonoff," Myra gushed. The agricultural experience had apparently affected her profoundly. "It was so nice of you to come by and give us this beautiful plant. I'll make sure to, um, monitor it? every day. As a matter of fact, I'm going to start right now."

Shraga extended his hand to Marvin, who accepted it with reluctance and said a curt "Good night."

The whole way home Shraga reviewed the evening's events — what he had done right and what he had said wrong. It was very reassuring to him that Marvin hadn't thrown him out in the end. Then again, the tyro marriage counselor reminded himself soberly, he was *already* outside by the time he had left.

Despite his burning curiosity, Shraga stayed away from the Shapiros for the entire week. Only on Thursday night, after he had finished delivering his *shiur*, did he set off for the cul-de-sac.

With great trepidation, Rabbi Aharonoff approached the house and peeked into the garden, where he discovered, to his utter dismay, the Peace Lily in pieces. The leaves were shriveled and withered and scattered on the ground. Shraga was reminded of one of his father-in-law's little jokes: "Never go to a doctor," he used to quip, "whose office plants have died."

Suddenly the joke wasn't funny. During the course of the week he had fantasized that the Shapiro home had been transformed into a warm, loving household wreathed in harmony and graced by a giant lily bush in the garden. What a delusion!

He shrugged his shoulders and wanted to say, "I tried," but his conscience wouldn't allow him. The words of his sainted father-in-law began to chant in his head like a mantra: "...To make *shalom* you have to be like a kettle. For a kettle to be able to intercede between fire and water, it has to be willing to get a little *shvartz*. For the sake of *shalom* you too have to be willing to get a little bit dirty."

The message repeated itself until Shraga Aharonoff mustered enough nerve to knock on the door. It was then that he noticed the absence of racket or, for that matter, of shoes sailing through bay windows.

"Maybe the *Shalom Bayis Plant* worked after all," he dared to hope, "and the Shapiros are simply not aware of its demise." His visit would prove critical if he could explain away his ruse before the revelation would damage the interim harmony.

A red-eyed Myra opened the door. "Oh, it's you, Rabbi Aharonoff," she said noncommittally.

"I was... eh, in the neighborhood—"

"If it's that black-coated huckster with another plant, Myra," a familiar voice bellowed from the living room, "get him in here. I wanna give him a piece of my mind."

That should have been Myra's cue for "You can't afford to give away any pieces — there's little enough to begin with!" but she just let the opportunity pass right by. Shraga didn't know if that was a good sign or a bad one.

Marvin came barreling out to the foyer just as Myra tearfully announced the death of the Peace Lily. "Quit blubbering, will ya?" her husband implored, then he turned on Shraga. "Your begonia is be-gone."

In the brief space of time between Shapiro's close-quotes and Shraga's open-quotes, a number of profound insights flashed through the Rebbe's mind:

1. The Shapiros — both mega-mouthed Marvin and mean-mannered Myra — actually *cared* that the Peace Lily was now the Rest-in-Peace Lily, and

2. that could only mean that they had wanted it to live, and

3. that meant that they wanted their marriage to survive as well, and

4. so did Shraga.

This was no longer a matter of "communal responsibility," and remembering that he had embarked on this mission in order to "make his mark" made him feel more than a little ashamed. Now he wanted to help this couple find *shalom bayis* for the purest motive of all: not for his sake, not even for his followers' sake, but for the sake of Heaven. When a couple is united in marriage, the Talmud asserts, their union forms a vessel in which the Divine Presence dwells; when a couple divorces, the Divine Presence sheds a tear. This thought propelled the young Rebbe into creative-thinking mode.

"Of course the plant died," he said. "That's precisely why I stopped by. I just learned that the one I gave you was defective."

"Defective?!" Marvin exclaimed, all incredulity. "You mean, like it was missing a part?"

"Eh... I mean they issued a recall on this plant."

"They?" Shapiro repeated, his incredulity climbing an octave higher.

"I mean the nursery people. They put up notices that anyone who bought this, uh, model should bring it back or proof-of-purchase and they'll replace it on the spot." Nervousness made jagged sine waves of his voice pattern.

Myra didn't seem to notice. In fact, she was getting

all gooey-eyed, wishing to believe the most incredible yarn since the last one Aharonoff had spun, but Marvin was having none of this. "I had enough of your snake-oil spiels, Rabbi. I think it's time you hit the road. The plant's finished; our marriage is finished. And now, so are you. Why don't you just take a hike." Marvin had lost none of his charm.

"Do you have the replacement with you?" Myra quickly asked, looking behind the Rebbe for a plant-shaped package.

"I thought I should get the defective one from your garden. I, er, lost my receipt." He promised to bring over the new plant first thing in the morning.

"Does this one come with a guarantee?" Marvin asked, not without irony.

Shraga wasn't tricked by the question. "Same guarantee as before. If it flourishes, so will your marriage."

Despite Marvin's unflagging cynicism, Shraga noticed the sharp turnabout in the Shapiro household. If the plant was responsible for it he would never know, but the fact remained that the hostility which had been so palpable — and audible — the previous week and in the past, was virtually gone.

"Marv," Myra said ever-so-sweetly (the very sobriquet "Marv," Rabbi Aharonoff thought to himself, demonstrated the vast improvement on the home front. This was not just wishful thinking. Only one week earlier she could barely bring herself to refer to her husband by name), "Why shouldn't we give it another try? It can't hurt, can it?"

"Okay. All right. You want a dumb plant, you can

have a dumb plant. What do I care? Just don't expect me to take care of it!"

"Thank you again, Rabbi Aharonoff. Do you want me to pull out the dead one for the trade-in?"

"No, no, that's not necessary," Shraga assured her. "I'll get it on my way out."

❀

From the time Shraga delivered the new plant on Friday morning, he never had reason to visit the Shapiros again. As usual, he passed the house every Thursday night, but gone were the rancor broadcasts. The lights still blazed, but the house was as quiet and as tranquil as any other on the block.

Best of all, for someone who believes in omens, the plant was thriving. The last time he looked, little buds had sprouted all over and it must have grown at least a foot taller.

The Rabbi wanted to believe there was only one explanation for the phenomenon, but as time went on a tiny worm of doubt began to gnaw at his fantasy. Maybe, and he hated to even contemplate the possibility, the couple had in fact separated — which would explain the peacefulness of the cul-de-sac.

The following Thursday Shraga once again paused in mid-perambulation to inspect his *Shalom Bayis Lily* and smell its sweet fragrance. Just then, the door to the Shapiro home opened and Marvin poked his head out. "How ya doin', Rabbi?" he called, opening the door all the way. "Myra," he shouted over his shoulder, "look who's here."

Shraga walked up the path to the entrance and was swept inside like visiting royalty. Mrs. Shapiro dashed out of the kitchen drying her hands on her apron, and offered her distinguished guest a seat.

"Oh, Rabbi Aharonoff," she enthused, "we talk about you all the time, but we didn't know when we would see you next."

"Eh, I was in the..."

"Neighborhood," Marvin finished for him with a nod.

"Right, passing by... and I... er, well, I was wondering how things were working out?"

Myra's smile that stretched from ear to ear was answer enough, as was Marvin's embarrassed hue. Shapiro looked like an elementary-school kid whose chums had caught him polishing an apple for his pretty teacher.

"Go ahead, Marv, tell him," Myra prodded.

Marvin pawed the ground, turned a few shades redder, and cleared his throat several times until he was finally able to raise his eyes to meet the Rebbe's expectant look.

"Aw shucks, Myr, you tell him," Marvin said softly. Who would have believed that that voice belonged to the same throat which only weeks earlier had been a strong competitor with the runway at Dallas/Fort Worth Airport for the Maximum Volume Award.

Myra smiled again — actually, she hadn't *stopped* smiling — and said, "Well, Rabbi Aharonoff, a few nights after you gave us the replacement plant, I found myself unable to fall asleep. I, well, I starting thinking about what my life would be like without Marvin..." She paused and glanced over at her husband, who was totally absorbed in straightening a picture on the living room wall.

"Oh sure, it's been rough these past few years, and we have spent quite a lot of time and energy squabbling..." (*Squabbling*?! Shraga thought. Custer's Last Stand is a *squabble*? I wonder what their *real* fights must have been like!) "but we had some good times, too," Myra went on. "Still, it was Marv who wanted to get divorced, and every time I tried to reason with him he'd get mad and we'd end up arguing again. I was sure a silly plant wasn't going to change all that, but maybe, just maybe, if it did survive, I thought, maybe we could sort of... I don't *know* what.

"Suddenly, the plant's survival became really important, and at about two-thirty in the morning I tiptoed out to the garden to check on it. It was pitch black outside and I was afraid I'd trip or something, so I looked for a flashlight in the kitchen, and, while I was at it, the little watering can I always used for my houseplants. But I couldn't find either one. I almost gave up and went back to bed, but I just *had* to see how the Peace Lily was..."

"C'mon, Myr," her husband interrupted, "what're ya dragging out the suspense for? Just tell the Rabbi already." Marvin, after all, was still Marvin. But despite the gruff voice and short fuse, the vicious acrimony was definitely absent.

"You're right, Marv. I'm just being dramatic for no reason. Well, when I got outside I saw there *was* some light in the garden, and it was coming from our *flash-*

light, and the flashlight was shining on my *watering can,* and holding my watering can was..."

"A burglar?" Shraga asked innocently.

"No, you idi..." Marvin began and quickly caught himself. "No, Rabbi. It was *me.*"

Heard from: Rabbis Mayer Horowitz and Yaakov Shurin

Reconciled

THE CLICK OF MY PURSE was like a shot in the silent room, but the stone-woman at my side did not flinch. Thoughtlessly I had opened it to search for a hanky or tissue, and then remembered I'd used my last one and quickly snapped it shut. Perhaps it was better. My emotions were so raw that the mere thought of a tissue caused tears to well up in my eyes, the very *idea* of crying threatened to open the floodgates, and then what use would I be to Ilana?

I quickly berated myself for such arrogance: Of what use *was* I to Ilana, Woman of Stone, chiseled from granite, whose gaze never once so much as acknowledged my presence, whose unblinking eyes stared sightlessly at the mummified figure in the neatly-made bed before us? If only, if only those taut white sheets would come undone, even ever-so-slightly rumpled... That's it, I told myself: I shall not ask for much; I shall pray only for a crease to appear in the starched pillowcase beneath the mummy-head, and then I could say to Ilana, "Look! A crease! He moved — Yoni moved! He's going to be all right!"

But Yoni did not move, had not moved for three days and three nights, and there was nary a crease in the pillowcase, barely a dent where his tiny bandage-wrapped head seemed to lie with the weightlessness of the dead.

There. I'd said the "D" word. Well, not quite *said*, but certainly *thought*. I, for one, was reconciled to it. Was it so terrible, after all? Is the concept of death so fear-inducing to a believing Jew? All the homiletic platitudes came to mind: Life is only the antechamber of the World to Come; Death is but a bridge of life.

Would death not be a release — for Yoni, and for his mother? Who knew what agony the unconscious child was actually experiencing, or what fresh agonies would await him when he awoke — *if* he awoke. And Ilana, she would be freed from her spell, the curse that compelled her to sit in suspended animation, like the wife of Lot, to gaze for eternity, horror-stricken, at the sight of unspeakable destruction.

Between the gauze that encased the northern hemisphere of Yoni's head and the plaster cast that began above his chin and disappeared under the hospital sheet, a two-inch strip of what was once flesh bore witness to the fragility of human existence. Only last week that beautiful child had knocked at my door to ask if Danny could come out to play. His cherub-cheeks were sun-kissed and dimpled; tiny freckles danced across the bridge of his button-nose; a smudge of chocolate played at the corner of his sweet lips.

Cheeks. Nose. Lips. No more than a bit of skin and cartilage so delicate that a splinter of wood as thin as baby hair could draw blood from them. Or the wheels of a bus obliterate them. In that two-inch strip of former flesh there remained not a hint of the beauty and promise it had borne for four years. Against the backdrop of white gauze, white plaster, white sheets, white walls, that two-inch strip was a hellish slash of purple, crimson and black, a technicolor nightmare, a glimpse of Armageddon. It was not the color of anything live I had ever seen.

And yet, Yoni was, amazingly, alive, or so the machines claimed. The *whoosh* and *beep* of respirator and cardiac monitor testified that the body to which they were attached still breathed oxygen and pumped blood, just like any other living creature. But could it think? And could it feel? Would it ever see again, or speak? The steady *whoosh* and *beep* filled the room with white noise but no answers.

I wanted desperately to believe it was all a mistake, but the mind-numbing scene that had unfolded on the street below my apartment had not been a figment of my imagination. Now I tore my gaze from the mesmerizing IV drip and looked out the window. The weather was glorious and Jerusalem glistened in the late spring sunlight, just as it had on that fateful afternoon. Despite the climate-controlled, antiseptic odor of hospital that filled my nostrils, I could still smell the fragrance of oleander and jasmine that wafted into my kitchen from the patch of garden near our building.

❀

It was only out of long habit that I paused in the midst of my cooking to watch the little *cheder* boys alight from the school bus. Danny had a touch of flu and was safely tucked into his bed that day, so he wouldn't be among his young classmates frolicking on the sidewalk. There was redheaded Yitzie; tall, tow-haired Sruli; serious Dovidl, his tiny eyebrows knitted in concentration; and there was Yoni, unquestionably the most beautiful child on the block, although the whole gaggle of four-year-old *yingelach* was a joy to behold.

This particular foursome, plus my Danny, had been inseparable for some time — their fathers, and therefore they, all davened in the same shul. All except Yoni's. Yoni's Abba davened with the angels, in the *Gan Eden* minyan, surely leading the Heavenly Assembly in prayer as he had led the earthly one for so many years. Yoni's Abba, *z"l*, had been on a routine patrol with his army reserve unit in Gaza when a live grenade was lobbed at them and landed at his feet. Instinctively, he had thrown himself on it, rescuing his companions and blowing himself to bits in one split-second of literal *mesiras nefesh*.

Danny's *chevreh* now stood on the pavement together, huddled in serious discussion, gesticulating as though they were debating the meaning of an essential *sugya*. I laughed softly, knowing that the terribly serious topic under consideration was "Rebbe cards," which the youngsters swapped, collected, counted and evaluated with the intensity and devotion of philatelists or art connoisseurs.

In the stillness of the midday air, a sudden gust of

wind breezed by and each of the four put a pudgy hand on his *kippah*. It was an unconscious, automatic gesture, but from where I stood it appeared almost funny, as though they'd rehearsed it repeatedly until they could do it with perfect synchronization. Breeze — hand; breeze — hand.

Yoni missed by a fraction of a second. The wind caught his *kippah* and tossed it aloft. It landed in the gutter, behind the school bus.

Ilana was there, on the sidewalk. The scream that poured out of her heart ripped the neighborhood in two, but it could not tear up the *gezeirah*. As Yoni stooped to retrieve his *kippah*, the driver backed up to pull away from the curb, carefully checking his mirrors and signaling with his blinker. Oh, yes, he had always been a cautious one, our *cheder* bus driver.

I don't know if I heard the horrible *crunch!* or merely imagined it, but it's a sound I shall never forget, a sound I would rather die than hear again, the sound of every bone in a tiny body being crushed, every delicate organ in a 40-pound child being compressed to bursting point by two-and-a-half tons of steel school bus.

❀

I felt a fury surge inside me, charging through every atom of my being. Not a day passes when we do not hear of horrible traffic accidents, of mangled bodies and lives snuffed out in a moment of recklessness. How many of those victims are sweet innocent Jewish children? Few accidents in this country are caused by drunken driving; most are perpetrated by daredevils and scofflaws. Our driver was neither, but he *was* the driver nonetheless. I willed him to come here, if he dared, to see with his own eyes the havoc and suffering he had wrought.

How Ilana must despise him, I thought, this man who had turned her to stone. Could he not have spared just a few more seconds, just one quick glance to make sure all those little ones were on the sidewalk where they belonged, before he backed his bus onto Yoni?

Again I chastised myself. It was because I needed to blame someone that I poured my anger on the bus driver, when in fact he had only served as a Divine messenger. For reasons known only to Him, the Almighty had heaped disaster once again on Ilana, the driver had been charged with carrying out that horrid mission... and I had been sentenced to witness its execution and aftermath.

The door to Pediatric ICU opened on hydraulic hinges and I shuddered with dread that indeed the driver had dared to come. My anger was so intense that I feared what I might do to him. "This is *your* doing!" I would scream. Unbidden my hands clenched into fists with which to pummel him, I who shrank from any sort of violence and rarely even raised her voice.

But it was not the driver. Instead a flock of white-coated men and women swooped in, the requisite stethoscopes casually draped around their necks or dangling from their pockets: the medical team had arrived. I tried to make myself small, to dissolve into the background somehow. It was suddenly very important to me that I not be mistaken for the mother, or even a relative of their patient, although I loved Ilana like a sister. "Please," I thought desperately, irrationally, "do not address your dreadful prognosis to *me*. I'm only a friend. *My* little boy is okay. Danny is fine. And he would have managed to catch his *kippah*, I know he would have, I just *know* it."

But my uncharacteristic anxiety was unwarranted; the doctors ignored me. They ignored Ilana as well, and focused their attentions on Yoni, or rather, on the machines and tubes and monitors to which his body was connected. Peering at the peaks and valleys inscribed on the long ribbon of EEG-printout, adjusting wing nuts on the plastic tubing, tapping the respirator valve, scrutinizing the hieroglyphics on Yoni's chart, the team functioned with the detached efficiency of maintenance personnel at NASA. *Whoosh, blip-blip, beep, click, whirr.* The only sounds in the room were the other-worldly voices of those infernal machines, and the silence of the doctors was deafening.

As quietly as they had entered, so they left, exchanging not a word or even a glance with the stone-woman. What could they say anyway — that it was hopeless? No. These weary-eyed and worldly-wise physicians had seen, time and again, hopelessness turn to hope, and hope to salvation. Jewish doctors, particularly in Israel, know better than to disparage or underestimate the power of prayer. And prayer was all Ilana had left.

The door opened again and a nurse abruptly called Ilana's name. I touched her gently on the hand and she started, looking around in confusion as though I'd roused her from a deep sleep. She followed the nurse out to the corridor. Even before the door swung shut, the pent-up tears began to cascade down my cheeks. I buried my face in my hands and sobbed. Why? Why? He's so young, and he's all that Ilana has left. Please. Please! Don't call this child yet — let him grow to learn

Torah, to follow Your loving ways and to bring comfort to his father's soul. Make him whole again — or, if You must, take him swiftly, while he sleeps.

A shout came from the corridor. Ilana! They've told her, I thought. I grabbed a scrap of gauze from the nightstand and mopped my eyes as I ran to be at her side, to hold her in my arms and comfort her. Blindly I pushed aside a chair and anything in my path, but my feet felt leaden. I was swimming in a sea of glue. Ilana! I'm coming!

A very peculiar sight greeted me in the hall. Ilana was there of course, and her eyes streamed with tears, but she was not on the verge of collapse. On the contrary, she had an arm around the shoulders of a young teenager whom I did not recognize and she was smiling through her tears. The shout had not been a cry of anguish, but of... joy?

"Thank you, thank you," Ilana was saying. Her voice was ragged from disuse, yet tender and warm. "And please thank your father for this *kame'ah*.* Imagine, in his condition, to go and see Rav Kadouri,** to wait for so many hours to get a blessing from the saintly *Mekubbal!*"

"My... my father... my father w-wanted you to know," the girl stammered with embarrassment, "he wanted you to know tha—"

"Oh, but I *do* know, dear," Ilana soothed. "I know your father is a caring, cautious bus driver, and a man

---

*A Hebrew inscription composed for the recipient by a Kabbalistic authority and containing mystical formulae designed to protect and heal.
**Rabbi Kadouri is a renowned Jerusalem Kabbalist.

who loves children. I know that he must be tormenting himself over this tragic accident. But it was not his fault. You must tell him that. Man does not so much as stumble in this world if it is not so decreed on High."

The driver's daughter wept softly. "He hasn't eaten, he hasn't slept... All he c-can talk about is... is Yoni."

"You know, dear, all this time I've been sitting by Yoni's bedside, and thinking about your father and how much he must be suffering. Hashem knows my prayers for my baby; He can read my heart. Yoni's fate is in His loving hands. But each of my prayers for Yoni has been accompanied by one for your father, that he may realize his innocence and that his anguish be relieved. Please tell him that."

"But... but..." With great effort, the girl composed herself and looked straight into Ilana's red-rimmed eyes. She cleared her throat and swallowed hard. "My father wanted you to know," she said at last, "that Rav Kadouri assured him that the child... the child will live."

"Who knows why we say *Modeh Ani* when we wake up every morning?" The Rebbe was introducing his *cheder* class to the *siddur* and this was the way that he always began.

A hand shot up from the third bench. For four-and-a-half months that seat had been vacant, but *Rephael Yonasan* was back now and he — better than anyone else — knew the answer to that question.

Heard from: Sheindel Lopian

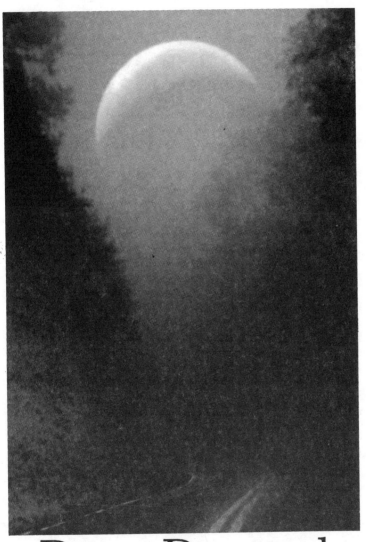

Peace Proposals

Awesome Reunion

THE LATE afternoon bus from Haifa stopped to pick up some new arrivals at Ben-Gurion Airport before continuing on its journey to the capital. As it drew nearer its destination the view became more picturesque with each passing kilometer. Honeysuckle hedges and vales of pebble dash lined the route, and lush fields gave way to rolling hills, olive trees, and craggy outcroppings. The landscape pressed Biblical cadences upon the passengers.

A wan sliver of dying sunlight dappled the brow of Erez Hadani. Lost in thought, he was oblivious to the rich past he was traversing and equally inattentive to the mottled cows meandering with lazy industry by the side of the road. Clusters of sheep on the other side bleated an ovine chain letter from hilltop to hilltop, but

Erez heard nothing, saw nothing.

The man was visibly depressed. With profound sorrow he focused his brooding on abiding relationships, the most elusive element in his life.

Self-righteousness being the mightiest mode of survival, Erez readily placed the blame squarely on his former partner, Rafi Katz. Rafi was the one who was too driven, too impetuous, too fickle. It was Rafi who had tossed his life into the blender and pressed the "SHRED" button.

Erez and Rafi had been mere teenagers when they were first united. Sharing the same bunk in the crack Golani brigade's boot camp, they took an instant liking to one another and soon were fast friends. For three years they drilled, fought, and solved the world's problems at never more than an arm's length apart, and on the day they were discharged, RafEz Enterprises came into being.

Within a year, the company had grossed over half a million dollars and by the first quarter of their second year they posted a profit of more than double that. Everything had been going great, and yet, and yet...

One of the cliches of business partnerships of the yuppie eighties was that you "grow up together," the irony being that growing up can also mean growing apart. The friendship survived nine years, the partnership six, across many terrains, at home and abroad, in good times and bad.

Moments of doubt, however, are inherent in any close relationship. Rafi had begun to doubt, and doubt is contagious. Once the infection spread, it established colonies of hostility and distrust, punctuated by chilly, prolonged silences. Silence speaks for itself, of course, and before their very eyes the fast friends watched themselves becoming sworn enemies. One explosive confrontation followed another, and yet the partnership remained intact, buffeted by blows from every side but still resilient... until the final betrayal.

The trauma of the ultimate break-up was certain to last far longer than the partnership itself had. The anger, bafflement and pain threatened never to go away, the scars engraved in Erez's heart forever.

Rafi had precipitated the final split, but Erez had seen it coming months before. It was written on the wall and reflected in the washroom mirror, where the glassy image had a complexion sallow as parchment, rings under the eyes like obsidian blisters. Erez had feared, indeed known, that he was losing not only the business he'd built from scratch, but his pride and his dignity, most of his money, and six years of life.

Now, three weeks after the demolition of his world, Erez was still diligently trying to consign Rafi to oblivion, but it wasn't working. There descended on his betrayed spirit a bizarre, enveloping jealousy, an acid envy, and tortured images of Rafi picking up the pieces with a new partner.

❧

Simcha Bunim's six-foot-two, two-hundred-and-fifty-pound frame stretched across two seats on the bus. His carry-on luggage occupied another two.

Years ago Bunim's *cheder* chums nicknamed him *Der Groisse*, and viewing him from any angle the sobriquet fit. He had a prominent hooked beak set over a persistent scowl; his eyes were fierce, tempered only by their hazel color; and his bushy untamed brows were chronically arched. Wiry salt-and-pepper strands, in collusion with a pot-sized velvet yarmulka, halfheartedly shielded his balding crown.

As humorless as his personality was his attire: basic chassidic black. And although Bunim was notably intelligent, he was not particularly articulate. Whenever he spoke — and with his formidable form, verbal communication was a rare necessity — his eyelids would flutter like stuttering butterflies, and his sentences would tumble out in a pattern that defied the laws of nature and comprehension, as though his syntax had been randomly plucked from a Scrabble board.

The Holy City was Bunim's home, but all the world was his stage. He could make himself misunderstood in six languages, a trait which had rendered him an unqualified success at fundraising. Today he was returning from a whirlwind four-country, twenty-four-city tour that would lay to rest his yeshiva's fears of collapse for the foreseeable future.

No sooner had Simcha taken his seats on the bus, than he spread a religious newspaper over his eyes as if to declare: "When Jerusalem we are getting to, wake me up."

Towards the rear of the bus huddled two teenagers, bowed under backpacks and bedrolls the size of telephone booths. They too had boarded at Ben-Gurion Airport, sporting identical hairdos and outfits — iced denim jeans and T-shirts — that rendered Doug and June indistinguishable from one another. Tzion, the bus driver, at first couldn't tell which, if either, was a he and which a she, but the earrings clued him in. June had three in one ear and one bead-and-chicken-feather gizmo dangling from the other, while Doug had only one tiny gold hoop.

Doug was telling his companion, in a voice that carried all the way to the driver's seat, about getting high on Jell-O shots. Tzion didn't have to wait long for an explanation, as the young man began to hold forth on this latest American fad. With Jell-O shots, Doug proclaimed, the Stupid Drink Syndrome had reached its apogee, crossed the river of no return, and reductoed all the way to absurdum. In upper Manhattan, he had heard, post-teens craving new stimuli and new cavities would spend entire evenings mainlining the colorful, high-carbohydrate globs from little paper cups like the kind delis serve coleslaw in. "Who would have thought that American youth would sink to such depths," he lamented.

June tried to console her fellow traveler. Jell-O shots, she maintained, did not signal the end of civilization. It wasn't even a symptom of fin-de-siècle cultural decay, much less a harbinger of protofascist stirrings within a disaffected generation whose expectations were being strangled by political corruption, ozone depletion, insufficient dietary fiber, and a realignment of global forces. "It's harmless," she argued, "a silly, stupid craze, no worse than goldfish-swallowing or flagpole-sitting."

Doug and June had a lot of vital information to share — with each other, with the youth of IsREAL, and with all of humanity.

❀

For a man who offers many clues to his personality, Zev's yellow-and-black *Kum!* (Arise!) T-shirt was out-and-out explicit. A feisty Yosemite Sam kind of guy, he had the political leanings of Attila the Hun, the supportive nature of Bluto, and the compassion of the shark in *Jaws*.

Zev hadn't quite gotten over World War II. Disturbed that some parts of Japan had managed to escape the effects of atomic fallout, he was far more irritated that Germany was still on the map, and hoped one day to personally right these two wrongs.

Those bus passengers in close proximity to Zev could not help but notice not only his argumentative tendencies but also his galling habit of rolling his eyes when someone disagreed with him and acting as though the person were severely retarded. Occasionally he would merely display extreme, almost pained boredom when someone else would try to articulate an alternate opinion.

It became abundantly clear to the passenger unfortunate enough to have taken the seat next to Zev when they both had boarded in Haifa, that the man was never wrong. That was the first rule he learned about him; rule two, of course, was to refer to rule one. Attempts at casual conversation were an exercise in futility (also nearly impossible, as Zev was thoroughly enamored with the sound of his own voice). During the relatively short ride to Ben-Gurion, the seatmate discovered that Zev embraced individuals with differing views in about the same way that the eighteenth century welcomed lepers. To his profound relief, Motor-Mouth was *not*

getting off at the airport, but traveling on to Jerusalem
for a — what else? — *Kum!* rally.

Vladimir Lazanskaya had gone all the way to the
airport earlier in the day to greet a comrade who never
arrived. "Maybe *Intourist* planned khis itinerary," he
rationalized as he boarded the bus back home to Jerusalem. "Khe will come when Khe comes, and not before."

A peasant's son from the grain belt of Russia,
Vladimir had delivered his measure of political hokum
for decades as a squat functionary for the Communist
party. In the style of all apparatchiks of those days,
Lazanskaya spoke like a character out of Orwell, turning language to dust. Who could understand the degra-
dation of public life quite as well as a man forced to
degrade himself on its stage?

At the beginning of his career there had been nothing but the hermetic, sometimes brutal regimen that
valued competence without brilliance, and obedience
above all. Accordingly, Vladimir had mastered the
world of codes, humiliations, favors, and "party disci-
pline." A prized product of the Communist-party apparatus, Lazanskaya was not blind to the fact that he had
been bred in one of the most debased institutions in the
Soviet Union. That's why he was always able to see
through every radio broadcast and *Pravda* headline
pronouncing the goodness of the Leader and Teacher of
the Workers of the World, the Greatest Genius of All
Times and Peoples, the Mountain Eagle and Benevo-
lent Friend of All Children.

Nauseous from the Marxist hype, he had craved an
existence with greater purpose than to just refuse, to

rebut, and to stall, and a life which did not require maintaining a dour and blank expression.

In Israel he had yet to find it.

❦

For the three German nuns who occupied the rear seat of the bus, this trip had been a mistake from beginning to end. Hilda von Hassenfeld, Gretchen Freidrich, and Berthe Blutwort, on their very first pilgrimage to *Das Heilige Land*, had been advised by *Schwester* Agathe to wear comfortable, casual clothing, and quite by chance the three nuns had ended up looking like triplets: plain white blouses, pastel cardigans, pleated plaid skirts, sensible shoes, and, naturally, the requisite black headscarf. *Schwester* Agathe had given them her own map, which she had inherited from old *Schwester* Marthe, and the three had followed it carefully, but almost nothing they saw was on that map, and vice versa.

This bus trip was a continuation of the previous three weeks of utter frustration: the nuns had not set out for Jerusalem at all; they were supposed to be en route to Nazareth. But frustration was *nothing* compared to what lay ahead.

It was the 20th of January, 1991. The Mother of All Battles was under way.

❦

"*Yah Saddam!*" Tzion growled as the air-raid sirens began to wail. His nine passengers went into total panic; pandemonium reigned on the Haifa-Jerusalem bus. It took the driver but a minute to analyze the situation, a minute of staring into the rearview mirror, his brow creased in concentration. Fortunately for all, the particular stretch of road he was on was straight and nearly deserted.

Tzion yanked his gas mask single-handed from its box and plonked it on his head. The goggles were now set midway on his broad forehead, the air intake filter perched approximately between his prominent eyebrows, giving Tzion the look of a deformed rhinoceros. That done, he jammed his meaty foot down on the gas pedal, pressing it to the floorboards, and the bus hurtled along the now dark, virtually empty highway towards the capital.

"Stop the bus!" Zev, the first — and, so far, only — to regain his composure, as it were, knew the Civil Defense regulations by heart. "You're supposed to stop the bus and get us to safety!"

Tzion responded with a finger drilling a mock-hole in his temple. "*Attah normali?*" he asked rhetorically.

"Stop the bus! Stop the bus!" the others chorused hysterically.

Tzion slammed on the brakes and the bus lurched to a halt, dumping the nuns unceremoniously to the floor.

"Look — there is khouse!" Indeed there was a khouse, er, house, a dilapidated but nonetheless solid-looking little house, standing in solitude near the side of the road where Tzion had pulled over. It was the only house, the only structure of any sort, for as far as the eye could see.

The passengers quickly grabbed their belongings

and lunged for the exit, with feisty Zev leading the charge. He tugged out and donned his gas mask without breaking stride and raised a — what else? — clenched fist to pound on the wallpapered front door.

A bright voice sang out from behind the floral print: "Morris? Ken you gettink it? I tink ve heffink company!"

The wailing sirens rose and fell eerily. Darkness closed in around the frightened passengers as they waited for the door to open, and when it did at last, they stormed in, rather rudely pushing past their diminutive hostess.

"Vell, vell, vell, vell. Vhat haf ve got here — Rinklink Brudder's Tzircus?" she asked, all smiles.

"Dontcha hear those sirens, lady?" Zev shouted through his grotesque mask. "It's war! Iraq is bombing us! With chemical warheads! Turn on your radio! Where's the sealed room? Quick — get your mask on! Open up your atropine shot — we could all be dying already!"

The rest of the group cowered in the center of the room; some were whimpering like children, others seemed merely bewildered, but most were gripped with fear, fueled by Zev's histrionics.

"Morris, vhat you sayink to soch ah poisen, hah?" Morris was nowhere in sight. "Vhere's your menners, yonk man? Dun't you sayink 'Hallo' vhen you comink in somevone's house? Your mama is not teachink you you say 'Hallo, mein name is...' — vhat is it, Kum? — 'mein name is Kum. Pliz ken I comink in?' Now you tryink it. Come on, let's hearink you."

Tzion, meanwhile, was lumbering about, opening

closet doors and peeking behind curtains. Simcha
Bunim likewise needed no invitation. He deposited
himself in a club chair, flipped open his *Tehillim*, and
began reciting Psalms at random in an unintelligible
chant. Hilda, Gretchen and Berthe began clicking their
rosary beads and mumbling their, presumably, salva-
tion-seeking prayers.

June and Doug were too freaked out on the decor to
notice anything else. It was an eclectic hodgepodge
of Early Transitional European Immigrant Neo-
Levantine Kitsch, with enough overstuffed davenports
and wing chairs, inlaid end tables, tasseled lamps,
pseudo-Persian rugs and assorted bric-a-brac in the
eight-by-ten-foot living room to fill a furniture warehouse. "Isn't this totally awesome?" June whispered.
Doug, totally awed, could only nod his assent. The
couches and club chairs all wore snowy antimacassars
over their shoulders like Spanish dueñas; the dark-
hued lampshades had sufficient gold braid to outfit the
admiralty of the Sixth Fleet. At the windows, the heavy
draperies hung in deep folds and fanned out at the base
like a bride's train, overflowing onto the rugs. Tzion, at
present, was wiping his grubby shoes on them.

Erez decided to take matters in hand. "I apologize
for our intrusion," he began, "but it seems there's an air
raid going on. We were all on a bus to Jerusalem when
the sirens started and we need shelter. My name is Erez
Hadani." More or less in unison, the others volunteered
their names.

"Mein plezhur," their hostess acknowledged. "Vel-
come to Goldie's house — dat's me, Goldie. Mein Morris
is somevhere. Morris? Come sayink Hallo, vill you?"
Morris had yet to make an appearance.

"I'm sorry, Mrs., er, Goldie," Erez interrupted, "but please understand — this is an emergency! The country is under attack. We must all go into your sealed room. You do have one, don't you?"

"Sealtroom?" Goldie laughed. "You tink ve vas goink in ah sealtroom in Lomza vhen der Nazis, *zollen oisgerissen vehren*, is bombink us? Now *dat* vas 'under ah teck'! Dis? Dis is *noddink*! You tink ve vas goink in ah sealtroom vhen ve vas in der kemps? No, tenks. Not if ve ken helpink it!"

Zev, grasping the situation, began to empty his oversized canvas backpack on the pseudo-Persian rug. "Good thing I came prepared," he muttered. Rolls of masking tape and plastic sheeting materialized, along with scissors, bags of bicarbonate, bottles of mineral water and canned goods. "You — with the earring — get moving! We've got work to do!"

Doug was galvanized into action. While Tzion fiddled with the transistor radio he'd found (lodged between a model of Rachel's Tomb constructed entirely from seashells and an olivewood clock with Hebrew letters where the numbers would be, bearing the portrait of a tight-lipped chassidic Rebbe in the center, arms outstretched to indicate that the time was *gimmel* after *heh*), Erez, Doug and Zev made quick work of sealing the windows in the bathroom and the two tiny bedrooms.

"Pliz!" Goldie implored them. "Vatchink out for der paint jop! *Gutt in Himmel!*"

Hilda, Gretchen and Berthe, who hadn't understood anything that was going on, lit up at what sounded like their mother tongue. "*Sprechen sie*

Deutsch?" Schwester Gretchen asked hopefully.

Silence fell on the crowded room.

"I do *not* sprechen any Deutsch," Goldie replied indignantly, drawing herself up to her full height of four feet, six inches. For the first time she noticed the nuns' necklaces and rosaries. "I vas talkink to *mein* Gutt, not *yours*, so pliz I vill tenk you not to eafsdroppink." She turned to Simcha and said, "*Ah chutzpah! Drei Nazishe goites in mein hoiz,* and vearink ah disguise like *frimme veiblach mit tichlach!*"

Simcha paused in his *Tehillim* recitation to reply, "On their heads is called wimples," he bellowed, eyes blinking rapidly. "Germans they are, but Nazis?" He shrugged with great eloquence, a dismissive gesture that included a raised eyebrow, a sweeping hand movement, and a modified "Bronx cheer."

"Comrade Goldieyeva," Vladimir interjected. All eyes turned to the bald-pated man with the medals. He had been so quiet until now that he had gone virtually unnoticed. "I too am khating Nazis. In name of all Russians People and noble Proletariat I say we throwing them out of khouse and letting Saddamski Khussein dropping on them nuclear war-kheads and then we taking tractor and..." Vlad's eyes were glittering with hope of retribution.

Goldie put up a hand to halt the flow of Communist rhetoric. "It's ah vunderful plen, Ivan," she soothed, "but I'm not heffink ah trector." Vlad's disappointment was keen, as was Zev's. "Mebbe ve chust mekkink dem listen to der radio," she suggested brightly, eyeing the nuns. "I tink dey playink your sonk!"

Indeed, Tzion — with the aid of a bent wire hanger

— had succeeded in operating the radio and tuning it to the channel designated for calming the frightened public (or vice versa). Inexplicably, the station's disc jockeys had selected a mournful piece perpetrated by Rita, a local superstar whose banshee wailing could easily have replaced half the malfunctioning sirens in the country.

"Nein, nein!" Hilda pleaded. *"Keine Nazis!"* She held up her crucifix as evidence and pointed frantically to her wimple. The three fell to their knees in supplication and began to intone a fervent prayer in Latin.

"Gutt in Himmel!" Goldie exclaimed, rolling her eyes Heavenward in very Zev-like exasperation.

"Sprechen sie Deu—?" Berthe ventured, but Goldie cut her off in mid-query. "Knockink it off, Rapunzel. You gettink on mein noives."

"Okay — the rooms are sealed!" Zev announced, his sparse, droopy handlebar mustache twitching with excitement. "Quick — everyone take cover!"

No one budged.

Simcha let out a loud *"Mizmor l'Dovid,"* and continued his mumbled recitation of Psalms. Tzion played with the radio dials. The nuns did their *Ave Maria* bit while Vladimir explained his medals to June: "This for I am being khappiest worker in *kolkhoz*; this for I am being khappiest interrogator for KGB; this for I am being khappiest tank commander in Ukraine..."

"You were the khap... er, *happiest?"*

"Others are defecting, so I am getting khonor."

"Look, would you can the socializing already?" Zev roared. "Everybody — get into the bedrooms!" Eight out of nine made a beeline for the sealed rooms. (Tzion, heaving his beefy shoulders from side to side in time to Rita's warbling, chose to stand pat.) With a speed that belied her years, Goldie flew across the parlor to bar the way.

"Chust vone minute!" she commanded. "In mein house is nubbody goink boys and girls in de bettroom togedder! De girls vill goink in vone room, and der boys in de udder."

"But Doug's my life companion!" June protested. "This is totally Victorian! I refuse to spend what are possibly my last moments on Earth with a bunch of Nazi frauleins!"

"*Keine Nazis!*" the trio cried.

"Don't freak, June," Doug remonstrated. "Where's your brotherly, er, sisterly love? Besides, as long as our Karmas remain in synch, we can never be truly separated. This phantasmagoric experience will help us get in touch with ourselves and with our transcendent souls, and before the night is through we'll know if these minute stirrings are merely a blip in the cosmic abyss or something we'll be able to engrave on the time capsule of posterity."

Zev's eyeballs threatened to soar right through the roof, but, somehow, Doug's oration had a calming effect on his life companion. The team divided itself along gender lines and prepared to spend the next who-knew-how-long in Goldie's sealed rooms.

Suddenly there was a knock on the door.

"Morris? Ken you gettink it? I tink ve heffink more company!"

Morris was still nowhere in sight, and Goldie did the honors. On the other side of the wallpapered door stood a young man, about as well-attired and groomed as they come in this casual country, medium height with an astonishing growth of beard that dominated his pleasant face. There was a *kippah* on his head and sandals on his feet, despite the January chill and the slight drizzle. "I'm terribly sorry to disturb you," he said politely, "but I was driving to Jerusalem when the sirens went off. It seems there's an air raid going on. May I come in?"

"Of course!" Goldie said with a smile. "Tree more and ve vill heffink ah minyan!"

As soon as the new arrival entered the room, Erez froze. "You!" he exclaimed. Rafi Katz was too astounded to speak.

Erez stormed past him and sat himself down in Simcha's recently vacated club chair. "Even if it means risking my life," he declared, "I will not be in the same room with Rafi Katz!"

"Now look here!" Zev screamed, his voice high with an edge of hysteria. "There are Civil Defense regulations that we gotta follow. The Butcher of Baghdad is hurling everything he's got at us and we're supposed to get into that room and seal the door. If you think I'm gonna seal it up and then, when you change your mind and come banging on the door, I'll *un*seal it to let you in, well, Mister, you got another think coming."

Out of the corner of his eye, Simcha looked at Zev with profound disdain. He planted himself in Erez's path, folded his massive arms across his vast chest and boomed, "Out or in — your now decision."

"It's all right. Erez can go in. I'll stay out here."

Vlad, who had the utmost appreciation of power, gazed at Simcha with new respect. Rafi, however, had impressed him even more. "You are true khero of Supreme Israeli Republic. You are khaving real altruism — to sacrifice self for good of khoppressed Peoples." He kissed Rafi with feeling on both cheeks. "You are khinspiration to masses."

"Ivan, you are beink epsolutely right," Goldie said. Vladimir beamed. No one had ever agreed with him before, certainly not since his *aliyah*, and this gave him a wonderful sense of importance, although he had not the foggiest notion of what he had said that his hostess might be agreeing with. "If Rafi is not goink into sealtroom, nubbody is goink! So, Raffaleh, you vantink ve should all beink blested to shmiddereens? Or you goink to svallow your prite and go mit Erez, hmn?"

While Rafi translated and contemplated this choice, Rita's wails were cut off in mid-shriek by the all-clear siren. Zev whipped off his mask. "We won!" he shouted with glee, fist raised defiantly. "Yes! Yes!" The passengers all looked at him as though he were an escapee from a mental ward, which, come to think of it, he might have been. Tzion repeated his temple-drilling gesture and Simcha shrugged his eloquent shrug. The radio in Tzion's fist announced that everyone could remove their gas masks and come out of the sealed rooms, but the public was requested to remain indoors until further notice.

"Vell, I tink I vill mekkink some tea," Goldie said

and headed for the kitchen. "And den you two boys ken tellink us vhy you almost gettink everybody kilt for noddink."

A tense silence filled the overfurnished parlor as the adversaries glared at one another with overt hostility. Five full minutes ticked by on the Rebbe clock while Goldie puttered in the kitchen, and when she returned with a tray of mismatched yahrtzeit lamp glasses filled with tea, not one of her guests rose to relieve her of her burden: they were all mesmerized by the barely concealed hatred radiating from Erez and Rafi.

"So, you are tekkink vone sugar or two?" Goldie asked June.

"Multinational corporations exploit the downtrodden nations of South America, paying starvation wages and providing abominable, subhuman living accommodations throughout the sugar cane harvesting season. Impoverished and desperate to upgrade their lifestyle, young Colombians and Bolivians frequently turn to poppy cultivation, which pays better, and that's how they get sucked into the international drug industry. The leading..."

"Ah simple 'no' vould do," Goldie interjected. "Der tea is gettink colt. And besites," she added, turning to Zev, "I dun't know vhat is beink so bet about der druk industry. Mein oncle Zollie, he hed ah druk store and he vas doink very nice. Kum, you vant tea?"

"Do you have anything stronger?" Zev asked.

"Yeah, I am heffink stronk tea. Here — trink."

❀

By the time everyone was served, the tension in the room had eased slightly and Erez was ready to talk.

"That man," Erez began, pointing at Rafi, "was my business partner for half a dozen years. We had been best friends in the army and so it seemed only natural that we should go into business together, or at least that's what we thought at the time.

"God was kind to us and we became enormously successful in very little time. Our product, a hand-held muscle massager called 'The Pulsator,' became an overnight international bestseller, and our company grew to over a hundred employees. We had sales reps all over the world."

Erez's voice struck a wistful note, as though he were trying to recapture and relish the past. "The key to our success was the way we worked together. Rafi was in charge of production and I managed sales. But he couldn't leave me to it. Always questioning my decisions, meddling in my division. If only you had trusted my judgment, Rafi, none of this would have happened, and we could have kept on raking it in." Erez shook his head from side to side in dismay. Then he went on with his story.

"The nature of my job took me abroad often. New markets were being developed and each trip proved more profitable than its predecessor. To keep pace with sales, Rafi was always hiring and training more employees and purchasing additional equipment. By the end of our third year of operation we were Israel's fourth largest importer of rubber and polycarbonate, the materials Pulsator is constructed from."

"Decadent capitalist khogwash," Vlad remarked to

Simcha, who was still trying to figure out who would want to buy a massage machine.

"During my last trip to New York," Erez continued, "I got a call from Charles Harris, president of the largest chain of department stores in the United States. I had never dealt with Harris personally before, only with his buying agent. Harris asked me if I could meet him in his office the next day, and you can be sure I was there on the dot.

"Picture this: forty-two stories above Park Avenue with a panoramic view of the East River and virtually all of Midtown — I thought I had walked onto a Hollywood set. The carpet was ankle-deep and the upholstered chairs were so low and sleek, they looked like submarines surfacing. I sank down into a chair so deeply that I felt like I was below floor level. Believe me, I've never seen an office like Harris', not in Israel for sure, and not in any of my travels.

"First off, Harris tells me to call him Charlie. He's real friendly towards me, swears that he loves our product and personally uses it, and proposes a deal the dimensions of which turn my heart into a squirrel cage. He wants to buy 60,000 Pulsators at their full wholesale price, provided that I deliver them in two weeks — that is, by the first of January — and that he have exclusivity in America.

"It was the opportunity of a lifetime. Our largest order to date had been for 12,000 units, and that had been at a significant discount.

"I wanted this deal to go through in the worst way, but it would be up to Rafi to decide if we could swing it. I told Harris that I would have to consult with my partner in Israel and I would report back to him right away. I knew that the exclusivity issue was not a problem: at that price and with that volume, he was entitled to be the only kid on the block to have 'em.

"I called Rafi and he told me that we had only about 24,000 Pulsators in stock. I tried to convince him that if we could put on a double shift right away, it was do-able. But Rafi poured ice water on my enthusiasm: the staff wouldn't agree, the labor union would give us trouble, Harris would back down and we'd be stuck with a huge inventory. He had more excuses than Alibi Ike. Finally, after talking myself hoarse, he agreed. Right — he did me a whole favor and agreed to let me close the deal that would enable him to retire at 30!

"I reported back to Harris and he invited me back to his heavenly office to work out the arrangements and sign the papers. The next day, fifty percent would be deposited into our account, the balance on delivery. I'd never even heard of such terms before! I could have danced down the forty-two flights to the street, I was so excited.

"I had some other business to finish up in New York but I was in a hurry to get back home so that I could have the peace of mind of knowing that the order got off on time. I wound up my business and came home a little earlier than scheduled.

"I went straight from the airport to our plant. It was about 1:30 in the afternoon when I drove through the gates — into a ghost town! Everything was locked up and totally abandoned — two days prior to shipment!

"I couldn't believe it. Here I had given my word, signed an agreement and received a hefty binder, and instead of working into the night, Rafi had declared winter vacation!"

"Workers not filling quota?!" Vladimir commented wryly.

"I went into the warehouse and I thought I would faint! The place had been emptied out, every shelf was bare. The entire stock of 24,000 units, plus whatever had been produced in the interim, was gone."

"Perkhaps they take kheverything with them to dacha," Vladimir offered.

"Pesach cleaning?" Bunim suggested.

"I walked over to the factory and I was no longer sure if I was still alive or on this planet. Everything was gone. Even the heavy machinery — which had taken forever to install, and trucks and cranes and crews to deliver — was all missing!

"I raced to the nearest phone, which by some miracle was still there and still working, and called Rafi at home. I spoke to his answering machine; I must have spoken to that machine forty times that day.

"The office was also closed down, even *my* secretary wasn't there! By an act of grace — or negligent omission — the office had not been pillaged and everything was still in place.

"I had to find out where Rafi was and where my stolen company was. I thought of calling the police, but it would have sounded so ridiculous: 'I'd like to report a theft... My company, staff and all... No, this is not a prank call.' — I didn't even bother.

"I went over to Rafi's secretary's desk and looked

through his appointment book to try and find some lead. The last few days were blank, but nine days earlier I found a notation which made my head swim. Nine days earlier, *only two days after our phone conversation*, I saw that Rafi had a lunch meeting with Andy Gordon, the purchasing agent for Harris' major competitor.

"I couldn't believe it! Every second, things were getting worse. But the worst, of course, was yet to come. I then found in Accounting an invoice for 165 gross — that's 23,760 Pulsators — made out to Gordon's company, and at a 20% discount!

"This was too much to handle, not that anything before was bearable. Not only does he steal the company and renege on my deal and exclusivity arrangement with Harris, but he then goes and sells everything we have in stock to Harris' competitor, and at a discount, no less!

"I didn't know what to do with myself. I just wanted to run away and hide, but not before I mutilated Rafi. The January 15th UN deadline for Iraq to pull out of Kuwait was approaching and I figured it wouldn't hurt me to be abroad. I knew that if I did find my ex-partner, I could not be held responsible for my actions. Since my army unit hadn't been mobilized, there was nothing to stop me from leaving, so I called up my travel agent and asked her to book me a flight and a hotel room in Geneva.

"Out of missile range, I would have all the peace and quiet I needed to rethink my life and be able to determine when it would be safe to return home.

"So, after being back here for less than 48 hours, I took off again for overseas, only this time it wasn't a business trip. And just as Rafi didn't leave a message for me in the office, I left no message for him.

"Well, I spent the past weeks sorting out what I'm going to do with myself, and decided I really should be in Israel at a time like this, army or no army. A little over an hour ago I landed, and now, of all people, I have to meet *him!*" Erez aimed an accusatory finger at his ex-partner, ex-friend.

"Of all the self-righteous, arrogant..." Rafi spluttered angrily, but Erez had turned his back and was headed for the front door. The huge Bunim planted a massive body in his path. "The army is saying outside we going not," he rumbled, blinking rapidly. "Rafi now his side is telling." There was no arguing with Man-Mountain Bunim.

"Dat's right," Goldie concurred. "Ve listenink to you, now ve listenink to him. A lotta tinks mebbe vas heppenink vhile you vas eatink Sviss chocolates and crink over spilt cuckoo clocks..."

"Nothing that worm has to say could interest me," Erez said flatly.

"I'm with Erez," Zev declared. "Rafi obviously ripped him off on a grand scale. Probably the only reason he's still in the country instead of on the beach in the Cayman Islands, is that he couldn't get a flight out! If he had anything to say for himself, he had plenty of time to do it — he could have left messages for Erez. Erez is the one whose reputation is down the tubes. Why should —"

Working up a good head of steam, Zev was oblivious to the wordless exchange between Vlad and Simcha. At Bunim's signal, the Russian began to sidle over to the fulminating *Kum!* activist until he was positioned mere inches from the fellow's left ear. Then he pursed his lips and emitted a whooping/wailing sound that virtually duplicated that of the air raid siren.

In nanoseconds, Zev had his gas mask back on, effectively cutting himself off in mid-fulmination, and was striding resolutely into the sealed room. Bunim shook his co-conspirator's hand, pumping it up and down for good measure, and all eyes returned to their hostess.

"As I vas sayink," Goldie went on, not missing a beat, "ve giffink you ah chence to spik, now you vill giffink Raffaleh ah chence, yes? Who knows — mebbe you two boychiks ken mekkink peaz."

To everyone's amazement, Doug threw an arm around Simcha and Tzion and burst into song: "All we are sayy-ingg," he crooned, swaying from side to side, "is give peace a..."

Bunim shot him a threatening look and Doug's Golden Oldie died aborning. Hilda and Gretchen, picking up the cue a little late, were already applauding, but June leaped across the carpet and expeditiously clamped her hands over theirs. Silence reigned once more.

"Tenk you, dahlink," Goldie said warmly. "Now, if Hensel and Gretl are finishink mit der kloppink, and de singers, vhistlers, and ecrobets are heffink no more entertainments for us, ve ken mebbe vindink up dis business. Erez, your potner hez sometink to say, so pliz to beink qviet and listenink."

Outnumbered, and clearly outclassed, by this group of total strangers whom Saddam Hussein had brought together and who inexplicably seemed bent on mediating in his private war with Rafi, Erez reluctantly took a seat and resigned himself to hearing his ex-partner's litany of excuses, justifications and rationalizations.

"What I have to say is very simple, albeit not as pious or self-righteous as my former colleague..." Rafi began. "While you were gallivanting in Europe, Erez, I was practically killing myself to guarantee delivery."

Erez looked as if he were about to attack Rafi, but Bunim placed a mighty paw on his shoulder and applied a little pressure. Vladimir winked his approval and gave Simcha a thumbs-up sign.

"The night Erez called me about the Harris order, there was a tremendous storm which anyone in the Netanya area will remember for a long time. Gale-force winds knocked over trees, bringing down power lines with them and crippling our entire area. The electric company said that it would take at least four days to restore service, and I knew that four days could just as easily turn into two weeks.

"I realized that the most logical thing for me to do would have been to call New York and explain that without electricity there would be no way for us to fill the order. But I wasn't looking for an easy way out. I also didn't want to deprive Erez of the opportunity to go wading again in Harris' carpet." The dollop of sarcasm in Rafi's voice was almost palpable.

"I decided to go for this 'mission impossible.' It was a crazy idea, but once I'd agreed to it I was determined to see it through, and as you know, there was a lot at stake."

"You could have subcontracted and provided employment for countless impoverished immigrants," Doug offered, but even Vlad — who was related to or acquainted with a good number of the countless — groaned at such naivete.

"There was no way that the job could be subcontracted. Our product is unique and nowhere else in the country is there machinery that can make anything like the Pulsator.

"I called up every real estate agency in Israel and followed every lead trying to find a site large enough — and equipped with electricity — to temporarily accommodate our plant: I was going to move the whole operation, lock, stock, and barrel.

"Eventually I found a vacant factory building in Beit Shemesh that was ideal, but they insisted on our renting the place for at least a full six months, for a small fortune. Add to that what the moving and installation costs would amount to and it would total a *colossal* fortune, but our margin on this deal was so high that it was still worthwhile. I took it.

"With God's help, by 3:30 the next afternoon the assembly line was already rolling. Everything had gone like clockwork.

"Andy Gordon was a Godsend. He was willing to pay for the whole lot in cash, which is why I gave him such a special deal. His order financed the rent, moving out and moving back, with change left over to boot.

"And as to Harris' exclusivity clause, Gordon's company, as it happens, deals throughout the Americas, and what I sold him was on condition that it go only to Canada, Brazil and Mexico."

Erez turned red with shame and buried his face in his hands.

"I told the workers — who, by the way, were terrific — that instead of working double-shift I needed them to work *triple*-shift. There was no other way to replace all the units that I had sold to Gordon. Remarkably, each and every worker agreed. Machinists called their brothers-in-law, their sons, their neighbors, you name it, to join us, and many of us worked twenty hours a day for *five days*! Personally, I slept on the premises, and you can be sure I wasn't the only one.

"For the five days that we were at it, the Coke company delivered 600 cans a day! The pizza and felafel shop in Beit Shemesh also worked a triple shift, and I'm told the owner earned enough during that week to buy a yacht and take a leisurely 'round-the-world cruise.

"The place looked like a college slumber party: people working in their pajamas, in sweat shirts, in T-shirts, in no shirts. Regardless, three hours before Shabbat we got the job done and I gave everyone a week's paid vacation.

"I had no idea where you were all this time, Erez. You were only due back two weeks ago, and obviously before you were to return there was just one thing on my mind.

"Since I had privileges to the Beit Shemesh factory for an entire six months, I was in no rush to move everything back home, even though our electricity was actually restored in five days.

"I allowed myself a little vacation too and then got our operation back to normal. I took advantage of the fact that our plant was vacated, to do some internal redesigning which will make the operation run more efficiently in the future. I hired an architect to prepare the plans and a contractor to execute them. We're also expanding the facility and doing some landscaping.

"Only when we were back to normal production at the temporary site did I start looking for you. I phoned halfway around the world to find you, but no one knew where you were. Had Harris' order not been filled when it was, we wouldn't have a prayer now, with the war on. Who knows how long it will last, but if this past week is any indication, we're in for some serious production interruptions."

Erez stared speechlessly at his partner as the Rebbe's arm inched past *vav* o'clock. The radio announced that it was safe to go outside and Tzion, with a wordless salute to his hostess, lumbered out to his bus. Gathering their belongings, the rest of Goldie's Ad Hoc Multinational Peace-Making Forces followed, subdued into silence by the events of the emotion-packed evening. Only Rafi and Erez remained.

The ex-partners glared at one another for long moments.

"Can I give you a lift?" Rafi asked at last.

"Can you ever forgive me?"

The two friends embraced, pounding one another heartily on the back.

"Vell, gentlesmen, dis hez been ah lotta fon," Goldie said. "Now I am needink mein beauty slip, so pliz, if you dun't mind, you ken beatink eachudder op outsite." She opened the front door and ushered them out. "Tenks for der visit — comink again soon!" she called after them, waving.

A calico cat padded in through the open door. "Morris! Vhere hef you been, you bed ket!"

Heard from: The gentleman in seat 24E, El Al flight 008, NY-TLV, February 29, 1992.

Nothing but the Truth

SOME PEOPLE WILL sacrifice almost anything for the sake of peace. For some, seeking peace is a driving obsession; for others, it is a low priority. Some acquire this trait at birth; some only eight days later.

❀

The mohel finished the circumcision and the baby was handed to his maternal grandfather, who would hold the infant during the blessings. Mendy Fried, the proud father, gave his revered mentor the honor of reciting the blessings, which he did in his resonant, mellifluous voice. The rabbi paused in the middle of the blessing, for the father to tell him the name he had chosen for his new son. Mendy whispered the baby's name, and the rabbi continued, "Our God and the God of our fathers, preserve this child for his father and his mother, and may his name be called in Israel *Shalom ben Menachem Mendel...*"

No sooner had the name been announced, than the baby's paternal grandfather slapped his hand against his forehead and released an anxious "*Oy!*"

The rabbi completed the blessing as if nothing had happened, but directly afterwards the new father went over to *his* father to see what the problem was. The grandfather was virtually tearing his few remaining hairs out.

"You named the baby after Mama's brother, right? Your uncle Shalom?"

Mendy nodded.

"*Vey iz mir,*" groaned Mendy's father, who was now as white as chalk. "His name wasn't Shalom; he was simply *called* Shalom because he was such a peacemaker. His real name was Yitzchak Chaim. *Oy,* how could I have forgotten?! And now it's too late — as you know, once a name has been given it cannot be retracted."

Mendy looked at his father, not appreciating the damper that had been placed upon the *simchah,* and shrugged his shoulders as if to say, "How was I supposed to know?"

"*Nu, nu,*" Mendy's father sighed, reconciling himself to the situation. "There must be some reason that this name was given. Who knows — maybe it's an omen that he will follow in his great-uncle's footsteps and spread peace among his people."

❁

Judy Jacobson realized that she should be baking, or cooking, or mending, or doing any one of half a dozen domestic jobs. Dust and germs should be fleeing in panic from her presence, and everything in the kitchen should be arranged by height and expiration date.

"Should," of course, was the operative word. She always suffered these Attila the Housewife arrows of angst on Thursday nights, seconds before she would abandon her mess and Shabbos preparations to bury her head in *The Heritage Gazette* weekly. For two solid hours Judy's world would be encapsulated in about 70 broadsheet pages, as she skimmed the articles and read the advertisements figuring out who's who, what's what, and when it's all happening. Once she finished, she would regret the time she had wasted and how late she would have to stay up to complete her chores, and at 2:30 in the morning she would pledge that she'd never make that mistake again — until, of course, next week's edition of *The Heritage Gazette* arrived.

The up side of this weekly binge was that Judy was transformed into a maven on Jewish news and was at least a day ahead of her friends and co-workers. Accordingly, every Friday morning at work Judy Jacobson would become a star: the center of the staff's attention and a virtual font of information.

So here she was, preparing late Thursday night for her current-events coffee klatsch workshop at the office, when an item on page six jumped out at her and made her gasp. "Can't be," she muttered to herself, but the bold leader was explicit and the article beneath it was even more so.

Although most people claim that they don't believe what they read, in fact virtually everyone does. Judy certainly had no illusions about herself. She knew that even if a paper of lesser stature than *The Heritage Gazette* ran a story about, say, a boy born in darkest Africa with three heads, she would believe it.

That's why, she understood at once, she was shuddering. Hundreds, maybe hundreds of thousands like her, would believe the *Gazette*'s scoop, even though it was patently false. Worse still, she would not be able to lead a symposium on "What's the latest?" at work the next day. How could she be au courant with the news without having read the paper, and how could she read the paper without seeing the article about the company that employed her!

After hours of deliberation Judy decided that she had to show her boss the article, and then — in good conscience — she could discuss the news of the week in review.

Thus on Friday morning, Judy found herself at work early, anxiously waiting for her boss to show up. And when he finally arrived, on schedule, she sprang up to greet him.

"You're only my secretary," Shalom Fried said in a jocular tone, "not my disciple."

Judy had planned to break it to him gently, but she could no longer contain herself. With a quick, nervous glance around to see if the coast was clear, she whispered urgently, "Look at this!" and handed her boss the paper folded open to page six.

Shalom spread the paper across his desk, sat down and did as instructed. When he finished, he asked, in a weak attempt at humor, "This isn't the Purim issue, I gather?" Judy's expression remained grave.

Shalom flipped through the *Gazette* to the masthead, located the name of the publisher and editor, and instructed his secretary to get Sidney Soltawicz on the phone.

❦

"Good morning, Mr. Soltawicz. This is Shalom Fried of Kosher Kuts. You have a feature on page six in this week's issue claiming that non-kosher meat was found on one of our trucks. I don't know of any incident you might be referring to, since nothing like that has ever happened. You don't quote a source, or even hint at where your information came from, so obviously you didn't even try to verify your allegation.

"I assume that you made a mistake and didn't mean to libel my company. You must have confused our name with..."

"If the *Gazette* wrote it, I'm sure its authoritative."

"How can you be so sure about something that is absolutely untrue?"

"That's what *you* say. Mr. Fried, we are a newspaper and our job is to report the news and convey information."

"Information? But I know this is a mistake!"

"And I know that the Saudis aren't happy with our news coverage either, nor are the members of Congress we blasted in this issue, who blocked the Aid to Parochial Schools bill. But we are not in the business of pleasing people, Mr. Fried. We're in the news business and we report it as we see it."

"Mr. Soltawicz, in the last minute I told you twice

that your paper is wrong, and you still insist that you're right. What's the source of your information?"

"Our excellent team of reporters."

"'Excellent reporters' is the same as saying 'anonymous.'"

"Call it what you like, we stand by what we print."

"I just can't believe that you are defending an out-and-out lie. I'm sure you realize what the consequences of this article will be. I want to remind you of what Rabbi Yisrael Salanter once said: 'If you say of a rabbi that he does not have a good voice and of a cantor that he is not a scholar, you are a gossip. But if you say of a rabbi that he is no scholar and of a cantor that he has no voice — you are a murderer.'

"I'm in the kosher meat business, Mr. Soltawicz. People rely on my integrity. If *chas ve'shalom* a batch of *treifa* meat was ever mixed in accidentally with my kosher meat, I'd recall the entire shipment the minute I found out. But, thank God, this has never happened. To falsely report that non-kosher meat was 'found' on my truck makes it sound as if *treifa* meat was *hidden* there and discovered by the authorities! This is character assassination, or, as Reb Yisrael would put it, 'murder.' Such irresponsible reporting by your paper could ruin me! I demand that you print an immediate retraction."

"Listen, Fried, we stand by what we wrote. If you think you can prove us wrong, then sue us." The line went dead.

Judy had overheard the entire conversation and she felt ready to explode. She couldn't believe Soltawicz's arrogance! She knew Shalom and his business well, and there truly was no way that non-kosher meat could end up on one of his trucks. In the remote possibility that a mistake ever happened, Shalom would never conceal it. He really would issue a public recall until the entire shipment was accounted for and he was certain that the meat would not reach a Jewish consumer.

And yet, as angry as Judy was on her boss' behalf, Shalom was absolutely calm. He just sat there, casually skimming the paper, with a peculiar expression on his face.

Judy peered at her employer uncomprehendingly. It was obvious that something "not kosher" was going on, something she didn't understand. "Why wouldn't Soltawicz offer to at least look into the matter?" she asked.

Shalom motioned for her to come closer so that he could show her the answer. Judy approached the desk and Shalom turned the *Gazette* to page 8, revealing a full-page display ad for The Broadway Meating Place. At first Judy did not grasp her boss' meaning and she looked for a typo in the copy. She scrutinized the ad several times, trying unsuccessfully to find what error Kosher Kuts' major competitor had fallen prey to, until suddenly it hit her.

"I get it," she said. "Why, Broadway's been advertising in this paper for as long as I can remember!"

Shalom gave a slight nod. "Over the years a relationship develops..."

"Why don't *we* advertise in the *Gazette*?"

"They want to know the same thing. Every year their advertising salesmen approach me to place an ad;

in fact this year they turned to me twice, and as usual, I refused the honor. The guy who called me wasn't exactly thrilled when I turned him down. In fact, he practically threatened me that we would 'lose out' if I didn't take out an ad in his paper. At the time, I thought he meant that consumers always prefer to buy a product they are familiar with, that they've seen advertised in their favorite newspaper. I never suspected that he was hinting at dirty tricks."

"So now what are you going to do?"

"The thing that Soltawicz least expects... Kosher Kuts is going to call the mighty *Heritage Gazette* to a *din Torah*."

❀

Seven weeks passed and three separate invitations to a *din Torah* were sent to Sidney Soltawicz of *The Heritage Gazette*. Each went unanswered. In the intervening period, an advertisement appeared in *The Heritage Gazette* sponsored by the "Ad Hoc Committee for Halachic Conformance." The ad asserted that if religious consumers would be particular about patronizing only Halachah-observers, then firms such as Kosher Kuts could never hope to get away with dealing with non-kosher meat.

By this time even Mr. Equanimity, a.k.a. Shalom Fried, had lost his patience. He called Sidney Soltawicz and demanded to know who was behind this "non-profit" ad hoc organization that he had never heard of and which was not listed with directory information. Instead of a reply, the *Gazette*'s publisher and editor again invited Fried to sue him.

Shalom realized that Soltawicz would never make

such a brazen offer if he had even the remotest fear that Kosher Kuts would accept the challenge. It is one thing to seek redress in a *din Torah* where both sides are truly equal and the Halachah is the only deciding factor; proving libel in a civil court of law is quite another.*

"Libel," as defined by American law, is multi-faceted and includes any written publication, malicious or otherwise, which is injurious to the reputation of another. Malicious intent that has resulted in a loss is a hard claim to prove. Printing an outrageous lie that could possibly harm a reputation is not necessarily libelous enough to lose a judgment. Unequivocal evidence must be presented that the false reportage was intentional, deliberate, and indeed harmful.

These stringent restrictions protect newspapers from having to deal with lawsuits on a daily basis. Because proving a violation of each condition would require the involvement of an expert legal team at a prohibitive cost, with no assured results, few ever initiate libel proceedings.

Shalom did not decide to take on the newspaper mogul in order to settle a personal score; he was not vindictive by nature. He would derive no personal pleasure in seeing *The Heritage Gazette* humbled. His decision was purely pragmatic. His business-honed mind informed him that there were but two options: he could sue the *Gazette* and if he lost, hemorrhage all of Kosher Kuts' and his personal funds; or he could let matters ride and allow Kosher Kuts to bleed to death

---

*Halachah mandates that all disputes be adjudicated before a *beis din*. In the event that the Defendant refuses three consecutive times to respond to a summons from the *beis din*, the Plaintiff may resort to the secular judicial system.

from all of the bad publicity. Shalom preferred a swift demise over a protracted and torturous one.

Legal counsel did not concur with Shalom's gut feeling that he had an open-and-shut case. However, they believed he had a chance, obviously a biased opinion since the law firm stood to profit handsomely from this litigation. The major problem, as they explained countless times to their client, was that the chances of winning such a judgment against newspapers and other publications were slim — many had tried but almost as many had failed — primarily because of the difficulty of proving all of the conditions necessary for landing a libel decision.

Before the process got under way in earnest, Shalom felt that elementary ethics mandated his seeking an out-of-court settlement. Predictably, the *Gazette* did not want to hear of it; this did not prevent Shalom Fried from making several overtures, nevertheless.

Finally, he retained the legal firm of Eisenberg, Morgenstern and Vogel to sue on his behalf. Veteran of several libel suits, Gerald Morgenstern was well aware of the work that went into fighting what was always a formidable and arduous battle and, accordingly, set the terms at a hefty 40% contingency with a $50,000 retainer against it, the client agreeing to pay all of the costs on a monthly basis. To apprise Fried of what he would be in for, Morgenstern explained that there would be numerous depositions — 2,000 pages would be a conservative estimate, at $4.50 a page — and of course there were many other papers to file. Likewise, there would be significant court costs, the expense of an investigator, and last but certainly not least, the lawyer's fee of $350 an hour, charged against the retainer.

Shalom agreed, confident that he had hired the best counsel that his money could buy. He was less confident that he would be able to buy anything else once the litigation got under way.

In accord with accepted ethical practice, Morgenstern phoned Sidney Soltawicz to inquire who was his counsel.

"Whadja say your name was?... You're representing whom?... I can't believe he's doing this!" As soon as Soltawicz heard *lawyer*, "legal expenses" started running, somersaulting, and catapulting through his head.

"Mr. Soltawicz," Jerry Morgenstern intoned in that curious blend of gentlemanliness and legalese that forms an attorney's patois, "you invited my client to sue you. He accepted your invitation. I highly recommend that you confer with counsel who can competently advise you about the consequences which you face. Once you have, I would be eager to speak to your attorney so that we can settle the matter amicably without having to drag this mess into court... Certainly. My number is 555-5176."

Soltawicz did not call back and a few days later Morgenstern phoned again and repeated his message. The newspaper editor and publisher countered, "I'm a busy man. I have looked into the matter and after due consideration, I concluded it is not worth another minute of my time. The reporter who wrote the article has my complete confidence. His reportage is gold standard, absolutely unimpeachable, and certainly on par with the high level of journalistic integrity which is the hallmark of *The Heritage Gazette*. Since everything reported is true, you can tell your client he's welcome to go ahead and sue me."

Soltawicz was trying, quite effectively, to put up a brave front that would make Fried back down. Morgenstern informed Shalom of Soltawicz's response, but the decision had already been made and Shalom was determined to see it through. He wasn't going to capitulate now; he would call Soltawicz's bluff.

Two days later, a redheaded kid in his twenties, clad in a windbreaker and Reeboks, sauntered into the office of *The Heritage Gazette* and asked to see the editor and publisher. He was directed upstairs to a secretary, who was strategically seated in front of the office of the Editor-in-Chief.

"May I help you? Mr. Soltawicz is in a meeting now, and he cannot be interrup—"

Without so much as a thank you, the kid bolted through the door, pointed at the man behind the vast walnut desk and demanded, "Sidney Soltawicz?"

"Y...yes," admitted the startled publisher and editor, who regretted at once that he had revealed his identity, for before Soltawicz knew what had hit him, the kid had shoved a thick envelope into his hands and was out the door.

Bounding down the stairs like a mountain goat, the redheaded deputy sheriff pencilled on his duplicate of the complaint, "I served the defendant in person by handing him a copy."

To avoid a ruckus, Soltawicz instructed that the meeting resume, and of course the assembled staff did so without question. The paper's metropolitan editor continued to enumerate the stories she would be following, droning on as Soltawicz flipped through the pages of the complaint. Then he came to the final page. Suddenly the man lost all his composure. The ever-present cigar dropped from his gaping mouth and cartwheeled painfully across his expansive belly. "This Fried guy is nuts!" Soltawicz bellowed. "A million-five in compensatory damages?! And *eight*-and-a-half million in punitive damages!"

The *Gazette*'s publisher and editor needed no further encouragement to hire a lawyer. He grabbed the phone and within minutes retained the finest defamation defense counsel in the area: Campbell, Greenbaum.

According to the complaint, Soltawicz had twenty days to file an answer; his reply was filed in court less than two weeks later. In it he asserted that the *Gazette* had done a superb job of accurately and truthfully reporting the issue in question and was therefore filing a motion for summary judgment, seeking dismissal of the case.

The Plaintiff (Fried) filed a reply to the answer and the Defendant (Soltawicz) filed a rejoinder to the reply. A surrejoinder to the rejoinder and several papers later, the process was complete and the interrogatories began.

Scores of pages of questions went back and forth between the sides, but virtually every substantive question posed by the Plaintiff was stonewalled by the Defense under the Shield Law. Journalists are constitutionally protected from revealing their sources of information under the First Amendment, which ensures freedom of speech and freedom of the press. The Shield Law is derived from the First Amendment. If a reporter had to disclose the origin of his information, the theory goes, people would be reluctant to divulge what they know, and the news services would be inhibited.

By invoking the Shield Law, Campbell, Greenbaum had essentially created a peg on which to hang its hat, thereby blocking Morgenstern. But Jerry Morgenstern was unblockable. He decided to seek contempt of court penalties for the Defense's failure to fully answer the interrogatories, and filed for a hearing in Civil Motion Court.

At the hearing, Morgenstern argued that the Defense was playing games with the court process and should be liable for sanctions. Campbell smugly replied, "Whatever was not answered in the interrogatories is privileged information."

"What do you mean *privileged!*" Shalom's attorney shot back. "There's nothing protected here."

Oliver Campbell launched into a lengthy excursus about the function and legality of the Shield Law that guarantees a newspaper's ability to function. "My client's reporter gave his word to his source that his or her identity would not be revealed." Campbell, Greenbaum's senior partner, was as smooth, as suave, and as polished as they come.

Morgenstern knew all along that his client, like every other Plaintiff in a libel case, faced an uphill battle. It wasn't until he arrived at Motion Court that he realized how steep a hill it would be. Campbell would not let anything get by him and would do anything that an experienced and well-paid law firm could to quash the complaint.

The judge concurred that *The Heritage Gazette* was

entitled to First Amendment privileges. "The Court is duty-bound," he said self-importantly, "to uphold the freedom of the press, even in its broadest parameters. Nevertheless, the reporter may be questioned and he is instructed to answer the queries posed in the interrogatory about how many times he met with his source and if this particular source has ever given information before that was not corroborated. The Plaintiff," the judge explained, "has a right to know if the information was given orally to the reporter or if it was written. Furthermore, the Plaintiff is entitled to know if the reporter recorded the meeting with his informant or took notes; if the source's information is firsthand, if he or she has personal knowledge of what transpired, or if it was simply hearsay."

This was more than Morgenstern had dared hope for.

The Defense countered by claiming that answering most of the Plaintiff's questions would be tantamount to revelation. "If we reply, for example," Campbell pontificated, "that the source is a truck driver for Kosher Kuts, since there are only six such employees, the identity of the source can be easily discovered. This is a clear infringement of the Shield Law."

The judge rejected this argument. "The Court will determine what disclosure will be considered privileged information, Mr. Campbell." He peered intensely at the Defense attorney through bifocals that were half an inch thick. Campbell could not meet his gaze.

The session in Motion Court was viewed as a victory for the Plaintiff. Although Morgenstern was certain that the reporter would claim he had committed the information to memory (so that he wouldn't have to supply any documentation), at least he'd be able to get this guy on the stand and question him.

By the beginning of the following week Eisenberg, Morgenstern and Vogel had filed notice of deposition to a host of individuals. Only one day later, an even longer list was filed by Campbell, Greenbaum. Anyone familiar with Shalom's financial standing and any disgruntled customer who had ever stepped into Kosher Kuts was subpoenaed.

Two weeks after the depositions got under way, the judge scheduled a pre-settlement conference. The bench came down very hard to settle, and not bring the suit into court. Shalom was more than willing to accept, but the Defense would not hear of it.

"Under no circumstance," Oliver Campbell declared, "will *The Heritage Gazette* consider anything less than a full dismissal of the lawsuit."

A trial was scheduled for three months later, the honorable J. Franklin presiding.

As the burden of proof rested upon the Plaintiff, Fried's legal team had to prove that the article and suspect advertisement which appeared in *The Heritage Gazette* were false, intentional, or grossly negligent, that they had caused damage and that there had been no attempt by the paper to mitigate the damage, by retraction or otherwise.

During examination the Plaintiff proved each point. Even the toughest claim to substantiate, "caused damage," was corroborated by solid evidence. Shalom argued that his income had dropped by more than twenty percent in the nine months since the article had appeared in the paper, compared to the same period the year before. Depositions by other kosher meat wholesalers and retailers showed no significant decrease in their income between the two years; in fact, their revenues had increased, due most likely to their picking up some of Fried's ex-customers.

The Plaintiff called witnesses to testify that they used to patronize Kosher Kuts but when they read about the scandal in the *Gazette*, they had switched to other suppliers or retailers.

Morgenstern then called to the stand Bernard Rabinowitz, the reporter who had written the article, and began an assault on the man's credibility. "Obviously the court cannot force this reporter to divulge his confidential source," Morgenstern intoned with a slight dollop of cynicism, "but confidentiality has nothing to do with responsibility. This reporter, any reporter, must abide by minimal ethical and journalistic standards. It is through such integrity that a newspaper exhibits civic responsibility and achieves public trust."

At his signal, Morgenstern's assistant wheeled before the bench a cart stacked high with back issues of the *Gazette*. Appearing to be selecting copies at random, Jerry attacked article after article with the Rabinowitz byline, leaving the impression that the man consistently wrote about the sensational and showed blatant disregard for the truth. There were even items by Rabinowitz that were contradicted by other items that appeared in the very same issue of the paper!

"How in Heaven's name," Morgenstern asked rhetorically, "can we trust the reportage of a man who has no notes to submit to the court, who bases all of his stories upon uncorroborated information, and who has a reputation for, shall we say, sloppy research?"

The Defense objected to the accusation on the grounds that it was argumentative. Campbell's objection was sustained. Morgenstern switched tactics and began to discredit the reporter's memory.

Plaintiff: How many times did you speak to your editor yesterday?

Witness: Two or three.

Plaintiff: Is it two, or is it three?

Witness: I don't recall.

Plaintiff: Does the date "the second of April" have any significance to you?

Rabinowitz thought the question over for a moment before saying, "Two weeks to income taxes." This brought a titter from the court stenographer, but the judge's glare quickly silenced her.

"I repeat," Morgenstern went on, "*what* is the significance of April the second?"

"Nothing I can think of, except that it's two weeks before income tax returns must be filed."

Morgenstern went still. A perplexed look spread all over his face before he asked, "Isn't April the second your wedding anniversary?"

The judge, Joyce Franklin, a black woman with a medium-length Afro hairdo, part of it gone gray, laughed once, revealing a top row of oversized teeth.

"Mr. *Rabin*-owitz." Morgenstern's tone bristled with derision. The particular stress he gave to the witness' name caused a slight stir in the courtroom. "Would you kindly tell the Court the meaning of YH 23 07 63 24 77."

"I'm not sure." Rabinowitz's native arrogance was taking a beating. He could not figure out what Morgenstern was driving at.

"I repeat: YH 23 07 63 24 77."

No response.

"Is this not your license plate number followed by your telephone number, Mr. *Rabin*-owitz?" The journalist seemed to shrivel in his seat.

"As your memory appears to be failing you," Jerry oozed sarcastically, "I wonder if you would remember whether your competence as a reporter has ever been called into question. Has it, Mr. *Rabin*-owitz?"

Rabinowitz adjusted himself on the stand. The assault was in earnest. "No, sir," he replied, with as much self-assurance as he could muster.

Jerry's face registered mock surprise. "Really? Is it not true that over the years your paper has received numerous letters of complaint about the accuracy of your reporting?"

"I wouldn't know about that."

Morgenstern held up a plastic sleeve stuffed with clippings. He displayed the contents to Campbell and then presented it to Rabinowitz on the stand.

Averting his eyes, Rabinowitz muttered, "Only nuts write to newspapers." He immediately realized his blunder: the utter silence with which his statement was greeted told him that everyone present — including

Joyce Franklin — wrote letters to newspapers.

Morgenstern gingerly removed the sheaf from Rabinowitz's hands, as though it had become contaminated. There was an odd theatricality to Gerald Morgenstern — and he always played it so subtly that one could never tell when he was laying it on and when he was being sincere. Strolling back to the Plaintiff's table, he tossed a question over his shoulder. "Do you have any nicknames?"

Rabinowitz shifted in his chair, cleared his throat, and mopped his brow before replying. "Friends call me Bernie."

"Aside from that?"

"My mother calls me Berish."

"Aside from that?"

"I don't use nicknames."

"No, sir, not that *you* use."

"I don't understand the question."

"Has anybody ever referred to you as 'Rabid Rabinowitz'?"

Bernard Rabinowitz, a.k.a Rabid Rabinowitz, did some more shifting, throat-clearing and brow-mopping. "Could be," he mumbled at last.

"Let me refresh your memory. You acquired that nickname some years ago from one of the religious community's most distinguished leaders, Rabbi Abramson, in a somewhat unflattering context, did you not?"

"Your contention."

"Rabbi Abramson told you to your face, did he not, that you had caused immeasurable harm with your outrageous stories, and that in his opinion the only journalist as 'rabid' as you was Julius Streicher, editor of *Der Stürmer?*"

Laughter convulsed the courtroom. Even Franklin allowed herself a chuckle. This was the first time Morgenstern had abandoned his veneer of gentlemanliness; the kid gloves were off now and the witness reeled from the punch.

"I don't remember that," Rabid replied in a whisper when the room came to order again. He looked out at Morgenstern, cringing in anticipation of the next blow.

"I understand that you have a close personal friendship with Mr. Soltawicz aside from your business relationship."

"We're quite friendly." On this point, Rabid had apparently been well schooled. Feeling himself on safer ground, he visibly relaxed. He would acknowledge his closeness with Soltawicz to avoid being accused of deceit or evasiveness.

"How often have you discussed this libel case with Mr. Soltawicz since it began?"

"Many times." Rabid was taking no chances. He knew that if he quoted a numerical figure Morgenstern would trip him up somehow. Furthermore, subpoenas were out, and he had no way of knowing what records had been obtained.

"Did Mr. Soltawicz ever discuss with you why the feature which you wrote about Kosher Kuts was so important to him?"

"Pardon me?" Rabid puffed himself up, all self-righteous indignation. "The article elicited no more interest from the editor than any other investigative piece that goes into the paper. Mr. Soltawicz's concern for journalistic integrity knows no bounds and it is inconceivable that he would give one article particular weight for personal reasons." Rabinowitz looked over Morgenstern's shoulder to Campbell, who gave a small, almost imperceptible nod of approval.

"Mr. *Rabin*-owitz," Jerry continued, "is it your ambition, sir, to become the editor of *The Heritage Gazette?*"

"I would like one day to be the editor," Rabinowitz replied with remarkably little hesitation. "Of course," he added, rebounding quickly, "it would be nearly impossible to fill the shoes of Mr. Soltawicz, but when he eventually retires, I would hope to be a candidate."

"Mr. Soltawicz's successor, of course, will be determined exclusively by the paper's publisher — who happens to be the very same person. Would you agree, then, that it would be fair to say that if you stick your neck out for him now, you are doing more than just ensuring your present job, you are simultaneously investing wisely in your future?"

"Objection!" Campbell exclaimed and Judge Franklin quickly ruled, "Sustained." All the while, Rabinowitz blinked his eyes with apparent disdain.

Morgenstern wasn't about to lose the momentum. "You just referred to Mr. Soltawicz's journalistic integrity. Would you not consider tampering with news coverage in order to favor a patron as unethical?"

"Makes sense," Rabid agreed, but his answers were

coming more slowly now. He seemed unsure where Morgenstern was headed.

"Morally debased?"

"Er, I'd say so."

"Are you, as an investigative reporter, aware of any reason why Mr. Soltawicz would be interested in vilifying Kosher Kuts?"

"Mr. Soltawicz is a paragon of honesty."

"We are talking about a man who is on trial for libel! Now, please answer the question."

"No, I, uh, I can think of no reason or interest."

Jerry looked up at Judge Franklin. "Your Honor, may the court stenographer mark the last three questions and answers so that she can read them back later if need be?" Franklin so instructed.

Meanwhile, Rabinowitz conducted a slow study of the courtroom. He looked at the judge, the stenographer, finally the Plaintiff's table. He was actually grimacing now. The trap, whatever it was, had been set. Everyone in the room knew it. The stenographer attached a clip to the narrow scroll of notes.

"Is it your expert opinion as an investigative reporter, and one close to the inner workings of the *Gazette*, that Mr. Soltawicz would have no interest in promoting one 'Broadway Meating Place,' a patron of the paper, over Kosher Kuts?"

Rabinowitz looked at Morgenstern with narrowed eyes. He bent over the microphone before the witness chair and replied, "Yes."

"Please do not rush, Mr. *Rabin*-owitz. You are accustomed to working under tight deadlines and must digest a large quantity of information on a daily basis. Are you certain you do not wish to rethink your answer?"

"*The Heritage Gazette* is a newspaper and, as such, it is blind to who is a patron and who is not. Our job is to report the news, not to fashion it."

Morgenstern returned to the Plaintiff table, where his assistant was already holding aloft the document that he sought. Jerry dropped a copy with the Defense and delivered the original to Rabinowitz. "You are acquainted with Tova Lefkowitz?" he asked, glancing at the document.

"She's my secretary."

"Would you please read aloud the short passage marked by the paper clip on the deposition of Tova Lefkowitz taken on March 26." Morgenstern turned to Campbell. "Page 3, counsellor."

Rabinowitz had to change glasses. Donning the pair from his jacket pocket, he read: "'After Mr. Soltawicz left Bernie's office I was called in to take dictation. Apparently an ad had to go into the paper right away and they were holding the presses for the copy. I knew that there had to be a terrible rush, since although Bernie often writes the copy for ads, he usually does it by himself, and almost never gives me dictation for them.

"'He dictated an ad to me about strict halachic observance and after checking a piece of paper the boss had given him — I recognized Mr. S's handwriting — he told me to head the copy in bold letters: The Ad Hoc

Committee for Halachic Observance.'" Rabinowitz scanned the sheet from which he had just read and began to frown.

Silence descended over the courtroom as Rabid Rabinowitz and his testimony disintegrated before their eyes.

"That will be all," Morgenstern concluded.

Campbell saw little purpose in cross-examining Rabinowitz. He feared that so much damage had been wreaked during the examination, it would be hard to undo it with a witness whose credibility had been utterly shattered.

It was now the Defense's turn to call witnesses and Campbell launched a four-pronged, acerbic attack aimed at bouncing Fried out of court.

Campbell, Greenbaum had subpoenaed all of Shalom's financial records, and had scrutinized them carefully for evidence of a long history of poor financial standing. Naturally, they found suppliers to whom Shalom owed money. It was standard in the trade to have outstanding debts, but of course the Defense did not call upon witnesses who would testify that this was the norm. The Defense was so selective in the suppliers that it did call to testify that Morgenstern could not get even one to concede in the cross that delaying payment was an accepted practice.

Worse yet, Morgenstern realized that he had no way of neutralizing their damning testimony. Very simply put, he had underestimated his opponent in this regard and had overlooked this angle of the case. It was

Morgenstern's first mistake.

By the time the Defense had finished going through all of Shalom's financial records with a fine-tooth comb, it appeared that for years Kosher Kuts had been running a marginally profitable business with a bad name in the trade. Hence, argued the Defense, suing *The Heritage Gazette* for millions of dollars was Shalom Fried's potentially lucrative alternative to declaring bankruptcy.

The Defense had hired a team of investigators that went door-knocking throughout the neighborhoods where Kosher Kuts' customers lived. After canvassing several hundred people, they found what they were looking for. The first witness called to the stand was a rheumy-eyed, loquacious, septuagenarian.

Defense: Mrs. Halberstam, how long have you been shopping at the Kosher Kuts retail outlet?

Witness: Ever since it opened, about ten or eleven years ago.

Defense: Do you still shop there?

Witness: No, I stopped buying there about two years ago.

Defense: Would you care to tell us why it is that you stopped giving your business to Kosher Kuts?

Witness: Well, one day I walked into the store with my friend Elaine Plotkin, I always go shopping with my friend Elaine, and suddenly she, that is Elaine, sees a new sign displayed in the glass showcase. Elaine, that's my friend, doesn't make much of it, but she points it out to me. I couldn't believe my eyes! Without any warning the store switched it's *hechsher*...

"Switched its *what*?" Judge Franklin interrupted.

"Its kosher certification, your Honor," Campbell explained. The judge nodded. "Please proceed, Mrs. Halberstam."

"Well, as I was saying, Kosher Kuts had switched its *hechsher*. I told my friend Elaine that we had better get out of there.

"She, that is, Elaine, wasn't very happy about leaving because she wanted to buy some chicken livers. But I told her that if she wanted to be my friend, and of course she did, she had better not patronize a kosher meat store that switches it's certification overnight. The whole thing seems pretty fishy, if you ask me. It just doesn't sound reliable to switch like that, and my friend Elaine agreed in the end. I like to have the confidence that comes from shopping at a store that is predictable.

"As soon as we stepped outside, I saw Mildred Tauber about to enter and I told her what we saw. And you know what the funny thing was?"

"What?" asked Oliver Campbell, a bit disappointed in this witness' testimony.

"She *also* wanted to buy chicken livers!"

The next battery of witnesses was more convincing than Mrs. Halberstam. According to Shalom, the Defense didn't miss calling a single dissatisfied customer who had left him over the years.

Rabbi Rudinsky, the *mashgiach* who had issued Kosher Kuts its original *hechsher*, was called upon to testify. The Defense made it appear that Rudinsky had actually *withdrawn* his kosher certification. The rabbi, still peeved over his loss of business, and lacking *glatt*-kosher ethics, did little to imply that his *hechsher* simply had not been *renewed*; it had been replaced by a more widely known and more reliable *hashgachah*.

Rabbi Rudinsky sat in the stand facing Campbell with limp indifference. His hands at his side, his face placid, to the court he looked like a man without need of expression. Campbell touted him as a scientist, an unaffected observer of facts, and undeniably the world's expert on the laws of Kashruth.

Rudinsky's halachic terminology and his unusual speech patterns caused the court stenographer to interrupt a number of times to ask for answers to be repeated or spelled out. Although the man had no apparent personality, his knowledgeability and confidence made for very impressive and convincing testimony.

The scene in the court was moderately comic and extremely tragic: a gentile lawyer was arguing in front of a Black judge that Shalom Fried had a low standard of *kashrus*. "...Little wonder, that a man who lost his 'hekshaw' would carry non-kosher meat on his truck..."

Once Campbell established a basis for discrediting Shalom's financial standing and the *kashrus* level of his business, he proceeded to chip away at the individual.

"Kashruth," Oliver Campbell explained to the court, "connotes far more than conformity to dietary restrictions. It is synonymous with purity and integrity, and is the antithesis of mercenary and selfish incentive."

One would imagine that it would be impossible to sling mud at an honest and well-liked individual like Shalom Fried. Oliver Campbell Esq. proved, however, that if a legal team was well-enough funded it could penetrate the impervious.

Shalom's outspoken aversion to impropriety had caused him some detractors over the years, and it seemed that Campbell, Greenbaum Inc. knew exactly where to find them. Individuals with few scruples, they were eager to settle a score and allowed Campbell to weave from their testimony a tapestry which portrayed Fried as an "unkosher" wretch.

"You see, your Honor, the man lives a double standard. He claims to sell strictly kosher meat, but he has a strictly unkosher lifestyle, as we have just heard. For the man to sell *non*-kosher meat would be far more in consonance with his hypocritical personality.

"Mr. Fried has made a sham of our judicial system and clogged up our courts by protesting — as libelous, no less — a claim which so many would readily believe as true even if they had not read it in a quality newspaper. This case should have been dismissed long ago, but I have yet to prove with incontrovertible testimony that the story which appeared in my client's paper was factual."

Up until this point Campbell had presented no hard evidence to prove that non-kosher meat had actually been found aboard one of Kosher Kuts' trucks. Usually the thrust of the Defense is aimed at discrediting the Plaintiff where the accusation leveled against the Defendant cannot be solidly refuted. This was the track the Defense had followed so far, and the trial had proceeded by and large the way Morgenstern had predicted.

The mention of "incontrovertible testimony," however, put Jerry visibly on edge. What hard evidence could the Defense have mustered? Morgenstern feared his second mistake.

"The Defense calls to the stand Mr. Willie King."

"Who's that?" Jerry whispered to Shalom.

"One of the workers in my warehouse. I can't imagine he would say anything against me."

"Objection," Morgenstern called, rising to his feet. "Your Honor, discovery violated..."

Before he could finish, Campbell cut in with, "Your Honor, there were exigent circumstances. We just found out about this witness late last night, too late for me to call Mr. Morgenstern. We exercised due diligence and acted in good faith and surely would have made our revelation known earlier had we only known about this witness beforehand.

"And your Honor, we have another witness that we just found out about and did not list in our pre-trial roster. My assistant has this minute walked in and informed me of his existence. Here, too, we claim exigent circumstances and feel that it is vital for the Defense to hear the testimony of Paul Taliaferro, garage attendant for Arctic Refrigeration Services."

"Objection, your Honor." Morgenstern remained on his feet.

Judge Franklin held up her hand and addressed the courtroom. "As the Defense claims that it exercised due diligence and acted in good faith, coupled with the fact that counsel contends that this testimony is crucial, the court will allow these two witnesses to take the stand and testify. However, in order not to prejudice the Plaintiff, I will grant a two-day recess so that this matter may be investigated fully."

"Thank you, your Honor," Jerry said, and collected his papers as the gavel came down.

❧

Willie King testified that numerous times, virtually on a weekly basis, he asked the truckers to take packages for him to locations along their route, and they always obliged.

"Here is a worker," Campbell's intonation ascended for dramatic effect, "at a supposedly 'kosher' establishment, sending packages on a regular basis all over town aboard Kosher Kuts trucks. God only knows what Mr. King and others have sent aboard the trucks, but I don't think I will be surprising anyone in this courtroom if I reveal that Mr. King does not maintain a kosher diet." Chuckles erupted throughout the courtroom, especially from the Defense table.

"This trespass, obviously a minor infraction under normal circumstances, is a major violation when it comes to a kosher establishment. This has been done right under the nose of Mr. Fried for years, and he has been none the wiser!"

King was a very strong witness for the Defense. He was obviously neither schooled nor primed by counsel about how to testify and his testimony was very damning to the Plaintiff.

Morgenstern suspected that this witness had been suborned. Why else would he come forward when his testimony was certain to cost him his job? However, it was conceivable that he was close to retirement age, or possibly sightly past it, so that his pension was secure.

Jerry decided not to risk challenging him.

Willie King was followed by Paul Taliaferro, an attendant who worked for the garage that serviced Kosher Kuts' refrigeration trucks. According to the attendant, on February 14th, that is, just three weeks before the story broke in *The Heritage Gazette*, the owner of a meat packing company in South Hills phoned Arctic and said that he urgently needed to borrow a truck for the morning. All but one of his trucks were out of town and the one nearby had broken down on its way to an important delivery.

Taliaferro said that the owner of the South Hills firm was a very big customer of Arctic. He had at least one vehicle of his fleet in for repair once a month. Swearing everyone to secrecy, the superintendent at Arctic allowed a Kosher Kuts truck — whose repairs had already been completed — to be borrowed by the South Hills firm for the morning.

On cross, Morgenstern failed to shake Taliaferro's memory of the events. The only thing he did manage to prove — at best a Pyrrhic victory — was that Paul Taliaferro had never spoken to Rabid or anyone else about the matter.

The Defense now had the upper hand. No one was convinced that the *Gazette* article was honest reportage, but after what the court had just heard, it hardly seemed libelous. It may have been false, but not intentionally, nor had gross negligence been demonstrated. Without fulfilling *each and every* criterion of libel, a judgment would not be awarded.

Campbell had sufficiently undermined the Plaintiff's case to now call his star witness, the one who would leave the strongest and most lasting impression. Sidney Soltawicz, editor and publisher of *The Heritage Gazette*, took the stand.

In well-rehearsed testimony, the Defense established the integrity of the *Gazette*'s editor and publisher and his respected position in the Jewish community. Mention was made of numerous testimonials by communal leaders, elected officials, and editors of other publications which lauded the *Gazette*. The Defense also firmly established that Soltawicz had never met or spoken to Fried before the feature appeared in his paper. Personal malice seemed a remote possibility as a motive for the alleged fabrication.

After Campbell's and Soltawicz's masterful performance Morgenstern needed a miracle to win the court's agreement that all the conditions of libel had been fulfilled. For the first time Shalom Fried was truly concerned about the outcome of the trial. He had read once that a jury never looks at a man they are going to convict, and it seemed to him that from the time King had testified, Judge Franklin no longer looked at him. Remarkably, Jerry seemed less concerned.

"What are you going to do now?" Shalom asked his counsel.

"One of the first techniques they teach you at law school is to lay the foundation."

Shalom gave Jerry a quizzical look, begging an explanation. "I have to lay a foundation," Morgenstern explained, "so that I can get the witness to contradict himself on the premise that he has already agreed to."

"Can you?"

"Can I?" Jerry repeated the question. "I can. Will I? I don't know." On that sobering note, Gerald Morgenstern commenced his cross-examination by, as he had put it, laying the foundation.

"Mr. Soltawicz," the lawyer intoned, solemnly pacing before the bench with his hands clasped behind him, "it has been duly established before this court that you and your paper have high standards. Am I correct in concluding that the high standards are a direct result of your personal involvement and supervision of every aspect of the paper?"

"That would be a fair assessment."

"It would follow, therefore, that not only are you in strict control of the editorial and journalistic aspects of the paper, but that you also run a tight ship regarding all of the managerial matters related to the *Gazette*'s publication. Is this correct?"

Soltawicz, assuming that he had to maintain a front of total responsibility, agreed to this suggestion as well.

"How many full-time employees are there at *The Heritage Gazette*?"

"Fifty-six, including myself."

"Are you certain of this figure?" Jerry's questions were coming rapid-fire now.

"Most definitely — I sign their checks."

"Do you know how many printing presses there are in your press room?"

"Can you name the paper suppliers you use?"

"Have you any idea how many trucks are employed to deliver your paper?"

Soltawicz answered each question as if he had prepared in advance.

"About how many offices are there in your building?"

Soltawicz thought for a moment before replying, "Seventeen."

Jerry then moved back from the office details of the *Gazette* to the details of news coverage. So far there was little in Morgenstern's questioning that Campbell had not prepared his client for, not that a clever man like Soltawicz could be easily tripped up even without priming.

"Could a story go into your newspaper without your knowledge?"

"If I am not on vacation, at which time I delegate authority, this would be a virtual impossibility since I check over everything for accuracy and editorial content before the paper goes to press."

Having barely wet his feet in this area, Jerry did another one of his element-of-surprise shifts of subject. Apparently he felt that the foundation had been established.

"I understand that your sister is married to the owner of The Broadway Meating Place."

"Objection, your Honor!" Campbell rose to his feet. "What difference does it make whom his sister is married to?"

"Your Honor," Morgenstern interjected urgently,

"may I see you at a side bar?"

"Why a side bar?" the Defense attorney challenged.

"It will become abundantly clear."

The judge nodded for counsel to approach the bench. As soon as Morgenstern drew near he said that he sought greater confidentiality and wished to speak to the judge out of the witness' earshot. Franklin tossed him a dubious look over her half-moon glasses, but when Jerry stressed how important it was, she agreed to see both attorneys in her chambers.

Inside, Morgenstern pressed the judge not to sustain the Defense's objection. The line he was about to develop established the entire bias and malicious intent of the defendant. Considering the weakness of the Plaintiff's position, Franklin agreed.

Both parties returned from the side bar and the judge overruled the Defense's objection.

"Do you," inquired Morgenstern, "have anything to do with the business?"

"What business?" answered Soltawicz, all innocence and incredulity.

"The meat business."

"Oh... that. No, I have nothing at all to do with the meat business. I have more than enough to do taking care of my newspaper."

"If you have nothing to do with the meat business, how is it that there are no invoices or receipts for the ads which Broadway Meating inserts in your paper?"

"Objection."

"Sustained. I must caution you, Mr. Morgenstern, that this does not bear directly on the issue of libel."

As Morgenstern's questions grew increasingly more pointed, it became evident to the trained eye that Campbell was trying through subtle body language to counsel his client how to respond.

"I'm sorry, your Honor," Jerry apologized, and then, appearing to abandon the track he wished to pursue, he retreated to an area he had already covered extensively. "Mr. Soltawicz, would you care to tell me how many telephone receptionists your newspaper has?"

"How many phone lines are there in your office?" Again Morgenstern used his machine-gun technique.

"Who pays the phone bills?"

"The accounting department, of course." Soltawicz did not know why Morgenstern had reverted to beating a dead horse, unless, of course, he had nothing left in his arsenal and was stalling for time. If Jerry could get the case pushed over to the next day, some new insight might occur to him overnight. "I have already told you that I sign the checks, and that goes not only for the employees, but for machinery, the coffee and sugar, and also the phone bills."

"How many phone numbers are there at the paper?"

"Objection."

Jerry winced. Shalom couldn't tell if Campbell was objecting to whatever it was that Morgenstern was driving at, or to the repeated harping on a subject that had been adequately chewed over.

Morgenstern sought another side bar, realizing

that Franklin would not grant him a second audience *in camera*. He strode over to the bench and, in a hushed tone that would not carry to the witness stand, implored her Honor to permit him to pose a series of questions about the existence of a private phone line and who pays its phone bill. Campbell vigorously protested, but Morgenstern cut him off by saying, "My client's case is contingent on this point alone." Franklin gave him a skeptical glance. Under normal circumstances she would not capitulate to such hyperbole, but she had adjudicated in other cases where Morgenstern had served as counsel and she felt certain this was not a line that he would use lightly.

"All right," she said, "I'll indulge you this final time." As the two attorneys resumed their positions, Campbell began to communicate in a veiled way to his client.

"Objection overruled."

The Defense attorney then motioned for a recess, and simultaneously Soltawicz turned to Franklin and explained that he urgently needed to use the facilities. The judge was just about to agree when Morgenstern stood defiantly behind his desk and stated, "I respectfully request that your Honor admonish the witness not to discuss his testimony with anyone, including his counsel." And the judge complied.

Morgenstern instructed his investigator, whom he had made sure would be in court that day, to follow Soltawicz to the bathroom and anywhere else he might go. Jerry told his assistant to follow Campbell.

❀

The court reconvened and Morgenstern took a slow

walking tour of the court. His hand traced the polished wood railing over to the jury box, he turned to inspect Judge Franklin on her throne, he looked the witness over, and then he returned to the Plaintiff's table from where he had started. When he found what appeared to be a comfortable spot he repeated, "How many phone numbers are there at the newspaper?"

"Seven."

"Would you care to enumerate for us all of the phone numbers?"

Not wishing to make a gaffe even remotely related to Rabid's, Soltawicz pulled out a small diary from his breast pocket and read out seven different numbers.

"Could it be that you have forgotten any of your phone numbers?"

Soltawicz looked out to Campbell, but this time Franklin, thanks to a subtle hint Morgenstern provided at the side bar, was onto his little tricks.

"I think that's..."

He had not quite finished his response when the judge interrupted.

"Just a minute," Joyce Franklin bellowed. "Just *one* minute. Let the record show that Defense attorney Campbell has just made a gesture which is evidently a signal to the witness in connection with his last answers. Proceed, Mr. Morgenstern."

Campbell was crimson as he struggled to his feet.

"Why, your Honor, I really don't know what gesture you are referring to."

"I am not blind, Mr. Campbell." She raised the gavel, pointed it at Morgenstern and said, "Proceed."

"Does the phone number KLapton 5-5322 sound familiar to you?"

"I don't think so," Soltawicz replied, making a show of searching his pocket diary. "No."

Morgenstern seized the initiative. "Mr. Soltawicz, if you indeed have high standards, as you have taken great trouble to prove to this court, and, as you have also demonstrated, can remember the smallest minutiae with meticulous detail, what I am asking is not unreasonable. Based on what you have testified, you should remember, or at least have written along with the other phone numbers of your newspaper, this final, *unlisted* phone number."

Jerry paused for a moment, for dramatic affect, and then dropped his bombshell. "Is it not true, sir, that the KLapton 5 number, whose unlisted address is the same as that of your paper, is also the phone number of the Ad Hoc Committee for Halachic Observance?"

The stenographer looked up at this revelation and took in a quick breath of utter astonishment. Sidney Soltawicz looked as if he'd just swallowed a bottle of Tabasco sauce.

"And is it not true that the phone bills for this phone number are paid by The Broadway Meating Place?"

"I don't think that's relevant," the Defendant responded weakly.

"Well, I certainly do!" thundered the judge, her glasses virtually careening off her nose.

Campbell asked for a meeting in the judge's chambers. Jerry turned to his client and whispered triumphantly, "We've got 'em now, and they know it!" Morgenstern's jubilation was twofold: Not only had the case taken a decisive turn, that is, opened the way for a favorable judgment, but Jerry was also looking forward to the opportunity of humbling a libeler. The expression on Shalom's face, however, stopped him cold. Fried, oddly enough, looked as though he actually felt sorry for Soltawicz!

As the two lawyers adjourned to the judge's chambers, Soltawicz crooked a finger at Shalom, beckoning him to approach, and said condescendingly, "You have been pushing all along for an out-of-court settlement. I might be prepared to consider one now."

Shalom looked up at the man who had assassinated his character and had caused him so much harm, the man whose nonchalant response to protests that he'd printed ruinous lies was, "Sue me." This was the very same man who had refused adjudication according to Torah law and failed to heed three summonses from the *beis din*.

It was now clear that the only thing that could move Sidney Soltawicz to an act of contrition was fear of a major court loss and the notoriety that would accompany it. The loss wouldn't ruin him, but it would serve as a reminder and deterrent the next time he contemplated destroying someone's life with the stroke of his pen.

Shalom didn't hesitate for a moment. "All I want from you is a retraction, my legal fees, and a commitment that your paper will never again print libelous, unfounded, or biased reportage."

Soltawicz's eyes lit up. "I think it can be arranged."

Morgenstern emerged from chambers and headed towards Shalom looking very confident. But his satisfied smile quickly faded when Shalom informed him of the arrangement he'd made with the *Gazette*.

Morgenstern went from incredulity to rage. "You mean you don't want the money damages you've won?!" he spluttered. "But you deserve compensation! And how can you trust this shark to print a retraction? He'll retract by saying that an error was made and then somehow *still* figure out a way to blame you. This is crazy! What could possibly have prompted you to do such a thing?"

Shalom's answer was succinct: "Haven't you ever heard of '*shalom*' before? It's a tradition in my family!"

Heard from: Rabbis Ezriel Erlanger and Chaim Flam

Grave Doubts

LIBERTY, MONTICELLO, Swan Lake, Ellenville. This is the buckle of the "borscht belt." For most of the year this area is comprised of a series of sleepy little villages strung out alongside the highways and byways of the Catskill Mountains region of upstate New York. Typically, these samples of Americana consist of a main street, several shops, a gas station, and a special corner where bored kids and unemployed adults hang out.

From June to September, however, the Catskills — better known as simply The Mountians — undergo a dramatic transformation. Quiet country lanes turn into clogged arteries. Prices for food, clothing and rent skyrocket. Noise levels become higher, tempers shorter. And chaos reigns supreme: the Jews are back!

Like the swallows returning to Capistrano, thousands of Jews from all over New York City make a yearly pilgrimage to the land of their forefathers and country cousins. In its heyday, the Catskills had dozens of exclusive and expensive resort hotels where the well-to-do invested as much energy in their relaxation as they ever did in their work.

Today, only a few of these "international resorts" remain, but in their place you'll find summer camps, vacation homes, and bungalow colonies by the hundreds. You'll also find scenes that are hard to imagine anywhere else: chassidic men and women hitchhiking (in separate groups, of course) along Route 42; little boys with long *peyos* and woolen *tzitzis* sharing the sidewalk with the redneck natives of Ferndale and South Fallsburgh; empty parking lots turning into impromptu flea markets and swarming with transplanted bargain-hunting matrons from Queens and Brooklyn.

Max Weiss was an exception to the avalanche of humanity that hit the Catskills every spring and summer. He lived there all year 'round in a colony known as "Weiss Acres." In its previous incarnation, Weiss Acres was called the Dairyland Hotel, a rambling country house that had its own peculiar clientele — people who wanted to be *near* those who could afford the best. The Dairyland advertised that all the "big names" in entertainment had played there. And they may have — when they were little kids, not show biz celebrities! At the Dairyland Hotel, the only "live" entertainment you could find was shuffleboard, pinochle, mah-jongg, bingo and other low-impact athletics. It was a low-budget vacation geared to a generation that knew how to pinch a penny until it cried "Ouch!"

Eventually, the men and women of that generation passed on, and the Dairyland Hotel was simply abandoned. Max Weiss bought the property from the heirs of the original owners, not for the hotel, but for the bungalows that used to house the staff. He felt that they would make a good investment. And they did. For years, he rented them out to his *landsleit*: people who hailed from his hometown in Hungary. The money he made during the summer provided him with enough to live on for the rest of the year.

Max was married to Miriam Herskowicz, but they had found each other very late in life and to their regret never had children. Throughout their years as the landlords of Weiss Acres, Max and Miriam kept to themselves. It's not that they were unsociable. It's just that they got along best with one another. In time, they became so close that they could practically dispense with language; a word, a glance, an inflection was enough to communicate volumes.

"Papa..." Miriam would say in a special tone of voice.

"Okay, Mama, okay. I'll go into town to do the shopping," he would reply, "and then I'll fix the leaky roof."

For more than thirty years, Max and Miriam appeared to be as inseparable as a couple could be, and when Miriam died, a part of Max died with her. He became withdrawn, silent, reclusive — alone with his thoughts and his memories. Even the people who stayed at his bungalow colony could tell the difference, as Max became progressively more bitter. Many of them left in mid-season, and did not return the following year.

After the "regulars" stopped coming, new groups of

vacationers took their place, but with each passing year the groups grew smaller. There was virtually no repeat business, and nasty rumors about Weiss began to circulate. Many spoke of "Max the Maniac" — the short-tempered, mean-spirited old codger who ran the colony. They said he would stalk the grounds after midnight, a haunted look in his eyes and mayhem in his heart. Eventually the vacationers stopped coming altogether.

One spring day, a van drove up the winding road that ran off Route 42. It had been years since anyone had stopped by to inquire about renting a bungalow, and the whole place had a desolate feel to it. When Miriam was still alive, Max had always kept up the grounds, painting the exterior of the "big house" annually even though it was not in use. Miriam wouldn't have had it any other way. But Miriam was gone and Max had just let everything slide.

Max stepped out onto the porch, scowling at the approaching vehicle. The van came to a halt in front of him. The doors opened and two young men stepped out. "Shalom aleichem," the taller of the two said cordially. "My name is Yossie Schneider and this is Akiva Berg."

"Hmph. I'm Weiss. Whaddaya want?"

"Mr. Weiss, we're from Bnai Dovid — that's a yeshiva in Brooklyn. Our yeshiva is looking for a summer home. Mrs. Stein, the real estate agent in Woodbourne, told us about the Dairyland Hotel. Would you mind if we looked at it?"

"Suit yourself. But it's 'Weiss Acres,' and the hotel is closed. Hasn't been used in years."

"That's okay," Kivi said. "We need a place for our beis midrash and most of the properties around here just aren't big enough for us."

"If we could get it into shape, I think this place might suit our yeshiva very well," Yossie added.

Max let Yossie and Kivi tour the grounds on their own. They began with the main house. After passing through the "suites" and the kitchen facilities, they came to the dining hall, a cavernous, high-ceilinged room large enough to hold 250 people. Empty chairs were scattered around, some positioned at the few remaining tables, to ghostly effect. "If you listen carefully, you can almost hear conversations still lingering in the air," Kivi said uncharacteristically. The place is really getting to him, Yossie thought, if he's hearing voices. Maybe it was just the wind and the echo of their footsteps. Then Yossie imagined the whispered sound of conversation too, but to him, it wasn't voices from the past, it was voices of the future — the future of Bnai Dovid.

No matter how hard they tried, Yossie and Kivi couldn't hide their enthusiasm. "Mr. Weiss," Yossie exclaimed, "this is perfect!"

Kivi agreed. "It sure is. In fact, it's ideal. I can't believe it! Is it available?"

Max Weiss looked at the two boys and something stirred inside him. A tiny spark seemed to flicker in his eyes. "Maybe," he said gruffly. "Let's talk."

And so it happened that the Dairyland Hotel, that is, Weiss Acres, got a new lease on life as the summer home of Bnai Dovid Yeshiva. When Yossie Schneider said it was ideal, he had no idea *how* ideal, but he soon found out. Although the main house had been boarded up and looked a bit shabby inside and out, everything was in surprisingly good working order. A paint job and some minor repairs were all that was needed to render it habitable. The hotel dining room was able to hold the *beis midrash*, while the rooms and suites would accommodate the students. The "tea room," which was adjacent to the dining room and kitchen, had a huge terrace which, when enclosed and incorporated with the tea room, would create a space that was ample for the entire yeshiva to eat their meals together. The *rebbeim* and their families would enjoy the relative privacy of the bungalows.

During the winter months, Max would serve as the "watchman," keeping an eye on the place, but during the summer, he would have no responsibilities at all. In exchange for turning the property over to the yeshiva, he received a sizeable cash settlement, and would be entitled to free room and board for the rest of his life. The yeshiva undertook to see to his final arrangements, after 120 years.

From the moment the deal was done, Weiss Acres became a hive of activity as never before. Workmen assaulted the place and whipped it into shape. In a matter of days, the yeshiva moved in, settled in, and settled down to the business of learning Torah. But despite the dramatic changes, Max remained untouched and unmoved. He still kept to himself and avoided any social contact. If anything, his reclusiveness increased, his brusque manner intensified, and his isolation from humanity was total, or nearly so.

Yossie Schneider was the single impediment to Max's complete disengagement from the human race. When he wasn't learning or teaching some of the younger students, Yossie would often seek the old man out. "Mr. Weiss, please come to a *shiur*," he would say. "You'll enjoy it. You really will!"

Max's reply never varied. A grunt of scorn or a snort of disdain was the most Yossie ever got for his efforts.

"You can't fool me, Mr. Weiss, I've heard you daven," Yossie said one day, trying a new approach. "Come on, you belong with us." Yossie expected the usual response, but as he turned to leave, he heard Max clear his throat. Yossie froze in his tracks and dared not breathe, afraid any sudden sound or movement would deter the elderly Weiss from taking this first tentative step into the outside world.

Max cleared his throat again and said, "I appreciate your invitations, but I'm... I don't want company. Since my wife passed away..." — he winced as he said the words — "it's hard for me to... to be in a crowd. We were very close, Mama and I and, it, well..." Max's eyes brimmed with tears, and his voice cracked as he blurted out, "It's not easy... you understand."

"I'm sorry for your loss," Schneider said with feeling, "and I do understand, but please believe me, you are welcome to join us any time."

Max nodded his head, looked away, and shuffled off.

This conversation, and variations of it, were repeated for several years. When Yossie got married, Max didn't come to the wedding, but Yossie could tell that Max was happy for him in his own private way. When Yossie's son was born, he invited Max to the bris. Weiss didn't attend, but that was all right; Yossie had come to respect Max for his silent struggle. Although he had heard the "Max the Maniac" rumors, he himself had never seen Weiss angry — not even when some of the younger boys made a racket around his bungalow. And while the old man did take late-night strolls around the grounds, he never ever committed any "mayhem."

The passing years took their toll on Max, and Yossie was keenly aware of it. Max became even more withdrawn, if possible, walking the property for hours on end, talking to himself. Yossie wanted to slow down the march of time and hold on to his silent friendship with the old man, but it was not to be. One evening as he was putting his younger children to bed, he received a call that he had known would one day come. The boys had found Max by his bungalow, slumped in his chair. A rebbe had called the HATZOLOH rescue service, and although they arrived in record time, it was too late. Max was gone.

Quite naturally, it fell to Yossie's lot to make Max's funeral arrangements, but never having done this before, he took Kivi along for support. At the local Jewish funeral home they met Sanford J. Siegel, R.E. (Registered Embalmer to his professional associates; Rich Embezzler to those who were unfortunate enough to require his services).

A youthful overdose of comic books had painted a picture in Yossie's mind of the tall, somber funeral director, attired in black tie and tails, with dull slicked-back hair, pursed lips and receding chin. This image was off by light-years. Sanford Siegel was a Catskill Mountain version of a used-car salesman.

The glitter of greed that lit up Siegel's eyes when he found the naive-looking young men on his doorstep was all they needed to make them lose their innocence.

"Remember, you're not just buyin a box," Siegel

began in a gravelly voice, "you're makin a statement about your love for the dear departed. So lemme show you this here number." He had a way of imbuing the sad duty of choosing a casket with the atmosphere of Bingo Night in Brooklyn. "It's our top-of-the-line enamel job. Just look at this baby." He gestured with his rank-smelling cigar, showering ash all over his yellow-and-green plaid sports jacket. "Comes in four fashion colors: classic burgundy, which is the one everybody's buyin this year; indigo for that formal look; fire-engine red for people who prefer something a little more ah, if you'll excuse the expression... lively; and my personal favorite, ten-mile orange — it glows in the dark. We got matchin leather padding inside and a light that goes on when you lift the top."

"Please, please," Yossie begged. "We're only interested in a plain pine coffin, according to Jewish —"

"Or how about our nautical model," Siegel interrupted, clearly carried away by his own sales pitch.

"You have a *nautical model* casket?" Kivi asked, stunned at the thought that something like that could actually exist.

"Yeah — it's got portholes! The dear departed can look out and see all those who came to wish him *bon voyage* on his last journey! We call it the Titanic Ta-Ta." Siegel huffed on one of the round windows and polished it with his sleeve.

"That's a very comforting thought," Yossie said dryly.

"Comfort? You want comfort?" With sausage-like fingers he patted a stainless steel sarcophagus. "This here's our orthopedic model — Spinal Taps — specially designed to give the dear departed the rest of his life, for the rest of his li—"

"Mr. Siegel!" Yossie cut him off. "I want a plain wooden box. Do you understand? A plain wooden box."

"Okay, okay, wood. How bout the Bobby Fischer Bye-Bye, for chess enthusiasts. Made of wood, of course, and it comes in your basic black — African ebony — or basic white, from American birch."

"Stop! Please! No LeMans, no Titanic, no Bobby Fischer. Plain wood."

"Will that be Philippine mahogany, Indian teak or Brazilian rosewood? I can get you walnut, if you like. The pecan is nice, but it takes a couple weeks. As long as you're waitin, for just a few grand more, we can even have a biography of your loved one carved on the outside for future generations."

"How about a pine box. No handles. No power steering or power brakes. No wall-to-wall carpeting or fancy upholstery, or tinted glass. Just plain, simple pine — the kind that is kosher according to Jewish Law."

"Okay, okay. You win. Plain, simple, no scrollwork. The Woolworth Special. I can't guarantee that it'll hold up, you realize. Now, the fiberglass numbers..." he added, his voice rising with enthusiasm, "those things are made to last. Guaranteed to protect your loved one from fire, wind, earthquakes, hurricanes and other natural and man-made disasters for a period of seven hundred years or your money'll be cheerfully refunded to whoever is left to receive it."

"The discussion is closed. I've made my decision," Yossie stated sternly. "Now Mr. Weiss is making his: he wants to be buried next to his beloved wife Miriam."

"Yeah, yeah, beloved wife," Sanford Siegel sneered, clearly put out at not being able to sell Yossie a $22,000 casket. "I know all about it. What I don't know is why he would want to be buried next to her. I mean, I've known Max Weiss for maybe a hundred years, and believe me that was no lovin spouse, if you get my drift. He didn't even come to her funeral. And far as I know, he never visited her grave. Now don't go givin me that 'you-shouldn't-speak-bad-about-the-dead' look. I knew Miriam when she was still single — Herskowicz, her name was — and she was a good woman. But since she died, Weiss forgot all about her."

"What are talking about?" Yossie felt his face burn with anger. "There must be some mistake. He loved his wife. He told me so."

"If you ask me, he told you what you wanted to hear. He didn't even care enough about her to go to her funeral. He didn't visit afterwards. And he didn't even pay for perpetual care. See for yourself — the grave's Weed City."

"I don't believe you," Yossie said hotly, appalled at the slander Siegel was dumping on Max.

"So don't believe me. I was at her funeral. Max wasn't. You don't trust me? Ask Clara Shulman. She lived at Weiss Acres for years. She left because she couldn't stand the way he treated his wife."

"Mr. Siegel, I don't want to hear any more malicious gossip. The funeral will be tomorrow and you will do as Mr. Weiss instructed. Is that clear?"

"Yeah, sure it's clear. But I'm gonna give you Clara's

phone number anyway."

All that afternoon and on into the night, Yossie Schneider debated with himself. Why should he listen to that *lashon hara*, that scandalous, libelous talk? It was all a pack of lies. On the other hand, why would Siegel be willing to give out that lady's phone number, if it weren't true? And if it was true, why would Max Weiss pretend to have loved his wife if he hadn't?

Finally, Yossie decided that he would call Mrs. Shulman to let her know about Max's death and the time and place of the funeral, and if she had something to say about Max, this would give her a perfect opening.

❦

"Mrs. Shulman?"

"Yes?"

"My name is Yossie Schneider. I am affiliated with the Bnai Dovid Yeshiva which took over the Weiss Acres hotel and bungalow colony from Mr. Weiss."

"I see," she said cautiously.

"Well, I'm calling to tell you that Mr. Weiss has passed away and the funeral will be at two o'clock tomorrow afternoon at Beth Abraham Cemetery. As someone who once lived at Weiss Acres, I thought you might want to know about it."

"Thank you, but I doubt you'll see me there. I was very close with Miriam, his wife, and I can tell you..."

Yossie didn't want to hear what she had to say next. He wanted to put the phone down and run away, but it was too late.

"Max Weiss never once visited his wife in the hospital when she was dying. He didn't show up to the funeral, either. So as far as I'm concerned, no one should show up for him. Good day."

Yossie slowly replaced the receiver, shaking his head from side to side. "For all these years, I thought he was a *mentsch*," he murmured. "Now, the truth comes out. Max Weiss was just using the memory of his wife to justify his antisocial behavior. Why couldn't I see that? How could I have respected him so much? How could I have been so naive?"

The next day, Yossie got up early to daven. The big round white-faced clock on the *beis midrash* wall threw minutes into the lonely hours of the morning. The clock seemed to be moving more slowly than usual. Eight o'clock. Nine o'clock. Ten. Ten-thirty. Yossie couldn't stand it. Eleven. Every time he looked up, the hands had moved, but just barely. By one o'clock, he was exhausted, irritable, and tense. "I don't *have* to go to the funeral," he thought. "I'm not related to the guy. I'm not his son. I've got better things to do with my time."

Akiva Berg burst into the room. "Yossie!" he called. "Don't you know what time it is? The van is full and it's waiting in the parking lot. C'mon, quick!"

"Kivi, I'm not going. I don't feel very well."

"What? You're the only *mishpocheh* he has!"

"I'M NOT MISHPOCHEH!" Yossie yelled. "I didn't adopt him and he didn't adopt me. Now, you heard what I said, so get in the van and go."

Kivi stared at him. Yossie glared back, perspiration beading his forehead like drops of rain. "Okay, okay, I hear you," Kivi said. As he walked out, he mumbled *"Refuah sheleimah,"* and shut the door behind him.

Yossie felt his heart had turned to lead. He tried to convince himself that there was no reason for the heaviness he felt, but it didn't help. After what seemed like hours, he heard the van return from the cemetery and Yossie tracked Akiva down. "What happened? Did anyone come to the funeral?" he asked.

"It was small — like you'd expect. Nothing unusual. A niece from Cleveland was there. Her husband made a little speech. Rabbi Levensohn said a *Kel malei* and Kaddish, and that was it."

"You say the niece's husband made a speech? What about?"

"I don't remember his exact words. But he mentioned that Mr. Weiss was a special man who had loved his wife very much. So much so that his doctor wouldn't let him visit her in the hospital, or even go to her funeral, because they were afraid the shock would kill him."

Yossie gaped at his friend, his face ashen. "He said that?!"

"Yeah, and he also said that even after Mrs. Weiss died, Max carried on like she was always there with him. He just couldn't accept the fact that she was gone. But you knew that."

Yes, Yossie did know that. What he didn't know was why he'd allowed himself to be misled about Max. Why hadn't he trusted his own instincts? Weiss had certainly never done him any harm — or anyone else, for that matter. So he was a little peculiar; so what? Was that a reason for Yossie to have turned his back on him?

"Okay, Kivi, tell me the rest."

"There's n-n-nothing else to tell. Really." Akiva turned away.

Yossie looked his friend in the eye. He could tell there was something more. "Spit it out, Akiva. What else did he say?"

Kivi's voice dropped to just above a whisper and he lowered his eyes. "He said that Weiss had told him how happy he was that the yeshiva took over his place. And, and... he mentioned you."

Yossie's knees felt weak. "Me?" he gasped.

"Yeah. He said that Mr. Weiss was especially fond of Rabbi Schneider. In fact, the niece wanted to meet you and thank you for all you had done over the years. But I told her you were sick."

If he wasn't sick before, Yossie Schneider sure was now. He closed his eyes against the pain. A wave of nausea swept over him. "Kivi! What can I do? I didn't mean to..."

"I know. It's not your fault. You just weren't feeling well, that's all."

It was almost sunset when Yossie Schneider finally found the strength to go to the Beth Abraham Cemetery. The gates were locked, but that wasn't about to stop him. It had been a long time since he'd climbed a fence, or anything more strenuous than a flight of stairs, but he was determined to visit Max Weiss and beg his forgiveness.

After several false starts and a hard fall, he made his way up one side of the eight-foot-high chain-link fence. Slowly, he swung his right leg over the top. His pants ripped at the thigh. In seconds, he could feel a warm trickle of blood flow down toward his ankle, but it didn't matter. The pain in his leg couldn't match the pain in his heart. Yossie swung his body over and the other leg followed. Clutching the cold metal links with his fingers he slowly let himself down a couple of feet, then dropped to the ground.

The Beth Abraham Cemetery was not large, but it took him quite a while to locate the Weiss plot. He scanned one headstone after another, quickly taking in the names: Koppleman, Shuster, Zveig, Stein, Lasky, Levy, Shapiro. Working his way down the rows, he finally came across the name Weiss: Miriam Weiss. Next to it was a fresh grave with a little brass marker that read "Max Weiss, 5675-5750 (1914-1989)."

Yossie stared at the grave. After a few minutes, he began to speak. "Max, Mr. Weiss. This is... " His voice left him. He tried again. "It's me. Yossie Schneider. I wanted you to know how sorry I am for not coming. It wasn't my fault... I didn't mean..." Yossie stopped. Tears filled his eyes. "Believe me, I valued our friendship. Please forgive me! Please forgive me!"

Yossie searched desperately for some sign, some indication that Max heard and forgave. But there was only silence. How long he stood there, Yossie didn't know. Finally, in the fading twilight, he realized he had to start back. The wind whipped at his torn pants. He made his way to the fence and began climbing.

When he reached the top, he looked out across the cemetery grounds and this time he had no trouble picking out the headstone that marked Miriam Weiss's grave. As he looked at the two graves side by side, a sense of peace came over him. It was comforting to know that Max and his wife were reunited at last.

Yossie Schneider thought that the wound in his heart would never heal. But that very night at *Maariv*, when he stood up in the Weiss Acres *beis midrash* and began to discharge his duty as Max's surrogate son, the pain of his guilt ebbed. At first his voice cracked and he felt he couldn't go on. Then the words of Kaddish rang out clear and strong:

"Yisgadel v'yiskadesh..."

Heard from: Rabbi Yosef Mitnick

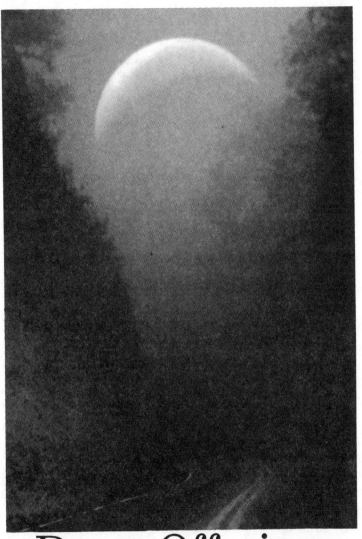

Peace Offerings

All from the Boss

O THIS GUY TAKES a plate full of steaming cholent and heaves it at Yaakov Yosef, scoring a direct hit. Can you believe it? His whole new beautiful *bekkasheh* is wrecked, probably stained for good. There are potatoes in his *peyos*, beans in his beard, meat in his mustache, grease on his glasses, and *kishkeh* all over his new *kappoteh*."

"So what did he do?" an avid listener asked. Everyone in the small crowd of worshipers standing in the hall of the Zichron Moshe synagogue was mesmerized. It was Friday night in Jerusalem, directly after services, and the speaker needed no encouragement from his audience. He had a story to tell and tell it he would.

"What did he do?! What do you mean, what did he

do? What does Reb Yaakov Yosef always do? Mind you, his son, Reb Nochum Dovid, wanted to tear the guy limb from limb. He had just bought his father the new *kappoteh* and it was the first time Reb Yaakov Yosef was wearing it.

"Reb Yaakov Yosef, of course, turns to Nochum Dovid and warns him, 'Not a word, not a move!' and so he should have no doubts that his father means business, Reb Yaakov Yosef puts his finger over his lips like this and 'whispers' a loud 'SHHA!'"

"So what did he do?"

"What did he do?!"

"Yeah, what did he do?"

"I'll tell ya what he did. He CALMLY, did you get that, *calmly* turns to the person who heaved the cholent, who you might have guessed is an extremely nervous individual, and I mean *nervous*, and he asks him, in *the* politest, *the* kindest, *the* gentlest way, 'Was the cholent not to your liking?'

"So Shebsl, that's the guy who threw the cholent, begins to fiddle with the silverware. Everyone knows Shebsl is real nervous. Even *Shebsl* knows he's nervous, not to mention a *shtickel* violent.

"So he's playing with the silverware, trying to stick the knife through the fork, and flip the spoon up from the table, you know, so that it lands in his glass, all the while getting everyone *else* real nervous."

"So what did he do?"

"I'm *telling* you what he did. Reb Yaakov Yosef is still waiting patiently for Shebsl to answer, and by this time the guy has missed getting his spoon into his glass at least a dozen times and bent at least two of the fork tines. There isn't a sound in the room, except the clinking of his spoon against the glass. Finally, Shebsl points a finger at the fellow fourteen seats down the table from him and charges, 'He got more than me! Why'd you give *him* more than *me*?'

"You see, Reb Yaakov Yosef always gives out the portions himself, so that no one will have a gripe against the Rebbetzin."

"*Ah chutzpah!*" one of the listeners protested at Shebsl's insolence.

"*Ah shandeh!*" agreed a second.

"Disgusting," moaned a third.

"What a *bizayon*. How rude can a person get!" a fourth and a fifth chimed in.

"Wait a minute," the storyteller resumed, "wait till you hear what Reb Yaakov Yosef did."

"What did he do?"

"I'll tell you what he did. He picks himself up, and goes into the kitchen. A minute later he comes out with a giant bowl filled to overflowing with steaming cholent which he puts down in front of Shebsl. Then Reb Yaakov Yosef apologizes for his 'lack of consideration,' and only *then* he goes to wash his face and change into his old worn-out *kappoteh*."

All of the listeners were shaking their heads in admiration when who should suddenly appear but the very man they had just been discussing: Reb Yaakov Yosef Herman.

After wishing everyone in the shul *"Gut Shabbos,"* Reb Yaakov Yosef started his routine roundups. The Hermans always had a number of regular guests who joined them each Shabbos for the meals, but this was not enough for Reb Yaakov Yosef. It was S.O.P. for this master of hospitality to make his way through the many pews of Zichron Moshe and the other *shtiblach* in the vicinity to see if there were any congregants who didn't have a place to eat, and one by one invite them to his humble abode. For twenty-seven years, dozens of guests would grace the Hermans' Shabbos table in Jerusalem, just as their American counterparts had done years before on New York's Lower East Side.

Reb Yaakov Yosef's technique was straightforward: He would approach whomever remained in the shul after services and inquire, "Do you have a place to eat?" Without waiting for a reply, he would direct the individual to his house, and then move on to the next straggler.

As Reb Yaakov Yosef worked his way through the sanctuary, he noticed huddled in the farthest corner of the rearmost bench of the shul, Shaya Newman, a well-known misanthrope with a vested interest in chaos. A noted genius, Shaya had crossed the line some time back between brilliance and sociopathy. The crossing had been far from tranquil, as virtually every resident of Jerusalem could testify. Accordingly, he was avoided by one and all like the proverbial plague.

Newman's reputation did not deter the intrepid emissary for "the Boss," Yaakov Yosef Herman. Undaunted, he deftly executed his host maneuver, but instead of graciously accepting the invitation Shaya merely looked at Reb Yaakov Yosef quizzically. "Are you nuts?!" his expression read. "You want *me* in your house?"

Reb Yaakov Yosef responded in body language *forte voce*, leaving no room for misinterpretation. His arm and forefinger extended like a Labrador retriever, he held the pose until Shaya began shuffling off in the right direction.

Reb Yaakov Yosef surveyed the premises one last time before he headed for Adler Street to join his guests at chez Herman.

As Reb Yaakov Yosef ascended the steps to his home, he was met halfway by the deafening din emanating from his dining room. Over a dozen conversations were being conducted simultaneously, but despite the racket Reb Yaakov Yosef was able to pick up several snatches.

"...I'm in the middle of davening and all of a sudden I find this watch, and of course I want to return it to its owner. So I look around and see this sign on the wall, written on the back of the lining of a cigarette box, saying: 'If you find a watch, return it.'"

"It doesn't say who to return it to?"

"It doesn't even say when it was lost."

"That reminds me of the story of the Jew who was walking down a cobbled street in Slutsk one Shabbos when he spotted a gold watch lying on the ground. He bent down to the ground and placed his good ear on top of the watch to hear if it was ticking. Once he determined that it was working, he stood up and stomped his foot in frustration, because he could not pick it up and carry it with him. Not knowing what to do, he commanded the watch, '*Oib du gaist, kim* — If you're going, come!'"

"That reminds me," offered a newcomer to the Herman household, "of the rabbi who fell to his knees on Rosh Hashanah and cried out, 'God, without You, I'm nothing.'

"When the *chazzan* saw the rabbi collapse in pious fervor, he too went down on his knees and exclaimed, 'God, without You, I'm nothing.'

"The *gabbai* picked up the cue from the *chazzan* and joined him on the floor proclaiming, 'God, without You, I'm nothing.'

"When the rabbi saw this, he turned to his *chazzan* and asked, 'Who does he think he is that he thinks he's nothing?'"

"Very good," laughed a third invitee. "It's like the story of the Jew who crossed the border into Russia. When the sentry asked if he was carrying any religious items, he placed a shofar to his ear as if he were hard of hearing and asked the guard to repeat the question."

"I understand, I think," reflected the man who had initiated the conversation,"what the connection of the gold watch incident was to the watch I found in shul. One story was about a watch and the other story was about a watch. Even though every time I hear a story about food, I don't think about every other story I know about food, and every time I hear a story about a car, I don't think about every other story I know about a car, nonetheless, let's say I hear the connection. I guess the same goes for the rabbi, the *chazzan*, and the *gabbai*:

the watch was lost in shul and their story takes place in shul. But what does a shofar have to do with a watch?"

"Just like the watch was *going*, the Jew was *going* across the border..."

As the scholarly symposium was reaching its zenith, Reb Yaakov Yosef reached the top of the stairs. Just when he was about to open the door Shaya darted out of the house, blindly shoving his host aside as he hurtled down the steps. Reb Yaakov Yosef quickly turned on his heels and chased after him. At the landing he caught up with his erstwhile guest and asked him why he was running away.

"There's no room for me at your table."

"There's always room for our guests," Reb Yaakov Yosef assured him in a soothing tone.

"Not for me."

"Oh, come on, Shaya," Reb Yaakov Yosef said, trying to lead his guest back up to the house, "I'm sure you can get along with the others just for one Shabbos meal."

Shaya looked his host in the eye and said, "*This* time the problem is not with *me*."

Reb Yaakov Yosef immediately grasped the implication of Shaya's words, but his determination was unshaken; dealing with an agitated Shaya Newman did, in fact, require a lot of determination. The two of them stood on the staircase arguing back and forth, Shaya invoking Talmudic logic, Biblical verse, and hyperbolic reasoning to support his contention, but Reb Yaakov Yosef could not be swayed. The persistent host would not take "no" for an answer and virtually dragged his recalcitrant guest up the stairs.

The moment the two of them walked in, the room fell silent, and like an eerie echo, the tension in the air was palpable. Reb Yaakov Yosef looked around at his thirty-odd guests and suddenly the spacious table at which up to thirty-five had sat week in and week out — the very table which always seemed to expand to accommodate whatever number of guests crammed into the apartment — appeared to shrink before his eyes. There was indeed no room for Shaya.

How could it be? Reb Yaakov Yosef glanced at the misfits of society, the poor and the downtrodden, the lonely, the disfigured, and the handicapped that filled his home. His table was a virtual Statue of Liberty, welcoming the rejected and the dejected, but none of the motley assembled that had flocked to his abode would meet his gaze.

Since no one seemed inclined to speak, Reb Yaakov Yosef decided to consult the Boss. Inspiration was swift in coming. In the jocular, self-deprecating manner he used so effectively to get a point across, Reb Yaakov Yosef began a sing-song monologue:

"Well, Yaakov Yosef," he intoned, "it seems like you've gotten carried away this time. There *takkeh* isn't an inch of space at your *Shabbos tisch*, so what are we to do? Should we uninvite one of the seated guests?"

The eyes of the guests nervously darted left and right, down and farther down — anywhere but at their host.

"No, Yaakov Yosef," he answered his own question, "it's unthinkable!

"Well then," he went on, "should we knock on all the doors of the neighbors and see if these families — which are halfway through their meal by now — will accept our overload?

"No, Yaakov Yosef, this is also unthinkable."

"Perhaps..." Reb Yaakov Yosef paused, *vey-vey*ing while he cogitated, "...perhaps it is my *own* seat that should be vacated for Shaya. After all, it was my overzealousness to fill my house with special Shabbos guests that caused this blunder in the first place. I am at fault here and therefore..." Reb Yaakov Yosef's singsong *niggun* filled in the gap.

At this point the eyes of the invited, which had momentarily been upwardly diverted, once again fell below table, as everyone checked to see if his shoes were tied and whether his socks matched.

"If only the Boss would send me a solution to my dilemma, and save me from the shame that I have brought upon myself. Here, I go and invite 35 guests and *each and every one* is equally welcome and certainly entitled to his seat." Reb Yaakov Yosef's *niggun* had now assumed a lugubrious tone, as mournful as a river sounds when it reaches a sharp decline and suddenly deepens. *Vey-vey* gave way to *oy-oy*.

Reb Yaakov Yosef halted his soliloquy abruptly, turned to his Rebbetzin, and in a flash a message was conveyed. Mere seconds later a small table in the foyer was set. Reb Yaakov Yosef had sensed that Shaya was about to bolt again, and he placed a firm, yet affectionate grip on his reluctant guest's arm.

Leading Shaya and escorting his wife, the threesome repaired to the foyer where the junior *Shabbos tisch* was adorned with challah, wine and place settings. They took their seats and no sooner had Reb Yaakov Yosef opened up his *siddur* to *Shalom Aleichem* than a thirty-four-man delegation appeared in the cramped foyer.

"Reb Yaakov Yosef," the self-appointed spokesman declared in a somewhat embarrassed tone, "of course there's room for you, and for your Rebbetzin, and for *all* of your guests."

From that night on, do you know what Shaya did? I'll tell you what he did: he became a "regular" at the Hermans', where he always felt at home. More importantly, he began to feel at home in other settings as well. The atmosphere and the welcome that he was given in the Herman house pervaded his being and transformed him into a different person. Gone was the bitterness and animosity that had fostered his degeneration into a social outcast. Shaya Newman was indeed a new man.

Heard from: Rabbi Moshe Aaron Stern

Bless This Match

I'M GOING TO tell you a remarkable story. It is remarkable in that it could only happen among the holiest people on earth, in the holiest city on earth. While the details may have been embellished a bit, due to the passage of time (over 90 years) and the nature of storytelling (and storytellers), the facts are undeniably true.

Our story begins with a boy, but not just any boy. Moshe ben Aharon Ha-Levi Katzover. Moshe was a *shadchan*'s dream. He was bright and studious, tall and good-looking, polite and self-effacing. The fact is, he had all the character traits a prospective mate (and even a prospective mother-in-law) would list on the matchmaker's application form. Except one: Moshe Katzover had no interest whatsoever in getting married. It's not that people didn't try. One of the most persistent was Rebbetzin Rachel Goldblum, a *Yerushalmi* mother, grandmother and *shadchante* par excellence.

One day, as Moshe Katzover was hurrying to night session at yeshiva, he heard a familiar voice. "Moshe, Moshe!" Rebbetzin Goldblum called out, quoting the Torah.

"What can I do for you, Rebbetzin Goldblum?" Moshe replied, knowing full well what she was going to say.

"For me, nothing. For yourself, you can find a partner for life! Don't you know what our Sages say? At 18, you're supposed to get married! What's going to become of you? You want to end up like Yitzchak *Avinu* and wait until you're 39?"

"Well, he didn't do too badly! Maybe I'm waiting for a wife like Rivka," he teased. "Believe me, when I'm ready, I'll let you know." Moshe started to walk away, but then an idea occurred to him.

"Rebbetzin, if you really want to do a mitzvah," he said, "maybe you could find a *shidduch* for my study partner, Avremie Gottlieb. He could *takkeh* use someone."

A gleam appeared in Rebbetzin Goldblum's eyes. "What kind of boy is he?"

"He's kind. He's honest. He's sensitive. And he's really smart. One of the best students in the yeshiva. Even Reb Yosef Chaim Sonnenfeld thinks so."

"But it sounds like you're describing yourself!" Rebbetzin Goldblum chided.

Moshe Katzover blushed. "No, no. You've got it wrong. *He's* really outstanding. Avremie's compassionate, a real kind-hearted person. I can't tell you all the times he has put himself out for other people. Why, just the other day, he helped me bring enough wood to Mrs. Bamberger's home to heat it for a month! In fact, he's always doing something for somebody. I mean it. He's really special."

Rebbetzin Goldblum thought this over carefully. If she couldn't make a match for the best young man in all of Yerushalayim, perhaps she could find a *shidduch* for the next one on the list. "Tell me more," she said.

"Well, I'm sure he's not interested in beauty or wealth. If I know Avremie, he's looking for a real *aishes chayil* — someone who will help him build an everlasting house in Israel."

All of a sudden, bells and whistles went off in the *shadchante's* mind. "Not interested in beauty or wealth, you say? Looking for a girl with excellent character? Wants a real *aishes chayil*? *Oy*, have I got a *shidduch* for him! She's a poor orphan girl, but believe me she's a real gem, a prize. She'll make any husband proud. She's sweet, kind, honest as the day is long. She sews, she cooks, she cleans, she works, she chops wood. She has no temper, she comes from a fine family, she..." The attributes, praises and compliments came cascading out in a torrent. "She'll wait on him day and night, hand and foot, left and right. She'll bear his children, mind his business, mend his clothes. She'll cook his kugel, steep his tea..."

"Wait a minute, please, Rebbetzin. Hold on. You don't have to sell *me*. I'm convinced. I really am."

"You mean you're interested?" she asked hopefully.

"No, no, not me. I told you that I'm not looking for

a *shidduch.* Avremie, my friend. He's the one who wants to get married."

"He does and you don't?"

"Listen to me. I told you that I am already married!"

"You are?!"

"Yes — to my studies. That's taking up all my time now and it wouldn't be fair to a *kallah* for me to be spending so much time in yeshiva away from home. But I'll tell you what. I'll mention this girl to Avremie. What's her name?"

"Baila Kreindel."

"I'll mention Baila Kreindel to Avremie. If he's interested, he'll get in touch with you..."

Later that day, Moshe Katzover took his friend aside. "Listen," he confided, "I was approached for a *shidduch.*"

"Again? How many does that make this week?" Avremie asked. "Seven? Thirteen? Forty-six?"

"Okay, very funny," Moshe responded dryly. "Listen, you're the one who wants to get married. I can tell by the way you've been studying. Your head is just not into it."

"Well," Avremie admitted, "you may be right. Perhaps I would prefer practicing Gemara *Kiddushin* instead of just studying it."

And so Avremie Gottlieb took the fateful step and got in touch with Rebbetzin Goldblum.

The Rebbetzin, as you may have guessed by now, was not the kind of person who needed to be asked twice.

Before Avremie knew what hit him a date with Baila Kreindel was arranged.

As Baila and Avremie looked out over the narrow alleys and streets of the Old City, Avremie Gottlieb thought about what Rebbetzin Goldblum had had to say about his match. He could tell that Baila really was exceptionally sweet, honest, and domestically inclined. Yet she was, to tell the truth, or at least she seemed to be, not the most intelligent person who ever walked the earth. She was also short and skinny — almost bony, and she liked to chew garlic and even wear it around her neck. ("It keeps me healthy!" she claimed.)

Needless to say, it was not what you might call love at first sight. One reason was that Baila Kreindel couldn't see. Her eyes had a tendency to water continually, distorting her vision so much that she was constantly walking into things. More than once, she ended up apologizing to stone walls, doors, and other inanimate objects that she had bumped into.

Baila Kreindel couldn't hear very well, either. The condition, she explained, was connected somehow to the watery eyes and runny nose, but whatever the cause, the outcome was that she was virtually deaf. "Whha-at?" appeared to be her favorite word.

Still, she radiated such an aura of naive innocence and good nature that everyone who met her took an immediate liking to her. Here was a poor orphan girl who didn't let the slings and arrows of outrageous fortune get her down.

Maybe it was the sense of hopeful optimism that

seems to bloom in the spring, maybe it was the thought of a new life together, maybe it was a combination of things, but Avremie found himself captivated by the thought of himself and Baila Kreindel as a *chasan* and *kallah*.

"Baila?" he asked nervously. "D-d-d-do y-y-you feel you're ready to get married?"

"Whha-at? Could you speak a little louder? I can't hear you very well."

"I said, 'Do you feel you're ready to get married?'"

"Whha-at? Do I feel harried? No, not at all. Why do you ask?"

"No, that's not what I said! Do you feel you're ready to become my wife?"

"Do I feel alive? Of course! This is Jerusalem! Look at the stars in the sky. Smell the honeysuckle in the air. Who wouldn't feel alive?"

Avremie took in a deep breath. All he could smell was garlic.

❀

The next day, Rebbetzin Goldblum was able to communicate to Baila the following:

"*Mazel tov*! You're a *kallah*!"

"Can I bake challah?"

"No! Repeat after me: I..."

"I..."

"AM..."

"am..."

"A..."

"a..."

"KALLAH!" Rebbetzin Goldblum shouted so loud, the news was all over Jerusalem. At last, Baila Kreindel understood. God had answered her prayers and the Heavenly petitions of her friends. Her dream of becoming a *kallah* had come true.

The next few weeks were busy ones for the entire community. Because Baila Kreindel was an orphan, the task fell to the *kehillah*. Rebbetzin Goldblum arranged for volunteers to sew the wedding dress and provide a trousseau, while Avremie and his family took care of the time and place, the music, the meal, and the living quarters. One of the most important aspects was deciding on who would officiate, and Avremie Gottlieb had someone very special in mind.

As the big day drew nigh, Moshe watched Avremie closely. He saw his friend become much more serious than ever before. "Avremie," he said, "you've been pretty tense lately. Getting married must be an even bigger deal than I thought."

Avremie laughed nervously. "It's not bad, really." Then he sighed. "Baila Kreindel's really terrific, but..."

"But *what*?"

"Do you like garlic?"

"Huh?"

"I can't stand it. Never could. I break out in hives whenever I even get close to it!"

"What has that got to do with anything?"

"Well, it's just that... oh, forget it. Forget I ever said anything."

Finally, the evening of the wedding arrived. Avremie Gottlieb looked positively regal, resplendent in the gold silk garments and fur-trimmed *shtreimel* of a true *Yerushalmi*. His bride was dressed in the purest white, her hair encircled by a band of fresh wildflowers plucked from the hills outside the Holy City.

All of Yerushalayim was there. Even Moshe Katzover's family had come, not only to honor their son's friend, but to show their esteem for the leadership and piety of the *mesadder kiddushin*. This wedding between one of Yerushalayim's brightest yeshiva students and one of its poorest orphan girls had brought this great scholar to stand under the *chuppah*.

Slowly, the formalities wound their way up to the climactic moment, the moment when man and woman become united as husband and wife, according to the Law of Moses and Israel.

Moshe stood under the *chuppah* too, as a witness to the *kiddushin*. The ceremony proceded as the venerable Rabbi took the ring from Avremie's hand, asked the groom if it belonged to him and examined it carefully. Then he passed it to Moshe so that he too should ascertain its minimal worth.

Turning back to Avremie, he solemnly ordered, "Place this ring on her finger."

Avremie took the ring from him and gripped it tightly in his trembling hand. "Place the ring on her finger," the kindly Rabbi repeated.

Avremie turned pale. Perspiration oozed from under his *shtreimel*.

"I-I-I-I...," he stammered several times. Finally, he managed to call out, "*I can't!*"

There was a gasp from those who were close enough to hear. A slight commotion stirred the assemblage. The *chasan* looked as if he were about to faint. "I *can't*," he reiterated. "I thought I could, but I can't! She's not for me." Slowly, with tears in his eyes, Avremie took off his wedding *shtreimel* and dropped the ring in it. He handed them to Moshe with a look of indescribable sadness, then broke through the crowd and fled.

By this time, the guests knew something was desperately wrong. "What is going on?" they asked each other. Those who fancied they could read lips or even minds conjectured, "Maybe the groom is sick."

Moshe watched his friend disappear, then turned to Baila Kreindel. In the commotion, she had been all but ignored. Blessedly hard of hearing and blurred of vision, the *kallah* had remained patiently composed. Moshe could smell the fragrant scent of garlic in the air. The Rav turned to the young girl who only now was beginning to understand what was happening. Her big brown eyes began to fill with tears. The sadness of this orphan's soul touched everyone in the room. "My daughter," he said tenderly, "for the moment, your wedding is off."

Moshe struggled with the lump in his throat. He swallowed hard and cried out, "No, it isn't!" People looked around, craning their necks to see if perhaps Avremie had returned. But he had not. The *chasan* was nowhere to be seen.

Moshe stepped up to the Rav. "If Baila Kreindel agrees, I will be her *chasan*."

The Rav looked at Moshe Katzover with incredulity. "Are you sure?" he asked.

"Yes," came Moshe's swift reply.

The Rav then turned to the *kallah*. "Are you willing to marry Moshe ben Aharon Ha-Levi Katzover? What do you have to say?"

"Whha-at?" Baila asked.

Now before you argue that there appears to be an infraction of Halachah, let me tell you that the *mesadder kiddushin* was none other than the Guardian of Jerusalem himself, Rabbi Yosef Chaim Sonnenfeld. Rabbi Sonnenfeld is perhaps best remembered for his zealous adherence to the Law, but in fact this zealousness was far more apparent in his boundless love for his people. Indeed so great was his love that he often took brave and unpopular stands in order to ease the plight of a suffering Jew.

Once, long before the wedding at hand, Rabbi Sonnenfeld was asked to select a new *baal tefillah* for the High Holidays. The *baal tefillah* who had previously held the position had passed away after many years of devoted service to the congregation, but there were plenty of new candidates blessed with beautiful voices and gilt-edged character traits. Rabbi Sonnenfeld, however, refused to reveal who would lead the congregation for the High Holiday services. During the month of Elul curiosity and tension rose every day, but Reb Yosef Chaim would not divulge his choice.

At long last, Rosh Hashanah arrived. Expectation hung in the air, as community members made their way to their seats in the synagogue. Rabbi Sonnenfeld stood at the head of the congregation, his presence assuring them that they need not worry — a proper delegate would be selected to lead their supplications. There was absolute silence.

Suddenly, the Rav walked over to a young man and whispered in his ear. A small discussion ensued, but in the end the fellow left his place and strode to the holy ark. Slowly, he began to sing. The crowd murmured, How could it be? The new *sheliach tzibbur* was the son of the *chazzan* who had passed away. Had the Rav forgotten that the son was still in mourning?!

Certainly Reb Chaim Sonnenfeld knew that it is preferable for a mourner not to lead the congregation. Certainly he did! And just as certainly he knew that given a choice, his congregation would find comforting a mourner an even greater preference.

In the balcony of the synagogue, her eyes squeezed shut against the pain in her soul, the wife of the deceased *chazzan* waited expectantly. For years, she had heard her husband's voice float above the congregation, carrying up to Heaven the community's Rosh Hashanah prayers and wishes for a healthy year. Now he was a member of the Heavenly choir himself. Who could replace her beloved husband, whose voice she so longed to hear once more? And then the first notes of *Hineni he'ani mi-maas* rang out, making her heart pound with pleasure at the sound of that familiar voice. Her eyes flew open, a tiny smile of pure joy played at her lips, and she was comforted.

❀

"Whha-at?" Baila Kreindel asked again. She turned and looked up to see a handsome young man standing beside her. She squinted hard. Who was he? Rabbi Sonnenfeld repeated his question, this time in a voice the entire congregation could hear. "ARE YOU WILLING TO MARRY MOSHE BEN AHARON HA-LEVI KATZOVER?"

Moshe Katzover? The most sought-after *shidduch* in Yerushalayim? Why would he want her? There must be some mistake. "Could you repeat the question?" she asked.

Guests and wedding party members alike burst into laughter.

"Excuse me, Rabbi Sonnenfeld, may I speak to Baila for a moment?" Moshe asked.

"Of course," Rabbi Sonnenfeld replied.

"Baila," Moshe declared in a loud, yet surprisingly calm, tone, "our Sages explain that a man without a wife is only half a man. I never understood that until now. I would like you to bring *sheleimus* to my life and *shalom* to my soul. In return, I will try to be worthy of being your *chasan*. Will you be my wife?"

For once in her life, Baila heard someone the first time around. "Yes, Moshe," she said quietly, then modestly cast her eyes to the ground.

"If you have a ring, we can proceed."

"I am giving mine as a perfect gift to Moshe." It was Avremie Gottlieb. He had regained his composure and returned to publicly apologize to Baila Kreindel and those who had come to the wedding. But instead of breaking up her *simchah*, he found himself witnessing it!

Without further ado, the ceremony continued and within minutes, Baila Kreindel and Moshe Katzover were wed. Before signaling the new *chasan* to proceed down from the *chuppah*, Rabbi Sonnenfeld turned to the assembled. "We have witnessed an act of such nobility that I cannot leave this *chuppah* without first adding my own personal blessing to the newly wedded couple."

The crowd watched in awe as the drama reached its peak. Rabbi Sonnenfeld smiled at Baila and her *chasan*. "To you, Baila Kreindel, may the Almighty grant good health, so that you have no further need of various medicaments and cures; and may you be privileged to raise a generation of scholars. And to you, Moshe ben Aharon Ha-Levi, may the merit of this mitzvah bring you many, many long and productive years of happiness. What you have done will surely stand you in good stead forever. Now, there is just one thing left to say... MAZEL TOV!"

And so Baila and Moshe were married. That wedding was the most joyous one that people had seen in many years. And sure enough, Baila Kreindel and Moshe Katzover enjoyed a long and happy life together. For once, every word that Rebbetzin Goldblum had said about the prospective *kallah* had been true. Furthermore, when Baila Kreindel's allergies suddenly disappeared, her hearing improved significantly and her eyes stopped watering so badly. She felt so well, in fact, that she even decided to get rid of the garlic necklace which a local herbalist had guaranteed would be beneficial to her health.

And when a robust and lucid Moshe passed away at the age of 104, great-great-grandfather of legions of pious descendants, people were still telling the story of his amazing *chassunah* and Rabbi Sonnenfeld's blessings that had been fulfilled.

Heard from: Mickey Rayde

Peace at Any Price

HISTORY acknowledges that the prime indicator of the development of a civilization is its establishment of the rule of law. A society that willingly submits to the rule of law — and it must be a fair and just law for the willingness factor to be present — is a society that rejects anarchy and actively seeks peace. When peace reigns, civilization flourishes.

"Mosaic Law," that is, the Written Law and the Oral Law which together form the Torah, is not only the pride of the Jewish nation but the foundation of the world's most highly esteemed secular legal systems. Yet history acknowledges another truth: It is not merely the lawgiver, or the lawmaker, but the law upholder — the judge or legal decisor — who is at the core of any legal system. Only he can apply the law and know which law applies. The body of law can provide examples and precedents, but 2,700 years after those precedents were cited, only the sagacious decisor can determine whether the driver of the car that struck someone is as guilty as the owner of the ox that gored. Twenty-seven hundred years down the line we may not encounter two men, each claiming ownership of a garment they found simultaneously on the road; more likely it will be a wallet full of money that they found, or a stray bearer bond. Does the garment precedent apply? Ask the *posek*.

One of the most celebrated and revered leaders of the Jewish People was Reb Chaim Volozhiner, who was the foremost disciple of the Vilna *Gaon* and founder of the famed Volozhin Yeshiva, the prototype of today's widespread yeshiva system. A Talmudist and author of renown, Reb Chaim was called "our great teacher, mentor of all Israel" in recognition of his vast accomplishments and erudition. Little mention is made, however, of his equally phenomenal achievements in halachic arbitration, an area in which his acuity and skill were unsurpassed. In fact, Reb Chaim Volozhiner donned the cloak of *posek* even before he donned the cloak of manhood.

[So ingenious was Reb Chaim's very first arbitration that variations of it have even found their way into contemporary books of "brain teasers" and mathematical riddles! See if you can solve "The Baron's Dilemma."]

On his way home from yeshiva one day, eleven-year-old Chaim was nearly crushed beneath the carriage wheels of the local baron's magnificent coach. Two pairs of perfectly matched, lavishly caparisoned stallions galloped by at top speed, hurtling past him and through the village square. They drew to a halt in front of Chaim's house.

Oblivious to the youth he had just barely avoided injuring, the baron alit and strode purposefully into the house, intent on finding young Chaim's father, a local scholar of note. It was the first time he had ever sought the rabbi's counsel, but his dilemma had baffled all of his advisers. They had no recourse but to direct their master to one whose wisdom and perspicacity was known far and wide (and, they admitted to themselves, exceeded their own).

The nobleman was swiftly ushered into the rabbi's humble abode, and Chaim followed, awed into silence by the baron's regal bearing and impressive attire. The nobleman wasted no time in presenting his case.

"It is a matter of distributing my family inheritance," he began, "and I, as the eldest heir, have been entrusted with the task." Before his passing, the baron's late father had written a will which instructed that half of his estate was to go to his eldest son, one-third to his second son, and one-ninth to his youngest.

"I had no difficulty carrying out my father's will with regard to the cash and properties," he went on, "but the stables are another matter altogether." He had doled out the cash according to the formula, and allocated the properties after calculating the number of hectares there were in each parcel of land. Any structures that stood on the properties were evaluated and distributed fairly, and whatever was not readily divisible, he had sold and divided the cash.

"It was my father's express desire, however, that the stables — that is, the thoroughbred horses — not be sold or exchanged. My father was very attached to his animals, and they are quite valuable. How can I divide them fairly among the heirs when there are *seventeen* in all?"

Although the distinguished guest had presented the case before Chaim's father, who was reputed to have a keen mind not only in matters of jurisprudence but in mathematical spheres as well, it was the pre-bar mitzvah *bachur* who came up with the immediate solution. At first the assembled were stunned at his audacity to answer in his father's place, but when they discerned the cleverness of the precocious boy's response, they could do no more than stand back in wonder in the presence of such brilliance.

"All you need do," Chaim said, "is add one horse to your father's estate, and you will have a total of eighteen horses to be divided. You, as the eldest, will take nine horses. Your middle brother will take a third of the total, or six horses. The youngest is to receive one-ninth of eighteen, or two horses. The remaining horse, which you donated in the first place, you can then take back, and each of you will have his proper share of the inheritance."

❀

Who can say how many predicaments, crises and vexing halachic dilemmas Reb Chaim Volozhiner resolved in the subsequent sixty years of his illustrious life? As the child prodigy grew to be a prominent rabbinic leader, and eventually one of the generation's most outstanding *gedolim*, one guiding principle informed his every action: maintaining *shalom* among his people.

Inspired, no doubt, by Jewish Law, Reb Chaim had an innate abhorrence of strife. He would go to extraordinary lengths, sometimes even taking an un"orthodox" position, in order to avoid disagreement or ill feelings.

When a resident of Volozhin departed for the Holy Land, the great rabbi urged him to adopt the local customs of Eretz Yisrael. By observing the practices of the local residents — even at the cost of discarding his own time-honored ones — the new immigrant would minimize the potential for dispute.

Reb Chaim was tireless in his pursuit of peace. It was not at all uncommon for him to visit the homes of quarrelling parties and devote many hours of his time — as long as was necessary — until the disagreement was resolved.

In his peace missions, Reb Chaim was guided by the words of the Gemara: "At the completion of the Prayer one should step three paces backward and then offer peace," which he interpreted to mean that everyone should, if necessary, step down three steps from his station in life in order to make peace and prevent a conflict.

Toward the end of his life, a complex case about a tidy sum of money came before Reb Chaim Volozhiner's court. One of the disputants was Reb Asher, a renowned *talmid chacham* who lived in a nearby town. The scholar's opposing litigant was a simple tinsmith.

Reb Chaim listened patiently as each side presented his case. The issue was indeed complicated, and Reb Chaim deliberated some time before ruling in favor of the tinsmith.

Upon hearing the *pesak*, Reb Asher gasped audibly, his eyebrows rising in surprise. Needless to say, he gave no voice to his protest, and meticulously heeded the ruling, but all the same it was clear that Reb Asher was taken aback and disappointed by Reb Chaim's decision.

Reb Chaim was not blind to the man's reaction; the pained look on Reb Asher's face had distressed him deeply. Still, he could not alter Halachah to accommodate someone's sensibilities. Nor could he hope to mollify Reb Asher by detailing the reasoning behind his decision: The man was genuinely learned and an explanation would only add insult to injury.

In time, the parties put their dispute behind them, and life went on.

Reb Asher worked in a shop located near Volozhin's coach depot. One winter morning, just as he was nearing his store, he almost collided with Reb Chaim Volozhiner who was rushing into the station. The two scholars began to apologize to each other when Reb Chaim stopped in mid-sentence.

"I am actually delighted to have bumped into you," he said, "as I must travel out of town on short notice, and I am scheduled to adjudicate a *din Torah* today. I will have to postpone the hearing... unless you would be kind enough to take my place in *beis din*? I would consider it a personal favor."

Reb Asher was honored by the offer and pleased to be of assistance. He readily agreed.

The next time Reb Asher saw Reb Chaim was at the beginning of the summer, one week before Reb Chaim was summoned to the Heavenly Assembly. Reb Asher, like so many others, had come to fulfill the mitzvah of *bikkur cholim* and, as much as he didn't want to admit it, to bid the great Reb Chaim Volozhiner farewell.

Despite the severity of his illness, Reb Chaim was remarkably lucid. When he saw Reb Asher enter the room, he raised himself up in his bed and spoke to him with sincere love and affection. Just before the visitor departed, the venerable *gadol* touched a finger to his forehead as if he'd just recalled a long-forgotten thought. "Tell me," he asked, "what ever happened at that *din Torah* that you adjudicated on my behalf?"

Reb Asher related what had transpired and how he had ruled, and Reb Chaim pondered his words at length. Reb Asher feared that the intense look of concentration on Reb Chaim's face indicated that he was displeased with the *pesak*. His fears, however, were immediately dispelled when the *gadol* opened his eyes and with a satisfied smile proclaimed, "Isn't that interesting! Do you remember, by any chance, the case which you and the tinsmith brought before me about a year ago?"

Reb Asher nodded.

"Think about it," Reb Chaim urged. "As dissimilar as the two cases appear to be, the reasoning in both rulings is virtually identical! Actually you and I both employed the very same line of reasoning. What an amazing coincidence!"

Reb Asher's face mirrored his astonishment as he grasped the truth of the great rabbi's observation.

Reb Chaim had spoken of "coincidence," but to Reb Asher it was a sobering and humbling lesson. He had had no right to be upset over Reb Chaim's ruling; instead, he should have realized that as a party to the litigation he could not be objective. His own self-interest had clouded his judgment and rendered him blind to the Halachah.

From the day of Reb Chaim Volozhiner's passing, time moved at a snail's pace for Lithuanian Jewry. The Father of the Yeshiva World had left a rich legacy, but the bereaved heirs were unable to appreciate it without their beloved and inspiring Rebbe sitting at the helm. As long as Reb Chaim Volozhiner was alive, it was as though the Vilna *Gaon* lived yet; but with the great disciple's demise, a void was created that it seemed would never be filled.

Reb Asher's mourning intensified when, several months after Reb Chaim's death, he encountered one of the parties to the litigation he had settled. Reb Asher was curious as to how his ruling had been carried out, but the response he received was entirely unexpected.

With a quizzical look and a deep sigh, the fellow told Reb Asher: "Now that our master is no longer here, perhaps *you* can explain to *me* what transpired. You see, the dispute which we presented before you was not a genuine one. We were merely following Reb Chaim's explicit instructions. He rehearsed us well in advance — so well that you couldn't tell — but all we were doing was repeating exactly what Reb Chaim had told us to say.

"We had absolutely no idea why he wanted us to

pretend to be litigants before you, but he paid us handsomely for the charade, and no harm was done as far as we could see. But truth to tell, I have been curious ever since."

Reb Asher froze, awestruck, and even the air seemed to be holding its breath until he responded, "Everyone talks about peace, but now that Reb Chaim Volozhiner is no longer with us, I see that he truly lived it! The void he left upon his passing is more vast than we mere mortals can fathom."

Heard from: Rabbi Gershon Chovsky

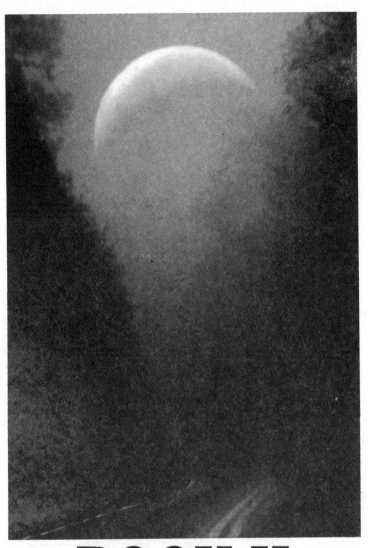

BOOK II

A Providential Coincidence

WHADDAYA*mean* 'there's no money in it'?"

"I already explained that. This is a non-profit operation."

"Hey, man, I always get paid. That's what it's all about. Mostly I work alone, y'see? But when someone else, eh, commissions me, we work out what you might call an equitable arrangement — usually on a percentage basis. I ain't never done it for *free!*"

"I told you, my friend. This is important stuff. Big time stuff. But there's no money in it."

"Look here, you put the word out that you were

lookin for a second-story man with class, and when our, eh, mutual friends contacted me, I told 'em I was your boy. But look, man, they didn't tell me this was *pro bono!*"

"Hold it — don't blame our friends. I didn't tell them what it was for..."

"Besides, I been thinkin about changin my line a work, maybe even goin straight. I'm gettin married soon, and my fiancée don't know what I do for a livin."

"Well, then, this is your opportunity to start paying your debt to society."

"Okay, lemme get this straight. You're a rabbi..."

"I'm not a rabbi."

"Anyone who goes around dressed like you must be a rabbi, or almost a rabbi, or somethin."

"Go on."

"Look, Rabbi, all I'm sayin is that here you are, almost a rabbi, right? And you want me to break into a synagogue. So what's your angle, and what's in it for old *numero uno?*"

"For *numero uno?* Well, Jimmy, I think there's a fifty-fifty chance that we'll be on television, and if we are, you'll be right there with us, see?"

"The tube? Really? I never been on the tube."

"That's right. Now, I've already explained my angle. The Grodno Shul is the oldest synagogue in Providence. A lot of Jews from Grodno settled in that part of town when they first came to America. In the beginning, they held services in all kinds of crazy places, but they always wanted to build a synagogue. So, when they got to be a little better off, they built one, see?"

"Yeah, I see. It was pretty much the same with my people."

"So all the Jews got together and built this synagogue and gave it this beautiful Hebrew name, which means 'brotherly love.' But since it was built by Jews from Grodno, everybody just called it the Grodno Shul, and that's how it's been known to this day."

"So Grodno is the name of a city?"

"Yeah. It's in Lithuania. Ever hear of Lithuania?"

"Sure. It's like a suburb of Moscow or somethin, right?"

"Yeah, well, more or less."

"Okay, so whydya wanna break in?"

"Well, Jimmy, all the old Jews that started the shul either passed on or moved away. So none of the original members go there anymore. In fact, it's been closed for about five years. There's one old fellow, the former president of the congregation — the last surviving member. He wants to sell it off, and he claims that he's gonna donate the proceeds to charities in Israel."

"Seems fair to me."

"Well, the thing is this: there are people who would still pray here if it stays; selling it means an end to Judaism in this area."

"Sounds terminal."

"We believe it's a crime to destroy or sell a synagogue. The person who wants to buy it plans to tear it down and build a parking garage and charge eighty thousand dollars for each parking space. It's a shame about the beautiful old building and the neighborhood. But now that the Jews are starting to move back and it's becoming a yuppie neighborhood..."

"Hey, you don't have to tell me, Rabbi. I've paid quite a few, eh, professional visits to the homes there."

"Be that as it may, there are Jews moving back in, and they could keep the old place going, easily."

"And that's why ya wanna break in?"

"Exactly. Remember, back in the sixties, when all the college kids were 'occupying' buildings?"

"Yeah."

"Well, that was their way of protesting, bringing their message to the public, see? That's what we want to do. We want to make a big fuss. Get the TV, radio, and newspapers to come down. So we break in and hold a prayer service."

"So how does the TV, radio, and newspapers find out?"

"We tell them, of course."

"Oh, I get it! You send out, like, press releases, right?"

"Right, and we've got just the guy to do it. This guy knows every reporter in town, all the TV types too, and he's going to call in a lot of favors."

"And what if the cops get wind of this? I ain't honeymoonin in the slammer!"

"Hey, that's why we're breaking in at midnight.

We're going to have this all-night prayer service, but the press conference is at ten the next morning!"

ND THAT'S what happened. We broke in at midnight, and at ten o'clock the next morning, we opened the doors to find...
Maybe I should back up a little. Baruch's the name, but my folks still call me Barry. I'm what you call a *baal teshuvah*. I became religious about ten years ago, although I never really got a chance to learn Torah as much as I wanted to. I won't bore you with the details.

I was the "street man" in the Grodno Shul thing — a job for which I had pretty good qualifications.

It all started after I met Itch Karlinsky. Since I'm something of a chess bum, I used to hang around the parks in Providence where people play chess outdoors. Hanging around the chess games was a good way of making friends, and it was over a game that I met this fellow Itch Karlinsky. Itch is a confirmed bachelor. Most of the year, he lives alone in a place that's something between a mansion and a palace. A couple of months a year, he lives in a very exclusive time-sharing place in Herzliya, Israel. He seems to be independently wealthy, and on the one or two occasions when I was forward enough to ask him what he does for a living, he mumbled something that sounded like "stock market." Personally, I never saw him work.

Itch and I hit it off right away, and before long we were studying together, making Shabbos together, and generally hanging out. No one could ever tell how old he is, and he's even more reticent about his age than he is about his income. He claims to have *semichah*, though he isn't like any of the Rabbis I've studied with, and he doesn't exactly have a "flock," at least not to my knowledge. He knows a lot, though, and he's got the biggest library of *sefarim* and books on Jewish topics, religion, and general philosophy that I've ever seen. He has a real Jewish heart too, always doing favors for some old lady or other, visiting handicapped kids in the hospital, and having all kinds of homeless weirdos for supper.

One day, after I hadn't seen him for about two weeks — he pulls these mysterious disappearances from time to time — he shows up in the park, and says, "Baruch, I gotta talk to you."

"Sit down, and we'll talk over a game," I tell him, but he says no, he's got to talk to me where we won't be overheard. So we go for a walk, and he asks me what I know about the Grodno Shul. Well, I had passed it once or twice before, but other than that, I didn't know much of anything about the place. So he tells me the whole story about how the last surviving member wants to sell it, and about how he, Itch, wants to save it, and then he asks me if I'm in.

"Sure, I'm in," I tell him. "What do you want to do?"

"Well," he says, "I thought we could break in, and just start running it like a regular shul. I've got plenty of friends to help us make *minyanim* from the beginning, and as time goes on, we'll draw members from the neigborhood."

So I tell him that's no good, that they'll go ahead and sell it right out from under us, and on the day they decide to knock it down, they'll come with cops, drag everybody out, and demolish the building before we even turn around.

"We've got to get the community involved," I tell him, "raise money and buy the place up before the developer does, or maybe get it declared a historical landmark."

"How do we get people involved?" he asks.

"Well," I say, "the first thing we need is publicity. We need to get the ball rolling, get all Providence up in arms about the Grodno Shul."

"Great idea. Yeah," he says. "Maybe we could get on TV, on the radio. Into the schools. Every kid in Providence contributes a quarter to save the Grodno Shul!"

"That's the idea."

"Yeah." He's starting to get excited, and those green eyes of his are starting to sparkle. "We need a big publicity stunt. Maybe we could chain ourselves to the mayor's desk, or stop traffic on I-95..."

"Whoa," I say. "Hold on a minute." By this time, I'm afraid he's gonna blow up an airliner or something to save the Grodno Shul. "Listen, Itch, if you know what you're doing, you can get plenty of publicity without doing anything crazy."

"How?"

"For instance, I'm just thinking out loud, you understand, but let's say we, uh, let's say, we break into the place one night about midnight, and start learning — we'll call it a Torathon or something like that. We'll daven at sunrise, and then have a big press conference."

"Right," he says, starting to pant a little (Itch is

pretty excitable), "a 'Learn-In,' a Thursday night Learn-In. And then, at the press conference, we invite all the Jews in the neighborhood for Friday night services! We plaster the community with posters explaining the situation! We get all the neighbors to come down! We set up a bank account for contributions! Set up an organization! Incorporate!"

"That's it," I say, "but slow down. Let's take one thing at a time. The first thing is the Learn-In and news conference. We've got to organize it."

"Okay," he says, "I can get the people, and the *sefarim*, and give the *shiurim*."

"And refreshments," I add.

"Yeah, I'll handle all the refreshments," he says. "What can *you* do?"

"I'll do two very important things," I say. "First, I'll talk to a lawyer."

"What for?"

What for? he asks.

"Whaddaya mean, 'what for'? Look, *boychik*, neither you, nor I, nor anybody else, for that matter, is getting involved in this until we know what can happen to us. I know it's a good cause, but if they're going to send me up the river for twelve to fourteen for davening in the Grodno Shul, well, you can count me and a lot of others out. So let's find out what's the worst that can happen to us, and make sure there's someone to bail us out if they decide to throw us in the hoosegow for a couple of nights."

"Uh, maybe you're right. You know somebody?"

"Branford Hainey the third."

"Who?"

"Branford Hainey the third. His ancestors came over on the Mayflower, and I'm not joking. But the guy's a Righteous Gentile if ever there was one. He studied under Dershowitz at Harvard. Bran's got a *Yiddishe kop*. I mean he's one smart lawyer, and he specializes in civil disobedience."

"Okay. What's the second thing you'll do?"

"I'll get us into the building."

"How? You know how to pick locks? I don't want any damage done to the place."

"I never picked a lock in my life," I say with my hand over my heart, and it was almost true, "but I have friends."

"What friends?" Itch can't stand to think that anyone is better connected than he is.

"Friends."

"Okay, you and your friends handle the locks."

"Now, who's going to get us the publicity?" I ask.

Itch thinks a minute, and then says, "That's easy. Moishe Greenbaum. He's in advertising, but he used to write news copy for WTVU. He knows all the local media people. He'll write the press release, and he'll see that it gets to the right people. With Moishe, who knows? We might even get national coverage!"

The break-in was easy. It took Jimmy the engaged-to-be-married, newly-reformed burglar all of 70 seconds to get in. He didn't leave a mark on the old place, and as a matter of professional pride, he didn't leave a fingerprint either.

At this stage, of course, we wanted to be as unobtrusive as possible, so just Itch, Jimmy, and I showed up at midnight. Since Jimmy's last name was Ryan, we needed eight more for a minyan. They waited at Itch's house, and once we were inside the shul, we called them on Itch's cellular phone and told them to come over. Moishe Greenbaum showed up about 9:30 the next morning to set up the news conference, and Branford Hainey the third came down a little later to handle the cops, should they arrive.

It was a jewel of a synagogue. High ceiling. Beautiful dark wooden pews. The aisles were carpeted and badly in need of a shampoo, but the flooring under the pews was terrazzo or something and surprisingly clean. The crowning glory of the old place was a really impressive one-of-a-kind wooden *aron kodesh*, which, as far as I was concerned, was worth the entire seven-figure price that Mr. Garage-Builder was offering for the privilege of knocking the place down.

We learned all night and davened at sunrise. Itch didn't look tired at all. He kept pacing, and sort of talking to himself. I figured he was preparing what to say at the press conference. Every so often, he would sit down next to me and ask if I thought any reporters would come. I told him I figured a few might show, and that, like I said, even if we make it to only one edition of the evening news, we would have what to build on. "If we get minimal coverage," I said, "we'll have to work a lot harder, canvassing the neigborhood, passing around petitions, going to city council meetings, and thinking up other publicity stunts, but if we get good exposure — maybe two TV stations and a little newspaper coverage — then we're home free."

"You think so, Baruch?"

"Depend on it, Itch. What's with Moishe Greenbaum? Did he do his thing?"

"Listen, Baruch, Moishe is going all out."

"So don't worry. Remember, you see one TV camera — just one — you know we're okay."

Did I say *one* TV camera? Try *five*!

Like everyone but Itch, I'd fallen asleep. About quarter to ten, Itch, who by now was flushed and perspiring with excitement, came around and nudged everybody awake.

All the guys, except Jimmy, who had slept since about one in the morning, were real groggy. We all straightened our clothes and ran our fingers through our hair. We collected our things, stashed everything near the door, and prepared to meet our public. "Please, God, let them be there," I heard Itch whisper, and that made something inside me go click.

I'm not much of a speaker, but suddenly I was angry, really angry. I felt the blood rush to my face and my whole body go cold. My heart started to pound, and my breath came in short gasps. I have a pretty loud voice, and as a result, I've taught myself to speak quietly over the years. I'm about six-three with broad shoulders. I played some varsity football in college in the

Midwest (where I come from) and I'm pretty strong, and more than a couple of pounds overweight. People sometimes call me "the gentle giant." And now, suddenly, I could hear myself bellowing.

I don't know who I thought I was talking to. After all, we were only eleven people, and everybody was standing right there next to me. All the same, I was shouting.

"Look here, people," I said. "You've all seen this beautiful shul. It was built by the sweat of our grandfathers, and it has stood on this spot for more than seventy years. This shul is a gem, and it's one of the most beautiful buildings in Providence." Who knows if that's true, but at the moment I *believed*.

"Now they want to tear it down, and that's wrong, dead wrong. This shul is history. It's part of the history of the Jewish People and part of the history of Providence. This shul is holy. It was made holy by the people who spent their hard-earned money to put it up and maintain it, by the people who davened here, and by the people who learned Torah here. History and holiness are more important than a parking lot, and we're not going to let it happen, because it's wrong. It's dead wrong."

And then I stopped, because I'd run out of gas. I didn't know how to finish, so I coughed a couple times. That was when I saw a fist shoot up. It was not a very big fist. Good second-story men are usually pretty small. The fist, it seems, was attached to the recently engaged, newly-reformed, Jimmy Ryan, and Jimmy was shouting, "It's wrong! It's dead wrong!" It didn't take but a second for everybody else to get the idea, and we all raised our fists and started shouting, "It's wrong!

It's dead wrong!"

We stood there shouting for a minute, our message penetrating our own consciousness and molding our faces into expressions of anger. Itch and I were still standing in front of our gang, facing them, when Jimmy Ryan pushed his way up through the little group, shouting all the time. He quickly wormed his way between us, spun us around, and slipped his slender arms through ours. I felt Jimmy begin to push us down the foyer, and I realized that all eleven of us were marching in time to our shouted chant.

And then we hit the door. I don't know who opened it, but I do know what happened immediately after. In my memory it's like a movie run in slow motion. First off, I went blind. The foyer had been quite dark, and now the morning sun smashed me in the eyes like a one-two punch. My left arm was still locked in Jimmy's right, so I opened my clenched right fist, and shaded my eyes. In a second or two my vision returned, and as soon as I could see what was going on, my knees buckled. There must have been a hundred people outside! I felt little Jimmy Ryan trying to keep me from falling, and I heard him say in a stage whisper, "C'mon, Rabbi, don't faint now. This is it, man!"

Directly in front of the shul is Moishe Greenbaum, wearing a business suit and little black leather *kippah*. He's got some sort of lectern affair, like they have at real press conferences, and he's leaning on it from in front, facing sideways and kibbitzing with one of the reporters. About ten feet away, standing around him in a small semicircle, are the reporters, technicians, soundmen, and so forth. There are five TV cameras. Five! Bran Hainey is standing unobtrusively off to the side.

We march over to the lectern, all eleven of us shouting, "It's wrong! It's dead wrong!" Moishe Greenbaum raises his hand for silence, and we quiet down. I hear the clicks of shutters and the whirrs of the motor drives on the still cameras, and I see the big zoom lenses on the shoulder-held television cameras going in and out.

"Ladies and gentlemen," I hear Moishe saying, his hand still in the air, "I would like to introduce to you Rabbi Yitzhak..."

Rabbi *Yitzhak*? I think. Yeah, a name like "Itch" would never play in Peoria.

"Rabbi Yitzhak," he says, "Rabbi Yitzhak Karlinsky."

Itch slips his arm out of Jimmy's, and Jimmy and I retreat a few steps as Itch approaches the *shtender*. Itch, his green eyes glowing like some religious ecstatic, takes a couple of papers out of his back pocket. The papers are folded together in half and again in thirds, and he opens them and smooths them down on the *shtender*.

"Ladies and gentlemen," he intones, "standing before you are the members of the Ad Hoc Committee for the Rescue of the Grodno Synagogue."

Where he got that one from, I'll never know — an ad hoc name for an ad hoc committee, I'm thinking.

"I am here to announce that the members of our committee have spent the night studying sacred texts and praying in this magnificent old structure, and that all of us have taken a sacred vow before the holy ark..." Sacred vow! Boy, is he laying it on. "...a sacred vow that the Grodno Synagogue, the oldest synagogue in the entire Providence area, will not, I repeat, will not be torn down to build a garage. We hereby declare the Ad Hoc Committee for the Rescue of the Grodno Synagogue to be the acting board of directors of this institution..." Acting board of directors — what a ham. "...the acting board of directors and as such, reject all offers for its purchase, no matter what the price."

Itch pauses for a moment, for dramatic effect, I guess, and clears his throat, but before he can resume speaking, one of the reporters — a hard-bitten New York type — shouts out, "You and yer committee got a lotta chutzpah, Rabbi. Whadda *you* care if the old place goes? Nobody prays here anymore, and all the money's going to charity."

For a moment, for just a moment, I see Itch's face flush with anger, but then it softens, and his eyes fill up. He looks down at the papers he hasn't finished reading. He clears his throat again, refolds the papers, and returns them to his pocket. Next he shoots a side-long glance at me and then rivets those big green eyes on the reporter. "My good man," he says calmly, "my friends and I have just spent the entire night inside the 'old place,' as you call it. And I would like to tell you, sir, that it is a gem, a jewel of a synagogue. It was built by the sweat of our grandfathers, and it has stood on this spot for more than seventy years. It is a gem, and it is one of the most beautiful buildings in Providence. Now they want to tear it down, and that's wrong.

"This shul is history," he says, his voice rising. "It's part of the history of the Jewish People and part of the history of Providence.

"This shul is holy," and now he's shouting. "It was

made holy by the people who spent their hard-earned money to put it up and maintain it, by the people who prayed here, and by the people who learned Torah here, including the members of the Ad Hoc Committee who studied, prayed, and took a sacred vow here last night." Again with the sacred vow.

"History and holiness are more important than a parking lot," he shouts, "and we're not going to let it happen, because it's wrong. It's dead wrong."

With that, we take up the chant again, and all the time I'm thinking that all this sounds pretty familiar. Anyway, with us shouting like that, the cameras all turn on us, but Itch is in control of himself and the situation now, so he waits a minute or so and then raises his hand for silence. "The acting board of directors of the Grodno Synagogue hereby announces that as of tonight, Friday night, the synagogue is again open and functioning..." I knew he was playing it by ear. "...open and functioning, and we hereby invite all of Providence to worship with us tonight, and to join us afterward for a festive *oneg Shabbos* party to celebrate the re-opening of the Grodno Synagogue."

Hey, I'm thinking, we never talked about *all of Providence*, and we never talked about an *oneg Shabbos*. What if all of Providence decides to come? What'll we do then?

❀

The rest, as the man said, is history. They interviewed every one of us separately and all of us together. They interviewed bystanders, each other, the rhododendrons — Greenbaum had them clamoring for the scoop within the scoop. The press conference and interviews took so long I was afraid we wouldn't make it onto the midday news.

But we did make it. Soon as we could, Itch and I jumped into his red Ferrari and with tires squealing, sped over to see ourselves on the boob tube. Sure enough, there was Itch inviting all of Providence down for Friday night services, and there was Jimmy Ryan stammering over the word "consultant" when they asked him who he was and what he did, and Branford Hainey, and all the rest of the participants. We had radio coverage every hour all afternoon, and our pictures appeared in the later editions of the afternoon papers.

All the neighborhood do-gooders wanted to get involved, and the non-Jews took an even bigger interest than the Jews. A lot of really sincere secular Jews from the neigborhood got involved too, and I figured that if they help save the place then they're going to have to support it, maybe come to services once in a while, maybe send their kids to the Talmud Torah.

On Monday, the Providence historical society contacted Itch and promised to lobby the city council to get the shul designated a historic landmark, and eventually it was.

The Ad Hoc Committee never met again, and after the midday news, I never saw Jimmy Ryan again. I think old Itch was actually a little disappointed. I know he enjoyed the notoriety, but he did have one more moment in the limelight, and that was at the Friday night services and *oneg Shabbos*.

But as you'll soon see, there's another reason why you have to hear about that party.

W HAT ARE YOU complaining about, Itch? It was you who invited all of Providence."

"Hey, man, I meant all of *Jewish* Providence, maybe a couple of non-Jewish bleeding hearts — okay, Bran Hainey — he's one of the family. You know. But not THIS!"

By "this," Itch was probably referring to the five hundred or so freaks, weirdos, beggars, shopping-bag ladies, crazies, communists, bikers, agitators, Moonies, and concerned citizens jammed into the little courtyard of the Grodno Shul. The Friday night services were clearly the side show here. The main attraction was everything else. The Grodno Shul party had made it onto the counter-culture calendar, and since by coincidence this was a pretty slow Friday night, Grodno, as it turned out, was *the* place to be.

Although the tables were set up and ready, in our attempt to maintain some semblance of order, we didn't put the food out until after we'd finished our own quick meal. I made Kiddush again, out loud, for all those who had just arrived, but my voice was challenged by the roar of Harley Davidsons and the chants of the Harry Kushners.* The food — in a moment of optimism, I'd planned for a hundred participants — disappeared faster than we could put it out, and afterward, Itch complained that he hadn't gotten to taste a thing.

The situation threatened to turn nasty when about fifty police officers arrived together with two empty school buses. There were plenty of experienced demonstrators and cop-baiters in the crowd, and by the taunts

---

* On the advice of legal counsel, the name of this cult has been disguised.

and epithets they started hurling at Providence's finest, some of them were evidently hoping to get a whiff of tear gas. I saw Itch shoot a glance towards Branford Hainey the third, who signaled him not to worry and mouthed the words, "Take it easy."

I was afraid of the crowd, though, so without thinking twice, I hopped up on a chair and switched my voice into bull-horn mode and began shouting. As I've said, I've got a pretty strong set of vocal chords, and standing on a chair, I didn't have much trouble getting people quiet.

"Friends and neighbors" — I told you I was from the Midwest — "a few officers of the Providence Police Department have just joined us." Shouts and groans from the crowd.

"Please, give me your attention!" With a voice like mine, they had little choice. "As I said, a few officers of the Providence Police Department have just joined us. I understand that they have come to protect the Grodno Synagogue, which we are here to save, and to protect us from ourselves." That got a few snickers.

"I have been assured by counsel," I went on, "that as long as this demonstration, uh, this Sabbath party, remains peaceful, we have nothing to fear. So in the name of the Ad Hoc Committee, I would like to request of all those who love the Grodno Shul to please, please help keep this a *non-violent* demonstration, in the spirit of our holy Sabbath.

"I would like to thank everyone for coming down and to assure you all that the Ad Hoc Committee will spare no effort to prevent the destruction of the Grodno Synagogue. I want to wish everyone a Sabbath of peace, understanding, and brotherly love. *Shabbat Shalom.*"

The atmosphere changed immediately, and the danger of a confrontation with the Men in Blue passed. The skin-heads demonstrating across the street with "America for the Whites" posters, also realized that they weren't going to get a rise out of this crowd and closed up shop.

Me? I was just standing there with Itch, Bran Hainey, and one or two others of the original Ad Hoc Committee. Then along comes this Harry Kushner dressed in the floppy robe they wear, his head — all except a thin little tail in the back — shaved almost to the skin, and some white stuff over the bridge of his obviously Jewish nose. He's got these thick super-nerdy-looking horn-rimmed glasses that are glinting in the light of the street lamps, and with this really nauseating other-worldly, I've-seen-the-light-and-would-like-to-show-it-to-you-too smile on his face, he extends a conch shell filled with change and bills, and asks for a contribution.

Itch apologetically tells him about our not handling money on Shabbos and then asks him his name.

"Nerunjanah."

"*Shalom aleichem*, Reb Nerunjanah," says Itch. "And what name did your parents give you?"

"Irv."

"Irv. You mean Irving?"

"Yes."

"Irving what?"

"Levine, Irving Levine," he answers with a nervous little laugh.

"Where'd you grow up, Irv?" Itch continues.

"Please call me Nerunjanah."

"I'm sorry, Nerunjanah. Where'd you grow up?"

"I was born and raised in Brooklyn."

"What part?

"Flatbush."

"Where'd you go to high school?"

"East Midwood."

"And college?"

"I dropped out of Brooklyn College when I became initiated."

"And where did you become initiated?"

"Oh, we have a big Ashram about twenty-five miles from Grandville, Florida."

Old Irv Nerunjanah Levine is looking a little uncomfortable. On the one hand, Itch, who really knows how to lay it on, is sounding so genuinely interested and solicitous, anyone would be flattered. On the other hand, Irv can't help but feel that maybe he's being set up for something.

"Anyway," Itch says, "what I wanted to ask was, what brings you down to the Grodno Shul?"

Here Irv brightens a bit, I guess because he's got a good answer ready. "Our leader here in Providence,

Kirtan Maharaj Goswami, said that this was a holy place, that your demonstration here is a holy event, and that we should be here."

"And what was Kirtan's name before he became initiated?" Itch asks.

"Um, Mark Goldstein."

"I see. Well, it was nice talking to you, Reb Nerunjanah. I'd like to invite you to come down for services some time, after we get the shul reopened."

"Oh, I could never do that. Not without Kirtan's approval. But I would like to invite you people over to the park on Sunday. We're having our annual Wonders of India Fair. I think you might enjoy it. Or, if you happen to be down Florida-way, you could come to our main event, on the Ashram."

Levine turns to leave, but then I hear myself asking, "What time does this fair begin?"

Irv turns around again, with that same unctuous smile, and I feel Itch, Branford Hainey, and the others staring at me like I've just gone completely off my rocker. "Oh, it's on from the early morning until sunset," Irv says, "but the one on the Ashram will be running all month long. I'll see you there."

Fat chance, I thought.

II

DEAR BUBBIE,

I guess you're wondering why this letter isn't coming to you from Israel. Well, a couple of days before I was supposed to leave, I started making the rounds to say goodbye to all my friends here in Providence. We were having an unexpectedly early spring. It was really warm outside, and all the trees had started to bloom. As you know, I'm a real sucker for a spring day. I was half drunk on the fresh air, and after visiting one of my buddies, I decided to walk home barefoot. I still remember how Mom and Dad used to get angry if I took off my shoes in a park or something, and now I'm beginning to see their point.

When I got home, everything was still okay. I

warmed up a TV dinner and settled down to eat it in my favorite easy chair. As I was sitting there with all the windows open, still grooving on the fresh air, my right foot began to hurt a little. I didn't think much of it, but pretty soon it began to throb, so I took off my shoes and socks again to get a better look. Well, the heel was all red and hot and swollen, and as time went on it kept hurting more and more.

You know, I'm no complainer, Bubbie. You remember when I broke my arm playing football? That hardly bothered me at all, but I never felt anything like this! So I hobbled into the bathroom and took a couple Tylenol, came back and put my foot up on the couch, hoping the pain would subside. Next thing I knew it was about 11:30 at night and I was lying there on the couch in a cold sweat, my foot feeling like it was about to explode. Please don't tell anybody, but by then, I was really scared. When you live alone, like you and I do, sickness can be really frightening.

So I got on the phone and called a radio cab, and moving all the time only on my good foot, inched my way along the wall and down the stairs. How long it really took that cab to come, I couldn't tell you, but to me it seemed like he must have driven in from California.

I passed out at the admissions desk, and when I came to, I was lying in a bed in the hallway of the emergency room, with an IV stuck into me. This doctor was telling me that I had some sort of insect bite, and that they would have to wait till the test results came back to know exactly what.

You're not going to believe this, Bubbie, but I was

a full week in the hospital. They told me I'd been bitten by a black widow spider, and that I'd have to take it easy for at least another week after I was released.

So here I am. In America and not in Israel. You're probably thinking that Baruch's just writing to tell you all his troubles, but I'm not. You see, this whole business left me feeling pretty depressed. I really wanted to be in Israel for Pesach. Ever since I became religious, I've been making the Seders with some of my friends, but there's nothing like family, especially when you're feeling down, and you're the only one who keeps kosher. So I was wondering if you might like a guest for Pesach?

> *Love,*
> *Baruch (Barry)*

❁

The letter was mostly true. I only fabricated on the wanting to be with family part. But I truly always feel guilty about my grandmother.

Don't get me wrong, she's an amazing lady, for her own age or any other. Like so many other Jews over the age of sixty-five, she and my grandfather retired to the sun belt. He died of a sudden heart attack a year or two later, and although it was a big blow at the time, she ended up handling it pretty well.

But she always says that Pesach is her loneliest time. My grandparents certainly weren't what you'd call observant, but they kept kosher and my Bubbie always put on a big Seder for the whole family. She won't come to my folks for the *Sedarim*, since they don't keep kosher, so every year since my grandfather died, my grandmother goes to a Jewish hotel with a friend of hers, for the whole week of the holiday.

I always felt bad about that, but since becoming religious, I've needed to attend other people's *Sedarim* until I knew how to lead one on my own. But when this thing happened to me, I decided that I'd spent enough years worrying about myself, that by now I knew perfectly well how to run a Seder. The time had come, I figured, to do something for someone else.

I took a bus down to Lauderdale. I know it's strange, but I like buses, and besides, other than hitchhiking, which I gave up when I turned twenty-nine, it's the cheapest way to travel.

I got down a few days before Pesach, and with my grandmother as straw boss, I cleaned while she cooked. Luckily I was feeling a whole lot better by this time, because you know how Jewish mothers of that generation are: everything had to be spick and span, squeaky-clean, and white-tornadoed. I never worked so hard in my life. And I never saw my grandmother so happy. At night, when both of us collapsed, she would tell me stories of how her parents had made Pesach. When I told her we were going to do *bedikas chametz*, her eyes filled up, and she told me that she hadn't seen that since she was a little girl.

She invited nine of her neighbors for the Seder, which I led. My grandmother *kvell*ed from *Kadesh* to *Nirtzah*. When a couple of the old fellows and I sang *Chad Gadya*, she *kvell*ed some more, and on the second night she *kvell*ed all over again. I guess grandmothers everywhere are the same.

It was a really great week. My Bubbie kept telling me it was the best Pesach she ever had, and I really felt like I'd done a big mitzvah. I also felt about ten pounds heavier after all she'd fed me. As I boarded the bus for the trip home with the turkey sandwiches, cans of tuna, egg salad, jelly, box of matzah, tomatoes, apples, cucumbers, oranges, carrot and celery sticks, peanut butter, dried figs, dates and apricots, sour pickles, green pepper slices, half a chocolate cake, paper plates and cups, and plastic flatware that my grandmother had packed me for the way home, I promised myself that I would be spending Pesach with her every year from then on. I fell asleep on the bus feeling overstuffed and happy and thinking that getting bitten by a black widow spider had its compensations.

It was a good sleep, filled with dreams of *matzah-brai* and *kneidlach*. I slept a long time too. In fact, I slept until the bus broke down just outside of Grandville, Florida's unforgettable bus station.

If you've never had the opportunity to visit the Grandville bus station, I would highly recommend that you not bother. This appears to be the place that the word "dreary" was invented to describe. Forget air conditioning. You know those old four-bladed drugstore-style fans from the thirties and forties? Well, that was what they used there to sort of circulate the stale tobacco/cheap booze/dirty bathroom smell that passed for air. I think the grime that was stuck to those fans was from the thirties too.

The ashtrays, as far as I could tell, had not been

emptied since the Civil War, and the floor, which may at one time have been some color other than black, seemed to have been mopped only once or twice since then. Somebody dropped a bottle of Dr. Pepper on the floor, and this old Black man came shuffling out with a big sack of sawdust which he dumped onto the puddle. Pretty soon the flies began to buzz around the sodden glop, but the man never came back to sweep the stuff up.

The few fluorescents still intact bathed the windowless waiting room in a kind of twenty-four-hour *bein ha-shemashos*. The dark green, molded plastic seats were arranged in facing rows and bolted to the floor. They were linked together by their rusting chrome arms, which had little curved plastic armrests screwed onto them about where your elbow was supposed to hit. At the end of each row was some sort of metal receptacle the likes of which I'd never seen before but I guessed must be a spitoon. What helped me figure that out, was this big sign on the wall: DO NOT SPIT ON THE FLOOR.

None of the seats looked clean enough to rest even my worn and faded jeans on, but that didn't seem to deter the five or six shopping-bag people — townies, apparently — from sleeping on them with their heads resting on their arms, resting on their knees. I discovered two soda pop vending machines in one corner and a candy machine in another. The third corner had a high four-legged wooden stool of prewar (Spanish American, I think) vintage, piled with newspapers on top of which sat a small cardboard box containing a couple of quarters. And in the fourth corner there was a display of dog-eared paperbacks on these revolving tree-like contraptions of black metal. Flanked by these on two sides, sat a cash register manned (or perhaps I should say womanned) by a twenty-year-old female who presided over a cracked and smudged glass showcase filled with cigarettes, cigars, Lifesavers, silver-paper wrapped chocolate mints, Tums, Alka-Seltzer, Bayer aspirin, and an unusually rich and varied assortment of chewing tobaccos.

First I spent my time exploring, then standing and shifting my weight from one foot to the other and back again. I walked outside. I walked back in. I walked out and in again. I walked up and down the platform and finally found my way to the garage, where I started a conversation with one of the local idlers. He assured me that his best buddy, an ambitious fellow who was waiting for an opening to become the assistant mechanic's deputy "gopher," had said that it wouldn't take more than three or four hours to get that baby — by that, I think he meant my bus — back on the road. I thanked him politely and strolled back to the bus station entrance. This time, I began noticing the posters that lined the walls of the bus terminal inside and out.

What a strange conglomeration, I thought. Good, wholesome American kids munching on hamburgers, happy faces promising the good life if only I would drink Coca Cola, You-Know-Who Saves (apparently on Sundays at the First Baptist Church of Grandville), the noble masculinity of an American cowboy filling his American lungs with American tobacco smoke, Mickey Mouse and Pluto beckoning me to join them and their pals at Disney World in Orlando, a Wall Street yuppie accessing the Dow Jones industrials on his Toshiba lap-top computer, and the smiling nerdy face and shaven skull of Nerunjanah Irving Levine.

Nerunjanah Irving Levine!? Hey, what's old Nerunjanah-from-Providence doing here in Florida?

But there he was, smack in the middle of a poster showing the smiling happy faces of about ten young men and women. The men were in robes and had white marks between their eyes, and the women, many of whom had little ornaments affixed to their nostrils and heavy bracelets on their wrists, wore saris. The men all had shaven heads, and everyone looked about as satisfied and transcendent as it's possible for a human being to be. They were photographed from the waist up, in a field of thick luxurious grass generously spattered with bright yellow wildflowers, and above their heads were the words PEACE LOVE BROTHERHOOD. No commas, I thought. At the very bottom of the poster, in much smaller but fully legible letters, was written, "The Society for Kushner Awareness (SKA)," and a telephone number.

I probably would have given this poster about as much attention as I had the one for the First Baptist Church of Grandville, but there was old Nerunjanah, and I recognized him right off the bat. I studied the poster more carefully, and the first thing I noticed was that the phone number at the bottom had no area code. I figured that they must have a local branch and looked again at those beatific faces.

Then it hit me. I'll say they've got a local branch! Grandville is where they have that big — what do they call it? Yeah, that big *Ashram*, where old Irv Levine said he became initiated. Itch had told me later on that the HKs had designated Grandville the home of the movement's American headquarters. Grandville...well, what do you know.

This is *some* coincidence, I thought, as that whole

silly conversation at the Grodno Shul came back to me, to be shipwrecked in Grandville, Florida only to run across a poster of my very own Harry. Is there really such a thing as a coincidence? I wondered.

That's when I heard the music.

SO HERE I AM, minding my own business, when suddenly I find myself encircled by an undulating, dancing, vibrating, chanting, singing, clapping, jumping, incense-burning band of bonafide SKA weirdos. And just as suddenly, there are *two* Nerunjanah Levines, the one on the poster outside the terminal, and the one leading the group.

I had to hand it to old Nerunjanah. He identified me immediately. That's how come they descended on me. "Oh wow, you came!" he said in his sweetest missionary voice, as he grabbed my limp right hand and began enthusiastically jerking it up and down.

Boy, did I feel dopey.

I like to think of myself as being able to land on my feet. But there I am with a terminal case of the post-Pesach bus-station-blues, and what I really do not, I repeat, DO NOT need at this moment is to have to give a polite brush-off to Irving Nerunjanah Levine at the head of a fanatical chanting gaggle of Grandville geeks.

But old Nerunjanah's pumping my hand, which I'm hoping that he'll let me have back some day, and he keeps repeating over and over again, "Wow, you came! I don't believe it! You really came!" At the same time, his left hand is on my right shoulder, like a scout master congratulating me on my first merit badge; all the faithful are smiling and nodding their assent, to what I don't know, and I, for some inexplicable reason, suddenly remember that I haven't eaten in hours.

Well, Nerunjanah finally realizes that he's been doing all the talking and decides to change course. "So how *are* you?" he asks, like we've known each other for just ages, and with that, the high-fidelity quadraphonic chanting starts up again.

"Hungry, mainly," I tell him.

"What?" he says, a little surprised at my answer, but right away he shifts gears. "Oh. You're hungry?" and his face goes all nerdy at the prospect of doing a good deed for a member of the unconverted.

"Me? Hungry? Nah." Leave me alone already, I'm thinking.

"You aren't?" He pauses to consider this latest development. "Well c'mon, then, uh, uh..." He's trying to get my name out of me, but I'm not helping. "I'm sorry," he says sweetly, "I forgot your name."

Forgot? I'm thinking. I never told it to you. "But I remember yours," I say. "You're Irv."

"Nerunjanah."

"Yeah, that's what I meant. Nerunjeleh."

"But I forgot your name."

I can see I'm going to have to make full disclosure, and I'm wondering if I should give him an alias, so I say, "Barry. I mean Baruch."

"What?"

Again with the "What?" "Baruch."

"Bur-*rookh*? Bur-*rookh*. Hanukah. *Bur-rookh at-tah...*"

"Right," I stop him before he can get to the Ineffable Name. "Ba-ruch. Just like when you light Chanukah and Shabbos candles."

"Gee, that's *great*," he enthuses, his eyes turning skyward. "Well c'mon, Bur-*rookh*. We've got a couple of vans here, and we'll take you back to the Ashram with us."

Now it was my turn to say, "What?" — not because I didn't understand, but because I did.

In Yiddish, they have a word for it. The word is *fumfit*, and, roughly speaking, it combines the meanings of the English terms splutter, mutter, and stutter. Be that as it may, standing outside the Grandville bus terminal that day with Kushner's Kossaks crowded 'round me, I *fumfit*ed like I never *fumfit*ed before, "Van? Ashram? Uh, you mean that you thought..." All the while Irv is giving me the big smile, and I'm inching backward till I mash firmly down on the bare foot of a very Jewish-looking Kushkette. She's wearing a really grubby Indian sari and has a red spot painted on her forehead and a pearl stuck in the side of her nose. She lets out a little scream, and I whirl around to say, "Oh, I'm so sorry," and whirl back to continue *fumfit*ing. "Uh, Irv..."

"Nerunjanah."

"Yeah, I mean Nerunjanah. Nerunjanah, you got this all wrong. I mean, I didn't come here. I mean, I *did* come here. But not *here*. I mean, you see what I mean?"

Of course he doesn't see what I mean, so he falls

back on his trusty, "What?"

"Look, Irv. Uh, Nerunjeleh. Could you and me maybe go inside and talk privately for a minute?"

"Sure, Bur-*rookh*." He's all concern and understanding.

We go inside, and I sit him down in a green plastic special. I excuse myself, and go over to the counter and buy a pack of Marlboros (I quit smoking ten years ago). I come back and offer him one.

"We don't smoke, drink, eat meat..."

"Right," I cut him off, as I light up. I'm really not ready for the *shpiel* just now. "Look, Irv, you probably think I came down to Grandville to spend some time on your Ashram and to find out all about, you know..."

"And I'm sure glad you did," he says looking like I'm his first case after graduating from social work school.

"Well, that's just it. You see, I didn't come for that at all. As a matter of fact, I had no intention of even stopping in Grandville."

"You didn't?" he says, his social-worker eyes widening behind the horn-rims.

"No, I really didn't." Finally got that out. "Look, Irv, Nerunjanah, do you remember what Passover is? The Seder? The Four Questions? Wine?"

"We don't drink wine, smoke, eat meat..."

"Yeah, I think we've been over that already. Do you remember what Passover is?

"Passover? Sure. Isn't that when the Jews came out of Egypt, and you eat matzah with cream cheese?"

"Yeah, that's it. Well look, Passover just ended, see? And I was down here in Florida visiting my grandmother for the holiday. Now I'm on my way back to Providence. You do remember Providence, don't you? Where we met at the Grodno Shul?"

"Sure."

"What" and "sure," I'm thinking. Come to glorious Grandville to build your vocabulary.

"Yeah, I'm glad you remember," I say, "'cause that's exactly where I'm headed. My bus broke down here in Grandville, see? And I'm stuck here for a couple hours. It's just a coincidence that I ran into you..."

"There's no such thing as coincidence," he says.

He's got a point, I'm thinking, but I say to him, "Sure there's coincidences, Irv. There's lots of coincidences, and this is a really big one. Just think of it. We get to know each other in Providence at the old Grodno Shul, and now I bump into you here in Grandville in the old bus station. Yep, this must be the grandaddy of all coincidences, see?"

I guess it's in the name of peace, love, and brotherhood that he doesn't contradict me again, I'm thinking as I hear the cadres outside slip into a new chant. I stand up, hoping that Irv will too and that I can ease him over to the door, so I can go and bury myself in a copy of the *Grandville Gazette* which I'll buy off the wooden stool. "So it sure was great seeing you again, Nerunjeleh. We really ought to get together next time you're in Providence."

But Irv's not listening. He's got his eye on the buck-toothed girl from behind the cash register who seems to be homing in on me from the other side of the terminal. "'Scuse me, Mister...?" Boy, do these crackers talk slow. "You on that there bus that got broke down?"

"Yes I am, Miss."

"Wey-ull, I'm sorry to have to tell you..." Uh-oh, I'm thinking. "I'm sorry to have to tell you that we can't fix it, and you can get your ticket refunded or a new ticket for the next bus to Providence."

"And when might that be departing?"

"Day after tomorrow, at ten A.M."

"Did you say the *day after tomorrow*?" My hands are starting to shake.

"Yes, sir, I did."

"Is today Thursday, Miss?"

"Yes, sir, it sure is. All day."

"So the next bus to Providence is on Saturday, is that right?"

"Yes, sir, that's what I said." And now I break out in a cold sweat.

"And when is the next bus after that?"

"Why, that'll be on Thursday again."

III

I DON'T KNOW WHY I said yes. I think it was Rabbi Nachman who said that the most dangerous thing is despair, and despair is about where I was.

My memory of what came after I got the good news about my bus is pretty fuzzy. I think that instead of me easing Irv out the door of the terminal, he must have eased me out. I seem to recall the chanting getting louder and louder and Irving Nerunjanah Levine clicking his heels together and repeating in a dreamy voice, "There's no such thing as coincidence. There's no such thing as coincidence."

I don't really remember much about the ride out to the church of the latter-day loonies. They sat me in the van between Irv Levine and the Jewish girl with the pearl in her nose and the (thanks to me) black-and-blue toes. The place where we were going was an old farm. It had some impossible-to-pronounce Indian name, but everyone just called it The Ashram.

It was getting dark when we got there. They offered

me something to eat, but I had the presence of mind to say I wasn't hungry. Irv said, "But you told me..." then stopped himself and switched to, "You must be tired." He led me off to this mobile home-type of affair, unlocked the door and let me in. I dropped my backpack to the floor. There was a freshly-made bed, but no sign that anyone else lived there. Later on, I found out that they had a number of these "guest houses."

Old Irv hit me with one more "There's no such thing as coincidence," said good night, and walked out.

Me? I davened, kicked off my shoes, put my feet up, and went to sleep.

When I woke up, I tried to put the events of the last twelve hours into some sort of order. I knew that I was alone in this mobile home thing and that for all intents and purposes I'd been spirited away by the men in the white robes. I wasn't frightened. Like I said, I played some varsity sports in college, and, as we say in the Midwest, I know pretty well how to handle myself.

I was angry, though. Not at old Irv Levine and his Ashram Astronauts. After all, they were only doing what Kushner had put them on this earth to do — persuade the entire world to trade their brains in for mush. I was angry at the idiot who had gotten me into this — namely, me.

I realized that I was doomed to spend Shabbos in Grandville, but I was determined not to spend it here on Kibbutz Kushner, so I figured that I might have some arranging to do. I hoped I might get my hands on a phone book, find the names of local synagogues, and just call around until I found an Orthodox rabbi who might be willing to put me up or find me a place.

I guessed that since Nerunjanah was the guy leading the infantry attack on the bus station, he was something like a sergeant, or if he was an officer, he wasn't a very highly placed one. I was certain they didn't send out the HK generals on such routine operations. I hoped that the higher-ups might be able to communicate with intelligent life from the planet earth (something which I was convinced was beyond Nerunjanah Levine's capabilities).

So, what I was looking for was the elite corps, the guys they must use to talk people into trying to be a Kishka for no more than a week or two "just to *experience* how great it is." Surely, those guys must know how we normals think, and I would explain to them that this was all a mistake and that I wasn't a candidate for a scalping or a mind transplant. And they would believe me, because they'd see right away that I'm too straight for all their nonsense. I'll just thank them politely for their hospitality, I reasoned, happily pay for my night's lodging, and ask when the next van leaves for Grandville. No van on Fridays, you say? That's okay, fellas; we can still be friends. I've got my thumb and the two feet that the good Lord gave me. And now, if you don't mind, I'll just be going...

But it would be awfully handy to make my phone calls from here, and for that I would need something like sympathetic cooperation.

After davening, I gulped down a can of pop from the fridge in the mobile home and polished off two of Bubbie's apples, so it was somewhere around six forty-five when I set off across the lawn for the nearest building.

❀

The Ashram looked deserted at that hour, but when I neared the building, I thought I could hear a low hum of human voices. I opened the door very quietly and found myself in a long, well-illuminated entry way with polished marble floor and walls adorned with strange-looking Indian art. At the far end was a very heavy, carved wooden door, which again I tried to open as quietly as I could. Luckily for me, it was well-oiled and swung open easily and in perfect silence.

At first, all I saw was people sitting on the floor in a large dimly-lit hall. All wore robes or saris and no shoes, and most had their heads slightly bowed as though they were reading something on the floor in front of them.

As my eyes grew accustomed to the gloom, I could see that what the worshippers were looking at on the floor were strings of colored beads. The sight of all those Kishkas sitting on the floor of a poorly-lit room, reciting their *mantra* and counting their beads to track the number of times they had repeated it, was mesmerizing, hypnotic almost. For a moment I forgot where I was.

You can imagine my shock, then, when my gaze rose from the nodding heads of the faithful to the wall opposite me, where I beheld a life-size, incredibly real-looking, wax model of none other than Kushner himself and some other of your favorite *avodah zarah* all-stars. At the time, of course, I had no idea what all those skin-heads were doing on the floor, or who the wax dummies on the other side of the room were. It wasn't long, though, before I found out.

I don't know if it was the frighteningly natural look of the idols, the mind-numbing scene unfolding right here in the American capital of idolatry, the shaven heads and pierced noses, or what, but I was gripped by a deep and very slow chill that started somewhere at the base of my neck and spread through my entire body, causing me to shiver all over. I needed air fast. I closed the door and turned to leave, but as I did, I thought I saw, out of the corner of my eye, a dark figure get up off the floor.

I headed for the exit as fast as I could, grateful that my sneakers made no noise on the marble floor as I ran. Once outside, I ran a few yards further and then lay down on the beautifully tended lawn. Hoping that the fresh air and prone position might calm my heaving gut, I inhaled and exhaled several times and then just lay quiet, my eyes shut.

Aside from the faint humming that I could still hear coming from the building, it was perfectly still. That's why I had no trouble hearing the soft padding sound of footsteps approaching me on the grass. When the steps stopped right next to me, I didn't bother opening my eyes. I thought that if I saw Nerunjanah at that moment we might both be in a lot of trouble.

There were two things that impressed me when the guy said good morning. The first was that he knew my name and, unlike Nerunjanah, pronounced it easily, accenting the first syllable in the usual way and not sounding as though he were a Hebrew-illiterate twelve-year-old preparing for his bar mitzvah. The second thing was that although the guy's voice had a real gentleness to it, he didn't come across like a first-year resident in psychiatry.

Once he spoke, I opened my eyes, but the Florida sun was where his head should have been, so I had to scrunch around a little there on the grass, lower my gaze, and put my hand to my forehead Native-American style. Given our respective positions and my lowered gaze, it's not surprising that the first thing I saw was the fellow's feet, which were bare, and his ankles, which disappeared not into a white robe but rather into the legs of what appeared to be a pair of dark-colored and very expensive suit pants. As my eyes continued up, they took in a very fashionable leather belt, a white shirt, a silk tie loosened at the neck, an open button-down collar, clean-shaven face, brown eyes and — Glory be! — mousey brown hair worn in a *regular* haircut.

"Uh, good morning," I answered him. "I don't think I've had the privilege," I said, trying to sound in control of the situation but not daring to stand up.

"Are you okay, Baruch?"

Okay? he asks! Okay?! I'm thinking. Does anyone who's okay travel between Fort Lauderdale and Providence by bus? Does anyone who's okay get off in Grandville? Does anyone who's okay say anything but "Beat it!" to a bunch of Krazies for Kushner? Does anyone who's okay help a bunch of refugees from the booby hatch kidnap him to one of the few places in the western hemisphere where Harry Kushner is king? But I'm stalling, trying to pull myself together, so I say, "Sure I'm okay, Mr. uh, I don't believe I caught your name."

"Oh," he says, still not introducing himself. "The way you were lying there like that, I thought you might not be feeling very well."

If only you knew, I think. "Oh no, not at all," I answer. "It's just that it's so nice out here in the early morning sun, I thought I'd just wait for you people to finish your, uh, your, uh, ceremonies in there, so I could talk to someone."

"Talk to someone?"

"Yeah, well, ya see, I need a ride into Grandville?"

"That's easy enough. I'm going into Grandville."

"And a phone book."

"A phone book? You have friends here in town?"

"Well, yes, as a matter of fact I do."

"Oh. Perhaps I know them and can take you over," he says, crouching down beside me.

"Oh, that's okay. If you can just help me with a phone book and run me back to the bus station, Mr. uh..."

"I'm sorry, Baruch. I really am being rude. My name is Janardhana Maharaj Goswami, but if that's difficult for you to pronounce, you can call me Bruce. As far as a phone book and a ride into town go, no problem. As soon as we finish our morning ceremonies, as you call them, I'll be happy to help you."

He really seemed friendly, old Janardhana Bruce, and a lot smoother than Nerunjanah Irv Levine. "Then we can arrange a time for me to run you back here to the Ashram before sundown, because I'm sure you don't travel on Shabbos."

Not only friendly and smooth, I think as this little

alarm bell starts to go off in my head, but a *talmid chacham* too. "Hey, that's great, Bruce, but I'll be staying with my friends for Shabbos."

"Oh that *is* a shame. A shame for *us*, I mean. I thought you would be our guest until Thursday when your bus leaves for Providence. I was looking forward to it. You know, a lot of people here have never met an Orthodox Jew, and I know that everyone will find you so *interesting*."

"Will?" I'm thinking, "*will?*"

"Would," maybe. *Would have found* me interesting.

But ain't nobody

gonna find nobody

interesting

'cause old Baruch

ain't gonna spend

one minute more than he has to

in this here domicile for displaced ding-a-lings.

Besides, how does this guy know so much about my travel plans?

That's what I'm thinking, but I say (in my best ecumenical voice), "Certainly, certainly they would, but if my friends heard I was in Grandville and didn't come for Shabbos, well, you can imagine... Anyway, Bruce, next time you're in Providence we'll have to get toge..."

"And believe me, Baruch. You will find the Ashram *fascinating*. You know we're an extremely pluralistic community. We learn from all faiths, and there are *profound* similarities between Kushner and Judaism. I've made a study of it."

Yeah, similarities, I'm thinking. We worship God, and you worship Barbie Dolls. We have a synagogue, and you have a wax museum. We study Torah, and you study Mannequins 101. But this isn't getting me anywhere, so I say, "That's terrific, Bruce. Now about that ride into Grandville..."

"And I was *so* hoping that my wife and sons would get to meet you. I thought you could come over Saturday night and..."

"Come over?"

"Yeah, come over. To our house. In Grandville."

"Grandville? You mean you don't live here on the funny far... I mean, you aren't part of the Ashram?"

And that was when I could see just how cool and experienced old Bruce Goswami was. I was sure he'd heard me say funny farm, but he let it go right by him. He just sat there in that crouch, being careful not to grass-stain his suit pants, knitted his eyebrows a little, and said, "No. Bhakti — you'd probably call her Beth — and I live together with our two boys in Grandville."

Now I was getting curious, and finally I sat up, my nausea subsiding.

"I'm a householder," he went on.

"A householder?"

"Right." Then he said some word in Sanskrit which I guess meant householder and continued, "Householders don't live on the Ashram. We marry, hold jobs on the outside, and don't take vows of celibacy."

Celibacy. Wow, I think, I didn't know they were into *that*!

"Of course, we maintain very close ties with the Ashram."

"Of course," I echoed solemnly.

"I'm out here every morning at four to wake up the gods."

"Wake up the gods?" I say with my jaw dropping. Up till now, I'd been thinking that Bruce might just come from this planet.

"Yes, four o'clock is 'waking of the gods.' We open the curtain which is drawn at night before they go to sleep.

As Bruce continued to explain the morning ceremonies that begin at four, I breathed a sigh of relief. Why? Simple. That was when I concluded that he must not have had any designs on me, because if he had, he would not have been hitting me with all *this* nonsense. Had he wanted to convert me, I was sure that he would first tell me all the wonderful things that Kushner and Judaism had in common, and then what a wonderful way of life it was, and then how their chanting would bring me tranquillity, solve the ozone problem, save the whales, etc., etc. But to tell me right off the bat all this baloney about how the idols go to sleep and wake up, well, that was the stuff they must keep in the bag at least until you've already reached a pretty high *madregah* of *meshugaas*. Anybody who heard about this stuff at the *beginning* would know right away that he was dealing with a bunch of U.S. Government inspected, Grade A goofballs.

❀

Well, that just shows you how wrong you can be. Here in the Kingdom of Kushner, I was designated a prime candidate for conversion, and Janardhana Maharaj Goswami — previously known as Bruce Albert Feldman — was doing a number on me. He was polite. He was subtle. He was respectful and friendly. Yes sir, I was getting the full treatment, custom-tailored for guys like me.

In any case, I didn't listen too closely to the whole description of the morning ceremonies until he said that they finished about eight-thirty, which gave him just enough time to get to his job in Grandville about a half hour's drive away. Believe it or not, he was an architect; he worked for a local firm, though he wasn't a partner. Bruce could pretty much make his own hours, but he usually managed to be there around nine o'clock.

Eight-thirty it was, then. At eight-thirty I'd be on my way back to civilization. Now it was about seven o'clock, too early to start my phone calls, but if I could get my hands on a phone book, I could make a list of numbers and addresses and then make my calls from a pay phone when I got to town.

"That's just fine, Bruce. It really is. Now about that phone book?" I said expectantly.

Well, Bruce was really sorry. He'd been outside of the ceremonies far too long already. At eight-thirty, he'd help me find a phone book.

"But isn't that when you have to leave for work?"

"Don't worry, Baruch. I told you I make my own hours, and if I can't take you, I'll have someone else drive you in."

As Bruce barefooted his way back to the morning ceremonies, the little alarm bell in my head started ringing again. I went over my options.

On the one hand, I didn't want to start scavenging for a phone book myself, because people might think I was trying to steal or something.

To pack up and walk away now would be simple enough. True, I didn't really know the direction back to Grandville, since I had been in something akin to a state of mental paralysis last night when they brought me here. But I figured that the first car I could flag down would tell me how to go.

On the other hand, flagging cars down wasn't what it used to be. How long might it take till someone actually stopped? Maybe I could lie down on the road; then someone would have to stop. If they saw me, that is.

And what about the alligators? Stumbling into the Everglades (wherever they were) was the one thing that did scare me.

On the third hand, maybe old Bruce was being straight with me. If so, all I had to do was wait until eight-thirty to get to a phone book and freedom.

On the fourth hand, if I waited till eight-thirty, and Bruce was still stalling, I'd have plenty of time yet to find my way into town, and there was no way they could stop me.

When I think about it now, I'm astonished at how foolish I was, and at how surprising Providence — and I don't mean the city this time — can be. To this day, I can't believe how many really dumb decisions I made.

Had I taken a plane (like any normal human being) to Lauderdale and back, I never would have landed in Grandville.

Had I not let my psychological guard drop to below my ankles there in the bus station, I never would have found myself weekending among the walking whackos.

Had I, at seven o'clock on Friday morning, collected my backpack from the "guest house" and set off walking, I most certainly would have made it back to town by early afternoon. Once there, I would have either found someone to take me in for Shabbos, or moved into the local flea-bag hotel. Sunday morning I could have checked out for either points north or for Fort Lauderdale, depending on the bus schedule.

No doubt about it. If then and there, I'd had the good sense to collect my things and walk off the Ashram, one way or the other, I would have been able to observe a restful Shabbos, and finally bid an unfond farewell to glorious Grandville.

But then, of course, there would not have been anything to tell.

HAVING GONE OVER all my options, those of the first, second, third, and fourth hands, I decided to wait until eight-thirty.

Bruce came out at eight-thirty as promised, found me a phone and phone book, and waited to transport me to town. He sort of hung around, but I suggested that if he had any business on the Ashram, perhaps he might like to tend to it, as it might take a while to locate these friends of mine, since they were new in town. I didn't want him around as I searched for shuls and rabbis. I asked if I could make a long distance call or two if I had to, hoping he would think I meant to call mutual friends somewhere else in my attempts to locate my Grandville buddies.

Bruce was really gracious about the whole thing, giving me the go-ahead on the long distance calls I had no intention of making, and then making himself scarce for twenty minutes or so.

But you know how it is. At this shul there was no answer. That one wasn't Orthodox. The third was called Temple something or other, so I didn't even bother. It didn't occur to me to try the Hillel house on the University of Florida campus, and before very long, I was out of ideas.

When Bruce came back, I was feeling more than a little chagrined. That I might strike out altogether was the one possibility I'd avoided thinking about. I told him that I couldn't reach my friends, although I'd found their number in the phone book. Again he asked me their names. I mumbled something like "Shechter" but quickly added that he probably didn't know them since, as I'd said, they were new in town. And even if they weren't new in town, I thought, there's no way you could possibly know my imaginary friends; after all, they'd be normal.

Bruce Feldman was at his soft-sell best. "Look, Baruch," he said in his most reasonable voice. "You have to do what God tells you, but I'm certain you'll want to be settled before sundown. You realize, of course, that you're welcome here. We won't interfere with your practices or ask you to participate in any of ours. Stay in the guest house for Shabbos — or until next Thursday. Come and go as you please. I know you won't eat our food, although we're strictly vegetarian. If you prefer, I'll take you into town, and you can look for kosher food in the supermarket. There's plenty of stuff with the little K's and U's on the packages."

And that was all he said. I found myself distracted, wondering how he knew about the K's and U's; but I knew I had to decide. Clearly, no one was twisting my arm here, and how I might pass the Shabbos alone in Grandville proper I didn't know. With Bruce's promise that they wouldn't interfere or pressure me and his generous offer to help me find kosher food, I felt more or less secure. At least I would have a roof over my head, I thought. On Sunday, I figured, I'll ask him to take me down to the bus station, and one way or another, I'll get a bus out of this nightmare.

"Okay," I said simply, and as I did, I had this fleeting vision of Nerunjanah Levine saying there's no such thing as coincidence. "In the meantime, I've got plenty of food to last me, and I think that on Sunday, I'll be moving on."

"Fine, Baruch," he said, being careful not to overplay his hand. "Whatever you like. I'm going to introduce you to Cho Ramaswami; he's the fellow in charge here. If you need anything, he'll be glad to help you. Here, take my card too. It has my phone number at home and at work. If there's any way that I can be of service," he added with a hint of satisfaction at his victory creeping into his voice, "please don't hesitate to call me. Bhakti, the boys, and I will drive out to visit you tomorrow, if you don't mind. I'd really like my family to get to know you."

By now, it was pretty clear that Bruce was a major *macher* around here. As I think back on the whole thing, I'm amazed at just how cool he was. "Keep trying with your friends," he said. "If you get through, just tell Cho, and he'll have someone run you into town." What more could he have said to persuade me that they only wanted to help?

True to Bruce's word, nobody bothered me on Shabbos. Without much to do on Friday, I walked around the place a little bit, and everyone I saw nodded and smiled at me. Whenever someone said hello, they always used my name; I guess news travels fast on an Ashram. From the looks of things, I estimated that somewhere between forty and sixty percent of the people I saw were born Jewish, and I trembled at the implication.

Nerunjanah stopped by on Friday afternoon while I was creating a lunch from Bubbie's goodies. I invited him to join me and he took a whole piece of matzah, but he wouldn't touch the tuna; I guess he didn't like the *hechsher*. Old Irv, I presumed, figured that he and I were fast friends by now. I didn't think that they'd sent him to work on me, though. If anybody was going to try to get me interested in having myself permanently committed to *Meshuganeh* Manor, I knew it would be Bruce or someone equally sophisticated. After all, I wasn't a post-doctoral dingbat, and I hadn't come here looking for PEACE LOVE and BROTHERHOOD, at least not the kind you get by paying homage to Madame Tussaud's handiwork.

Nerunjanah, as it turned out, was a good guy to answer my questions about the Movement. I could tell that from him I was getting the pure, unadulterated *narishkeit*, because it was clear that they had washed what little brains he ever had very thoroughly before returning them to him. We talked for quite a long time about his past, my past, Harry Kushner, Judaism, life, and so forth. He was nice all right, but totally programmed by the HKs.

Bruce and his family did drive out on Shabbos, but I wasn't the focus of their visit. Nerunjanah had explained to me that every Saturday afternoon about five o'clock they had a "feast" which was open to the public. *Seudah shelishis*, I said to myself. Anyway, it seems that Bruce, as the top ranking guru in Grandville, and one of the five or six chief Harrys worldwide, came out every Saturday and sat with his family at the head table. Bruce usually gave a *derashah* at these shindigs and made it his business to greet personally every new face he saw.

Bruce, as I learned, was a real master of warmth, charm, and sincerity, always shaking your hand in both of his, knitting his eyebrows, and looking you straight in the eye as though he could see into your soul that way. That I hadn't been subjected to that approach (at least not yet) was a measure of just how sharp Bruce really was. Talking to me, Bruce had been in problem-solving mode, because that was what I needed at the time and because under the circumstances, problem-solving rather than deep insight into my spiritual needs was the best way to ingratiate himself with me. There was no question that he was intelligent and smooth (not to mention good-looking), and that he'd achieved some sort of synthesis between good old American pragmatism and Eastern spirituality.

Anyway, a light knock on my door came about four in the afternoon, and on the other side was... I wasn't sure.

After a few long seconds, I was able to I.D. Bruce, dressed this time like the rest of the goonies. He had the white clay painted over the bridge of his nose and extending to the center of his forehead. He had not shaved his head, of course, but he was barefoot, as before, and wearing the white robe.

I guess I should not have been shocked when he said "Good Shabbos," but I *was* shocked, too shocked, at least, to answer back right away.

"Bruce?" I asked.

"Janardhana," he answered.

"Jana... Jana... Janard...," I stammered.

"Just joking, Baruch," he smiled. "You can still call me Bruce. Aren't you going to wish me a good Shabbos?"

"Sure, Bruce. Good Shabbos."

"You feel like stepping outside, Baruch? There are some people here I'd like you to meet."

My dear Bruce, kindly give me a break, I wanted to say, but "Sure" came out instead. After all, Bruce Feldman was my host here in Never-Never Land.

When I walked down the three stairs that led out of the guest house, I found the lawn bathed in an extremely pleasant late afternoon glow. A few feet away, stood the other members of Bruce's family.

Beth (Bhakti) Feldman was wearing a sari (quite an elegant one at that), nothing on her head or feet, and a tiny diamond affixed to the side of her left nostril in that way which seemed to me so very painful. Like all the HK women, her only makeup was the white clay over her nose and forehead.

Beth smiled a little stiffly and said some word in Sanskrit, to which I, having practiced on Bruce, responded, "Good Shabbos."

Standing with Beth were two boys. One looked to be about twelve or thirteen and was also barefoot and wearing clay on his nose and white robe on his body, but his head was not shaved. His face still had the smooth innocent skin of a child. He had an open inquiring look accented by the big brown eyes he'd inherited from his parents. The other boy had wavy hair down to his shoulders and looked to be about fifteen or sixteen, at the most. He was chewing gum and wearing a short-sleeved, button-down sport shirt, white Levis, and a pair of New Balance sneakers. In his hand was a paperback novel and on his face was that bored, I-wish-I-were-anywhere-but-here look of a teenager.

Although I later found out that on their birth certificates they were listed as Keith and Stuart, Bruce addressed them by their Indian names. It gave me something of a start when I heard Bruce say to them, "Kushner, Suraj, say hello to Baruch." Both said hello without looking at me, and Bruce said, "Baruch, meet Bhakti, Kushner, and Suraj."

"Hey, guys," I said to the boys, extending my hand in their direction. Neither bothered taking it, but the younger one, Suraj, said "Hi."

"Here, sit down, Baruch," Bruce said, gesturing with his hand. We all sat down on the lawn, the two elder Feldmans assuming the lotus position. There was a pleasant breeze that ruffled their robes a little. The boys each reclined on one elbow.

"So how's it going, Baruch? How are you enjoying your Shabbos?"

"Fine, Bruce, just fine."

"Good, I'm glad to hear it. Have everything you need?"

"Oh sure, Bruce. I'm cool."

"Great. And nobody's been by to bother you, right?"

"Right. Old Nerunjanah stopped by yesterday for some matzah..."

"*Matzah!*" Bruce exclaimed, glancing at Beth. "My goodness. How long has it been since we've tasted matzah? Gee, Baruch, I'll bet Kushner and Suraj would *love* to taste some matzah. They've never even *seen* any. And you could explain to them how it's made and what it symbolizes and all."

Kushner and Suraj looked about as interested as a couple of *Litvak*s stuck at a chassidic *tisch*. "Well, I can't carry it out here on Shabbos, but you're all welcome to come in and..."

"You also don't carry things on Shabbos?" Bruce broke in.

"Well, sort of. Inside the house it's permitted."

"Boys, you know that Grandma and Grandpa and Uncle Eugene and Uncle Stanley are also very religious

Jews. They act the same way on Saturday."

Kushner nodded, slightly more interested at the mention of his relatives, and Suraj said "Uh-huh."

"Almost everybody here at the Ashram was once Jewish, and some were even like my family and Baruch here," Bruce went on. "They're not only Jewish, they're *Or*-tho-dox. Do you know what that means?"

Suraj shook his head noncommittally, and Kushner went back to being bored.

"That means," Bruce enthused, "that Baruch keeps all the ancient observances and practices. It means he's a kind of priest. That's why he wears the beard and the skullcap — it's called a *yarmulka*. Judaism, you know, is almost as ancient as Hinduism."

I could feel my eyes roll skyward as I whispered to myself, "A break, just give me a break."

"For the *Or*thodox, every Saturday is Shabbos, and it's a *very* spiritual day for them. You must do a lot of meditating on Shabbos, Baruch."

"Well no, actually. Not exactly," I said. "We do pray a lot and study."

"Do the *Or*thodox fast on Shabbos?" — this from a guy who said he'd made a comparative study of Kushner and Judaism, and comes from a religious family.

"No, as a matter of fact, we eat extra special meals and usually catch up a little on our sleep. On Shabbos, we serve the Almighty with our entire being." How I ended up explaining that point, I didn't really know.

"Isn't that positively *fascinating*, Bhakti?" he practically shouted there from his lotus position. "You see,

Baruch? Another similarity!"

Tell me about it, I thought, but I was spared when Bruce said, "We *really* have to *continue* this, Baruch, but I have some things to take care of. Bhakti, you and the boys stay *here* and get acquainted with Baruch. He's really *so* interesting."

The boys, by this time, were maybe twenty feet away, sitting on the lawn and talking to each other in low voices, looking in our direction every once in a while and giggling.

"Meet you over at the dining hall at five," he told her. Then he turned to me and said, "Baruch, we're having our weekly feast over in the dining hall. You're welcome to come."

"Oh, I think I'll pass, Bruce," I declined emphatically.

"Have to have those little K's and U's, huh?" he smiled.

"Yeah, sort of," I answered.

Actually, it was a lot more complicated than K's and U's. Nerunjanah Levine had explained to me how all food has to be sacrificed first to the idols — he called them the gods, of course. They take all the pots in which the food is prepared and set them before the idols for a few minutes before serving, and, in good old Nerunjanah's words, "Anything the gods leave over, we are permitted to eat." I kid you not. That's what he told me.

That's not all he told me, by the way. He also told me that you can always tell if the people in the kitchen are really putting their souls into the work of preparing the food. When they put their souls into it, the food is tastier to the gods, and they eat more! I'm serious. He said this, and then he went on to say that the way they can always tell when the gods are eating more is by — get this: THEIR CLOTHES GETTING TIGHTER!!

That's right, friends and neighbors, boys and girls! The Kishkas who change the gods' clothes in the morning, at night, and on special occasions can always tell when the kitchen staff is goofing off, because the gods' clothes get looser as they lose weight! I wondered if they'd ever had to treat an idol for anorexia or send some god out to Weight Watchers, because the kitchen staff had gotten over- or under-conscientious.

I mean, these were people for whom reality was nothing but a minor obstacle! But the point was that the little K's and U's were no longer the point. What Bruce was inviting me to do was to eat food that had been sacrificed to idols! Believe me, before getting off the bus here in the Twilight Zone, that was one *aveirah* I never thought I'd have to watch out for, at least in America.

Anyway, not wanting to eat what the gods had slobbered all over, I politely refused.

With that, Bruce walked off, leaving me with Beth, who by the look of things was no more interested than her boys were in getting to know an *Or*thodox Jew. We talked uncomfortably for a few minutes, and I managed to find out that she was an only child, that her maiden name was Klein, that she'd grown up in the Jewish section of St. Louis, attended six years of Hebrew school, and had a lavish "bat mitzvah."

One thing I'll say about the HK's: I never met one who denied that he was Jewish or seemed ashamed of it. Not only that, contrary to my expectations, the Jewish ones were the kindest and most accepting of me. They were all completely open about their previous names and family histories, though they all seemed to think it was perfectly natural for Avraham *Avinu*'s heirs to toss four thousand years of spiritual progress out the window in order to worship a bunch of dressmaker's dummies.

Beth didn't find out anything at all about me. Like I said, she really couldn't have cared less. Her husband had assigned her to entertain me until five, so she sat. Otherwise, I'm sure she probably would have preferred to go and exchange recipes with some of the statues.

After a few minutes of really stilted conversation, I asked her if she wanted to come in and taste the matzah, but she told me that she remembered what matzah tastes like and that she never much cared for it anyway. I excused myself, saying that I had to recite my afternoon prayers. Beth looked relieved.

She mumbled some sort of farewell in Sanskrit, got up, and walked away. As she passed the boys, I heard her say, "Five o'clock, in the dining hall," her voice striking me as just a touch too strident.

Me? I went inside and davened *Minchah*.

WHEN I EMERGED from the mobile home, I saw the two Feldman boys still talking to each other, although it was already well past five. I walked over and said "Hi," and the older of the two grudgingly acknowledged my greeting with a nod.

"Pretty nice weather we're having," I said, stooping down next to them.

I got no answer, so I tried again. "Is this typical for this time of year?"

"I guess so," the older one finally answered, still chewing his gum.

"You're Kushner, right?"

"Call me Keith, will ya?"

"And he's Suraj?"

"You can call him Stuart."

"Okay, Keith and Stuart it is. That's a lot easier for me to pronounce."

Keith's eyes were saying, "Are we dismissed?" but I ignored them. "You fellas born here in Grandville?"

"He was. I wasn't," Keith answered with a great show of effort. Stuart was regarding me with his mouth about half-way open.

"I guess you guys have to commute out here to the Ashram for school."

"Nah," Keith said, sticking to the short answers.

"Don't they have a school here?"

"Yeah, they got a school here." Keith was still the spokesman for Feldman Bros., Inc. "But the kids are all geeks." A compound sentence! I thought. Maybe I had a chance to turn this monologue into a conversation. "And you, Stuart, do you go to school on the Ashram?"

"Nah," said Stuart, echoing his elder brother's eloquence.

"The kids your age must be geeks too, huh?"

"I guess so."

"I guess you guys must really be into this Kushner jazz."

"I guess so," said Keith.

"I mean, do you, like, say your *mantra* every day and study all the stuff?"

"Nah, not so much."

"But you *are* into it."

"Sure, sure, Mister. Hey, Mister?"

Now I figured he was going to tell me to get lost, but nobody calls me Mister and gets away with it, so I said, "Baruch."

"Yeah, Baruch. Tell me, what's a bar mitzvah?"

Irv, I thought, you're right. There is no such thing as coincidence. Here I am, Baruch the *baal teshuvah*, sitting on the lawn of an Ashram in Grandville, Florida, and a Jewish kid with an Indian name is asking me what "bar mitzvah" means.

"What?" I said. The whatting bit was contagious.

"Bar mitzvah... What's a bar mitzvah?"

I once read somewhere that you're not supposed to tell kids any more than what they ask, and I thought maybe that principle applied now. If there's anything teenagers can't stand, it's someone who talks too much.

"Well, *a* bar mitzvah is a Jewish male who's thirteen or older. When a boy is thirteen, he *becomes* bar mitzvah. The boy's family often makes a party to celebrate the occasion, and that's called a bar mitzvah too."

There was silence, and then, "But what does the *word* mean, Baruch?"

Here it was. I took a deep breath. "*Mitzvah*," I began, "is Hebrew for 'commandment.' *Bar* means 'son.' So when you're bar mitzvah, you're—"

"What's a commandment?"

He'd been reclining on his elbows. Now he was sitting up, using his tongue to tuck his chewing gum into his cheek and immobilize the stuff for the time being.

"A commandment is something God told us to do. There are lots of commandments in Judaism written in the Torah, our holy book."

Now his bored act was shed completely. He was actually looking interested.

"Hey, Mister," Stuart suddenly put in.

"Baruch."

"Baruch. Hey, Baruch, you come here to get initiated?"

"Nah," I said, trying to sound like the boys. "I came here by accident, and your old man's been nice enough to put me up here on the farm. That's all. Tomorrow, I go back home to Providence."

"Providence?" Something in the way Stuart said that gave me a little shiver.

"Yeah, Providence. That's in Rhode Island, way up north. That's where I live."

"So you're not joining the Ashram?" Keith asked.

"Hey, not if I have anything to say about it." I saw them both relax now.

❊

Since the boys were facing the direction of the guest house from which I'd come, they didn't see their mother emerge from one of the buildings behind them and begin walking towards us. "Kushner, Suraj, I see you're getting acquainted with Baruch," she said, her smile tense and her tone saccharine-sweet.

"I guess so," Keith said, returning to lie on one elbow and starting to chew his gum again.

"Well, come on now," Beth continued, still sweet but with a new note of firmness in her voice. "It's nearly five-thirty, and your father will be speaking soon. Besides, you haven't eaten."

"I don't like the food here," Stuart said in a kind of whine.

"Okay, okay, Stuart." She said it! She said Stuart, I thought. "We've discussed this before. We'll talk about it at home.

"Now come on, the two of you." This last line was delivered rather brusquely, and with it, Beth (Bhakti) Klein Feldman turned and walked back to where she'd come from. After five or six seconds had passed — enough time for him to retain his self-respect and not appear as though he had no choice — Keith punched Stuart in the upper arm, got up and followed, head down and looking at the grass. Stuart got up and walked after Keith.

"See ya around, you guys," I called.

They both turned in my direction for a moment. Keith looked at me for just a second in that way I later would see his father look into people's eyes and into their souls. Then his eyes fell back to the ground and his face resumed its bored-teenager expression.

"I guess so," he mumbled as he walked away.

IV

AND I WOULD like to propose a toast to Sam and Esther Feldman, the best mom and dad anyone could ask for. *Lechaim!*"

"*Lechaim!*" everybody, myself included, shouted.

Keith Kushner and Stuart Suraj Feldman were in bed, and Bruce's parents — Sam and Esther Feldman — and Bruce's two brothers — Eugene, the lawyer, and Stanley, the cardiologist — were sitting around Bruce's dining room table and celebrating the elder Feldmans' fiftieth wedding anniversary. Bruce and Beth were back in their straight clothes, and except for the profusion of Indian art on the walls, the funny little statues that adorned most of the horizontal surfaces in the house, and that perfect little diamond still stuck into Beth's nostril, the event seemed like a normal gathering of a normal Jewish sub-unit of the great American upper middle class (emphasis on upper).

My jaw dropped and remained that way when I saw

Bruce's family. They really were *frum*. Every male wore a yarmulka and recited the proper blessing before eating. Excluding old Brucey.

"Speech, speech," someone called, and everyone, except Bruce and Beth, laughed.

"I'm serious, Dad," Stanley said, still laughing. "Stand up and say a few words."

"Y'know I ain't from de big talkas," Sam said in his raspy, born-and-bred-in-Brooklyn accent. "Maybe yer mudda would like t'tell youse what an hona it's been livin' wid me f'all dese many years," he continued, getting to his feet.

That got a good laugh from all, but most particularly from Esther Feldman, who then shouted, "Some hona, pickin' up yer socks f'fifty years."

"Now, now, Estie," Sam said, pretending to chastise her, "I tought we wasn't gonna air no doity laundry t'nite, in fronna d'kids." D'kids got an even bigger laugh out of that one. It was clear that Esther had been playing an extremely competent straight-man for Sam, a retired printer for *The New York Times*, for most of their married life. It was equally clear that Eugene and Stanley could never get enough of Feldman & Feldman and that Bruce, the eldest brother, was having no part of it.

To me, the change in Bruce's demeanor had been nothing short of astounding. After the Ashram's Saturday banquet, which ended just about the time I finished *Maariv* and *Havdalah* in the guest house, Bruce — already back in his straight clothes — came and asked if I wouldn't like to continue our visit back at his house in Grandville.

I tried to refuse as politely as I could, but he told me that his parents and brothers were in town to celebrate the Feldman Srs.' fiftieth wedding anniversary and that he and Bhakti would just be *delighted* if I would join them. "They're not Harry Kushners," he added in a whisper.

I thanked him and said I really wanted to get an early start in the morning, but again he was asking me, practically begging me to come. It was the first time I'd seen Bruce anything but one-hundred-percent cool. Later that evening, I would see that little chink in his composure widen to a crack and finally to a gaping hole. But like I said, that was later.

Afterward, I figured the reason he wanted me around was that with a stranger present, the extended Feldman family might avoid another installment of the continuing feud that had begun some fifteen or twenty years earlier with Bruce's decision to join the HKs. There was a certain just-barely-detectable note of desperation in Bruce's voice there in the guest house that Saturday night, and that got me to thinking that since he'd been so nice about putting me up and had really kept his word that no one would bother me over Shabbos, maybe I owed him one.

As it worked out, my presence really did do some good for the Feldman family, though certainly not in the way that Bruce had hoped.

"Okay," I said, "but you have to promise you'll get me out of here tomorrow morning."

"After morning ceremonies tomorrow, Baruch, you

just tell me what you want, and I'll do it — even if I have to drive you to Atlanta."

We walked across the Ashram to Bruce's big station wagon, where Beth and the boys were waiting. On the way to his house, Bruce stopped off at an all-night supermarket. Knowing exactly which aisle to head for, he bought some properly *hechsher*ed junk food, cookies, pop and paper plates.

❀

Bruce and Beth were sitting woodenly all through Sam and Esther's comedy routine, not so much because they, like just about all HKs, were more or less devoid of a sense of humor, but because Bruce knew that once his Dad got started there was no telling where he might stop.

"C'mon, Dad," Bruce's younger brother Eugene was saying. "Be serious for a change. It's not every day you celebrate your fiftieth."

"Very sharp, Eugene," he replied, and then caught himself before finishing the wisecrack. Sam looked out at his kids and was suddenly struck by their expectant expressions. They really wanted him to be serious.

"Okay, kids," Sam began soberly. Clearly, the Jimmy Durante dialect was more natural for Feldman Senior, but now, with some effort, he was able to switch to more intelligible English. "Listen up, 'cause I really do have somethin' to say.

"You know that I never had a real Jewish education. But, nonetheless, my parents taught me proper Jewish priorities, and once you boys finally came along — after over ten years of waitin' — I tried to pass 'em on to you.

Who woulda known how successful, almost successful, I would be.

"I never thoughta sendin' you to Jewish schools. It was unheard of when I was growin' up. But the one thing I knew I *had* to do was give you all a bar mitzvah. So I hired a really good guy — you remember him? Of course you do. He was more interested in you becomin' good Jews than in gettin' paid. He brought you over to his house, introduced you to other kids your age, and before we knew it, all you could talk about was goin' to Day School, like the rest of 'em.

"Well, your mudda and me, we thought that was a pretty fanatical thing then, but today we know that that was maybe the best thing we ever did in our lives. When you boys got religious, you made us get religious along with you, which added a whole new, wonderful how-do-you-call-it? dimension — a whole new dimension to our lives. And we're sure one day *soon* you boys will marry terrific Jewish girls and raise beautiful Jewish families." The emphasis Sam placed on "soon" was not lost on the two aging bachelors.

There was a sudden catch in Sam's voice and he stopped abruptly. His eyes welled with tears and then he went on. "If only we'd had that teacher a few years before, everythin' mighta been perfect. Brucey, I'm talkin' to *you*. You were the only bad apple in the barrel. Mama and me, we could take it if you wouldn't be religious. The blame for that would be all mine. But this Kushner thing — it's just plain weird. You've torn our family apart with your weirdness.

"What's done is done, Brucey, and it can't be undone. But couldn't you at least do for your sweet boys what I did for you? Couldn't you at least give 'em a bar mitzvah? Let them know that they come from a long tradition, a *real* tradition, that meant somethin' to their grandfather and to *my* grandfather?"

"Dad," Eugene said, trying to calm his father. Beth's eyes were closed and her lips were moving. I think she'd begun saying her *mantra* to herself to avoid making a scene. Everyone else in the room was busy inspecting their fingernails as if they might hold the secret of how to keep *Sam* from making a scene.

"Those boys," the anniversary celebrant bellowed, changing his tone from historical narrative to anger and hurt, "those wonderful boys! Breaks my heart to see how you're raising 'em. You know they're ashamed to invite their friends over to this nuthouse. When was the last time either of 'em had a friend over here? Huh? You see? They're ashamed!"

"Dad," Stanley the cardiologist said with considerable firmness, "you know this is no good for your heart."

"My heart? My heart? I'll tell you about my heart! Whaddaya think it does to my heart to see how he's raisin' my grandsons? Feh! What's the use of talkin'? I said it all before."

"That's right, Dad," Stanley jumped in. "You've said it all before, so why don't you just..."

"But it breaks my poor heart," Sam shouted. "My own grandsons! Great-grandsons of Binyomin Feldman, he should rest in peace. He must be turnin' over in his grave. He built one of the first shuls in America; he was a real community leader, my father was. A pious man. He's turnin' over in his grave, I tell you. And you're gonna send *me* and your *mudda* to an early grave, Brucey. You don' know how your mudda cries herself to sleep over those boys, son.

"Those wonderful boys. Keith's almost sixteen, and he still didn't have a bar mitzvah."

"Dad, as your doctor, I must *insist* that you calm down!"

"Ah shuddup, Stanley. I didn't send you to college and medical school so you could tell me what to do!

"And Stuart, he's gonna be thirteen in just a coupla months. I guess he's not gonna have a bar mitzvah either. Right, Brucey?!"

By now, I and everyone in the room except Beth, who still had her eyes closed, had their fingernails committed to memory.

"Well? Is he, Bruce? Why dontcha answer me, son? Is Stuart gonna have a bar mitzvah or isn't he?"

"I don't know," Bruce whispered.

"You don' know. *You don' know*! I thought you knew everything. My son the architect who found religion! That you call religion? Bowing down to a bunch of grown-up Cabbage Patch dolls? You make me..."

The first thing I heard was the sudden scrape of Stan's chair being shoved back and the *bang!* as it collided with the wall behind him. I jerked my eyes away from my fingernails in time to see Sam Feldman, his hand at his chest, his face ash gray, lower himself *very slowly* into his seat. Stan was next to him in an instant, loosening his father's tie and reaching for the pulse on his throat while telling everyone in his calm, authoritative doctor-voice to please take it easy and move back.

He was nimble, Stanley, and before I knew what had happened, he had Sam lying on the couch, panting slightly and perspiring profusely, with his tie off and his shirt unbuttoned to his waist. "Beth, get me my black bag, please," Stan said, slipping a nitroglycerin tablet under his father's tongue.

"*Oy, Gutt in Himmel*," Esther was whispering to Eugene, who stood supporting her and holding her hand. "Why does he do dis t'himself?"

"He's going to be okay," Stan said, calmly applying his stethoscope to his father's chest.

"Should I... should I call an ambulance?" Bruce asked nervously.

"Not yet," Stanley responded. "I brought plenty of medication. Unless it's a full-scale coronary, I should be able to manage him here." Stan disappeared into one of the five or six bedrooms and returned with some sort of apparatus which he began attaching to his father's upper torso. "You just can't let yourself get excited like that, Dad," he cooed.

A minute or two passed during which no one seemed to breathe.

"It's just an angina attack," Stanley proclaimed, and everyone relaxed. Sam's normal color was returning as Stan asked him, "Have you been taking your medicine, Pop?"

"O'course he takes his medicine," Esther retorted indignantly. "If he don' take his medicine, I'll kill da bum!" That broke the tension and everyone, Sam included, had a good laugh. Unfortunately, Sam's laughter rapidly degenerated into a coughing spasm, but

Stan was there calming him, and before long, the coughing abated.

THE ROOM went silent for a moment, and then I heard Bruce hiss, "I *said* this wouldn't work, Gene. I *said* it was stupid to put the two of us together in the same room."

"Pipe down, Bruce," Eugene the lawyer ordered.

"Pipe down, yourself," Bruce shot back, still hissing. "This was *your* idea! I told you he can't control himself! Every time he comes here, it's the same story."

"Can we just talk about this later, Bruce?!" Gene said in a strident whisper. "Your *father* is having an attack!"

"Come outside," Bruce hissed one last time.

Nonplussed was the word that came to mind. I think I saw it once in a British novel. But it doesn't matter where I saw the word — this was definitely not the urbane, warm, friendly, understanding, problem-solving, in-control-of-the-situation Bruce Albert Feldman I'd come to know. The top HK in Grandville and one of the five or six head honchos worldwide had clearly been nonplussed all evening in the presence of his family. His wife, by the way, did not appear to be doing an awful lot better. Beth had disappeared into the kitchen, where she seemed to be busying herself in order to get out of an all-too-familiar situation.

Bruce and Eugene slipped outside, leaving Stan, Esther and me in the living room with Sam. Stan and his mother were sitting next to Sam now, talking to him, trying to calm him down, and I was feeling very much a fifth wheel.

It wasn't quite air conditioner weather yet in Grandville, which meant that just about every window in the house was open. I know it wasn't right, but from the easy chair I was sitting in near the window, I could make out just about everything the two brothers were saying.

Not to put too fine a point on things, I think I could reasonably describe Bruce as furious.

"For Kushner's sake, Gene, you promised it would be different this time!"

"Don't give me that Kushner tripe, Bruce Feldman. That's what started all this."

"What started all this is my parents' complete refusal to accept me and my family for what we are."

"And just what are you?"

"Quiet, Gene!"

"Quiet, yourself! Don't you know you're killing those two people?"

"They're killing themselves. All they have to do is accept me."

"That's an awful lot to accept, fella."

"What do you know?"

"I know you get up every morning at four o'clock to go count beads on that stupid farm! I know you go traipsing around Grandville in that overgrown nightshirt and without any shoes on! I know you think those large economy-size ventriloquist's dummies eat the food you make for them!" Now his voice dropped, sounding less angry than sad. "And I know that your own boys think you're off the wall, and I know that you're killing your parents."

"Look, Gene. You and Stan think I don't care, but I do," Bruce's voice was also softening. "I care very deeply for Mom and Dad, and for you and Stan too. But what none of you wants to understand is that my religion is my life. Besides, I've got a business to run here."

"What?"

"Never mind. Look, Gene, you said it was going to be different this time."

"Bruce, he promised me."

"It doesn't matter what he promises. He can't control himself. That's why the best thing for his health and my sanity is for us just to keep away from each other. Believe me, Gene, I never answer him back. I don't care. But it kills Beth, and it's going to kill him. He can't see me without losing his temper. I'm crazy about him and Mom, but he can't see that."

"Did you ever try telling him?"

"You gotta be kidding. That old goat hasn't listened to a word I've said since I became initiated back in 1970. Twenty years is a long time, Gene."

"Make your boys a bar mitzvah and maybe he'll start listening."

"Nothing will make him start listening!"

"He says you're tearing the family apart."

"I?" Bruce was squeaking now. "*I'm* tearing the family apart? Oh, that's a good one. Look here, little brother. All I'm doing is following my conscience, and if the small minds of this family can't accept my wife and me for what we are..."

"Who you calling small minds?"

"Forget it, Gene. Just forget it. I don't have time for this. I've got a business to run."

"What did you say?"

"Forget it."

"I don't want to forget it. That's the second time you said you have a business to run. You've got something on your mind, big brother, so why don't you just spit it out?"

"What I mean is that SKA is a big operation — bigger than you can imagine — and I'm into them for a lot of bread."

"And what's that supposed to mean?"

"Forget it, Gene. I'm sorry I said anything."

"No, Bruce. What does that mean, that you're into them for a lot of bread?"

"I said forget it!"

"I don't want to. Tell me what you're talking about."

"Are you sure you want to get into this?"

"Of course I want to get into it. We may have our differences, but you're my brother, aren't you?"

"Okay, Gene. Look, we've got huge expenses, maintaining the Ashrams and all. Half our people are totally supported by the Society. They're all supposed to be out on the street collecting alms, selling books, flowers, and stuff. We bring in a lot of money, but some of these coconuts are thoroughly inept."

"Coconuts, big brother?"

"Let's face it, Gene. Back in the old days, when Beth and I were initiated, we were getting the cream. For the past five or ten years, though, we've been getting the dregs. We used to get seekers, okay, but most of us were people who could make it in the real world..."

"Real world, big brother?"

"You know what I mean."

"I sure do."

"Lay off, will you?"

"Sorry."

"Anyway, I've always been in on the finances, and it's been a good deal for me. I've had more than a little to say about the salary they pay me. Today, I'm the chief financial officer of the organization, and my salary is commensurate. As you can imagine, I didn't pay for my house and car with beads and conch shells."

"Sounds vaguely Western."

"Are you going to close your mouth and listen?"

"All right, all right."

"Anyway, the Society for Kushner Awareness is building a theme park here in Florida. Of course, we're not going to call it the Harry Kushner Park, but it will have an Indian flavor. Indian decor, gifts, food, hostesses in saris; you know the shtick. We'll hand out our literature. There'll be plenty of our people around, but they'll blend in with the local color. Visitors will have their minds opened to the wonders of Kushner and get a chance to find out what nice regular guys we are at the same time. We hope to raise a lot of consciousness to the contribution Eastern spirituality can make to Western civilization."

"And save a few souls for Kushner."

"Anyone who wants to learn more about Hinduism in general and SKA in particular will certainly have the opportunity in our pavilion at the Park, at our desk in the hotel, and in the temple that will be on the grounds. There'll also be a 'non-denominational meditation room' with a library whose content we control."

"Right. Who's financing it?"

"We've got a couple of angels, and we've issued some bonds."

"Really?" Eugene raised an eyebrow.

"Don't get wise. Now, like I said, as a humble but pivotal servant of Kushner, I receive quite a generous salary from the Movement. My needs and the needs of my family are relatively modest. Even with the nice house, big car, and expensive suits and saris, we could never burn money the way a typical American yuppie does — no offense, Gene.

"Anyway, as a result of the salary I pull down from the Movement, and my job as an architect, I'm — or at least I *was* — pretty liquid."

"You know, for a Hindu holy man, Brucey, you seem to have quite a command of the Western financial idiom. Yes sirree, *quite* a command."

"Can it, counselor. I'm telling you everything now. As you might imagine, I managed to land the contract to design the theme park. I never wanted to be a partner in the firm, since my first priority is SKA. But it was a huge contract, and the architectural firm I work for gave me quite a bonus. Of course, all of this was done with Steve Jacobs' approval."

"Ah, yes. The holy Steve Jacobs Maharaj Goswami, your fearless leader."

"To get to the point, the bonus and a large share of my other assets were invested in the bond issue. That was part of the deal."

"And?"

"Well, things are getting bogged down. We always thought that we could meet our bond obligations out of the SKA budget. Over the years our revenues have been enormous. Between sales and alms, one member of the initiated can bring in forty thousand or more a year, and it doesn't cost half that much to maintain him. A lot of members signed their property over to the Movement too."

"So?"

"Well, that was in years gone by. Now the ranks are still growing — true, a lot more slowly than they grew in the sixties and seventies — but revenues aren't. The new people just don't know how to hustle, and they rarely have any property worth signing over to the Movement."

"In other words, your overhead is growing but your income isn't."

"Well, let's just say we're having a temporary cash

flow problem. We've even had to sell off some holdings. *I'm* the guy that has to balance the budget. *I'm* the guy that has to meet the bond payments. *I'm* the guy that has to pay my salary, and *I'm* the guy who stands to lose his shirt if I don't manage."

"And saying your *mantra* every morning doesn't seem to help?"

"Knock it off!"

"What does Beth have to say about all this?"

"She doesn't really know what's going on."

"I see."

"Yeah, well maybe you do, and maybe you don't. What I'm trying to say, Gene, is that with all this on my mind, I don't really need the old man having a heart attack in my living room. And if, Kushner forbid, he gets stuck here in the hospital in Grandville, and I have to get out to see him every day and entertain Mom to boot, well, I'll have a heart attack myself.

"Look, Gene, I love the old guy. He's *my* father too, you know. But I can't change what I am, and I certainly can't change how he feels about it. It's his *attitude* that's killing him, not me. So for everybody's good, don't bring him down here anymore."

"You know, Bruce, it's not true that you can't change how he feels about you."

"That's what you think."

"That's what I *know*. Like I said before, there *is* something you could do that would change your relationship with Mom and Dad, and overnight."

"Yeah, enter rabbinical school."

"Close. Look, Bruce, Mom and Dad mourn for those boys of yours. Make them a bar mitzvah, and your parents will die happy."

"Out of the question."

"How come? I've heard you say a thousand times that you learn from all faiths."

"Yeah, that's what we tell the uninitiated. But the leadership would have my head if I tried to pull anything so heretical."

"Doesn't your own family take precedence?"

"I don't have time for this."

"This discussion, or the bar mitzvah?"

"I don't know," Bruce said wearily.

"Tell me something, Bruce. How much are you down?"

"I don't know, Gene. Two hundred, two-fifty."

"Two hundred and fifty *thousand*?!" Gene let out a low whistle. I would have whistled for a different reason. I couldn't believe what I was overhearing. That someone in the Kishkas had to deal with cash flow, overheads, and bond issues, I could understand. What amazed me was that aside from the folly of the faithful, Bruce's only problem was that he didn't have the *time*!

"What kind of time does it take?" Eugene was saying. "It's the boys that have to give up their time."

"Oh c'mon, Gene. I don't even know where to start. Where would I find someone to teach them? They don't even know what the Hebrew alphabet looks like.

They've never seen the inside of a synagogue. And what synagogue would handle it? Everybody in Grandville knows who I am — who's going to bar mitzvah the kids of the chief Kushner?"

This was getting more fantastic as time went on. I mean, he was rejecting the idea, but he was talking about it seriously.

"All those are problems that can be solved," Eugene said quietly.

"Yeah, but solving them takes time, and time is what I haven't got. Don't you see, Gene, I'm in way over my head. I'm busy every minute of every day. Besides, who's going to pay for a party? I'm really short just now, Gene."

"Who says you have to have a party?"

"I thought that was part of it."

"The main thing is the learning before the actual bar mitzvah. You should remember that."

"The guy who taught you and Stan wasn't the same guy that taught me. My 'teacher' was inept and bored with the whole thing — he kept falling asleep during the lessons. As much as I care for Mom and Dad, this entire plan is impractical — make that *impossible*. There's no synagogue that would undertake it and no one to teach the boys."

"Hey, what about that Baruch fella?" Eugene suggested. "Maybe *he* could teach the boys for their bar mitzvah."

GULP! I thought. How did *I* get into this?

"Him?" Bruce sneered. "As far as I know, he's nothing but an Orthodox hobo, got stuck in Grandville. One of my birdbrains — that's what I was talking about — thought he was a serious candidate."

"Never mind," Eugene said. "I'm sure we could work it out. Send the boys to me for a month or two. I'll find someone to teach them."

"Right. Send them to you for a month or two and I can save on a round-trip ticket. Forget it, Gene. The boys are not leaving here without me."

"You're being stubborn, big brother."

"I'm not being stubborn. I'm trying to dig out — I can only concentrate now on my financial problems. For me to bar mitzvah my kids is a major religious decision, and I just can't think about it now. Come back in a year or so after I've gotten things squared away and my head together. We can talk about it then."

"A year or so? That could be too late!"

"What do you mean too late?"

"You know what I mean. Mom and Dad are not getting any younger."

"Guilt trip?"

"I didn't think you could experience guilt where the family's concerned. But I'll be delighted if you prove me wrong."

"It won't work, Gene. I don't accept the challenge."

❀

S INCE IT was late, Bruce put me up for the night at his place. He had to leave for the Ashram at three-thirty every morning, so I thought it wouldn't be very nice to insist that he take me back at night. He promised that he would do everything he could to get me on my way the next day, and I took him at his word.

On the way out to the Ashram, we didn't talk much —I was too groggy — and once we got there, Bruce went his own way, telling me he would see me about eight-thirty and that I was invited to eat breakfast in the dining hall. "K's and U's," I said as I walked off towards the guest house. Four or five minutes later I was asleep again, dreaming of theme parks, heart attacks, and bar mitzvahs.

Bruce showed up about a quarter to nine, having awakened the gods and, I presume, eaten breakfast.

"What's your pleasure, Baruch?"

"Drive me to Atlanta."

"Uh, Baruch, I said I'd drive you to Atlanta, and if I have to, I will. But maybe there's an easier way to go about this. Maybe there's a bus."

"Okay, Bruce. If you don't want to drive me to Atlanta, I *will* make it easy on you. Just tell me how to get in touch with your brothers, Eugene and Stanley."

"What on Kushner's good earth for?"

"Well, Bruce, I guess I owe you an apology, but you know the windows were open last night, and I couldn't help but overhear your conversation with Eugene."

Bruce's face flushed, but he held his temper and said nothing.

"Bruce, you've got a couple of real nice boys there. It'd be a shame if they never had a bar mitzvah. It'd give your folks a lot of *nachas*, and what's more, I think your boys want it."

"Baruch, please." Bruce was back to his smooth self, "I feel bad that you had to be burdened with the contents of a *very* personal conversation..."

"Bruce, I'm really sorry. I really couldn't help..."

"No, that's all right, Baruch. I'm not blaming you. After all, the windows *were* open; I should have been more discreet. Off the record, I'm not really myself when my family is around."

"Listen, Bruce, if I took care of all the arrangements, would you consider making a bar mitzvah for your boys and inviting your brothers and parents?"

"If, as you say, Baruch, you heard that conversation last night, and if you understood it, then you must realize that I'm in no position to *consider* such a thing just now. By the way, I must ask you to keep everything you heard and saw last night completely confidential."

"Sure, Bruce. But I have an idea that could help you. I really want to see those boys of yours have a bar mitzvah."

Much to my surprise, Bruce had not socked me in the mouth yet.

"With all due respect, Baruch, whether or not Kushner and Suraj are bar mitzvahed is not really your affair."

"You're right, Bruce. I know I'm out of line, but will you answer me one thing?"

"Okay," he said with a sigh of resignation.

"Is there anything in your religion that would *prevent* you from giving your sons a bar mitzvah?"

"I don't think so, but I'm not the final authority."

"If you could get it cleared, would you agree to let your sons have a bar mitzvah?"

"Baruch, my friend, I've been around far too long to answer hypothetical questions."

"Okay, but are you willing to give me Eugene's and Stanley's phone numbers?"

"Sure," he said, taking a very fancy leather memo pad and gold pen from his inside suit pocket.

"These are their numbers at home," Bruce explained as he wrote. "Stan is taking Mom and Dad home, then going straight to the hospital for his rounds and afterward to his office. Eugene will also go straight to his office from the airport. So you can't reach them until the evening. Use the phone that I showed you on Friday as much as you like. You have enough food?"

"Yeah, I'm good for another couple of days."

"Okay," Bruce said as he turned to leave. "I'll have Cho Ramaswami send over some more pop. Sorry I can't get you any beer. We don't approve."

"Beer?! You think I'm a redneck?"

That got a laugh out of old Brucey. As he walked away, I realized that in the subtle chess game that was developing between us, he may have just won a small advantage from his point of view. By giving me his brothers' home phone numbers only, he'd made sure that I had to stay on the Ashram one more night, at least.

❀

My idea was to get Eugene and Stanley to bail Bruce out. I could see that both were doing well, and I figured that between them, they could handle it. I knew they weren't going to put up a penny for the SKA operating budget or buy bonds, but I thought they might be willing to help their brother directly. With his bankbook back in the black, Bruce might be able to think things through. He claimed that he cared about his parents and bringing the family together. If his brothers were willing to put their money where their mouths were, maybe Bruce would do the same.

Just to make sure the whole idea really *appealed* to Bruce, I would ask the brothers to condition their six-figure gifts to him on his agreement to have Keith and Stuart bar mitzvahed.

In the meantime, though, I was stuck for another day in the monkey house. Food was no problem, but all the clocks seemed to be moving in slow motion. Boy, was I bored! So bored, in fact, that I was actually happy to see Nerunjanah Levine when he stopped by to say good morning. I invited him in for some more matzah — I was hoping he might get addicted — and the two of us sat and talked for a while.

Nerunjanah asked me if I would like to spend the day with him, and thinking that anything was better than sitting and staring at the clock, I agreed. We started strolling around the Ashram. Old Irv didn't act as though he had anything in particular he had to do, although he'd explained to me on Friday that everyone had his appointed tasks and that all the whackos were required to work.

At one point, Nerunjanah stopped, bent over, and picked up a rock about the size of a man's fist. It was round and smooth like the rocks you find in a dry river bed. "Oh, Baruch," he said. "This is terrific. You've brought me..." and he said some word in Sanskrit which must mean luck or success or something. With me tagging along, Nerunjanah took his find and walked to one of the buildings. We went inside, and he led me to a room that looked like a kind of arts and crafts workshop, with all sorts of tools and materials.

Nerunjanah took a new brush and opened a little bottle of the kind of paint kids use on model airplanes. Very carefully, but with not too much talent, he painted a face on the rock, and then we sat down to talk for about fifteen minutes while the paint dried. "What are you doing?" I asked him.

"What?" Old Irv was still whatting me.

"I asked what you're doing."

"Oh. You'll see."

"Okay, I'll wait. Tell me, Nerunjanah, how is it that you don't have anything you have to do right now?"

"What?"

"I was wondering how come you don't have anything you have to be doing."

"Oh, but I *am* doing something. I asked if I could be your spiritual guide for the time that you're here."

"What?" Now it was my turn.

"I said that I asked if I could be your spiritual guide for the time that you're here."

"Spiritual guide?" It was all I could do to suppress a groan. "Who'd you ask?"

"Cho Ramaswami."

"And he agreed?"

"Yes."

I could see that this was a private initiative. Bruce would never have paired me up with one of his "bird-brains." Truth is, I didn't much mind. For me it was a diversion, and I knew that old Nerunjanah was certainly not the one who could charm me into a thirty-day, money-back-guaranteed, free trial of idol worship.

"Does Bruce know that you're my spiritual guide?"

"What?"

"I said, Does Bruce know you're my spiritual guide?"

"Bruce? Oh — you mean Janardhana Maharaj Goswami?"

"Yeah."

"I don't know. I suppose Cho Ramaswami will tell him."

"I see."

After the paint dried, Nerunjanah started rummaging around until he found some good strong cardboard. He cut it in the shape of two ears and glued them onto the rock. We sat and talked some more.

282 / GIVE PEACE A STANCE

When he was satisfied that the glue was completely dry, Nerunjanah picked up his kindergarten project as carefully as he could and carried it into another room in the same building. The lighting was dim, and the room had a very strong smell of incense.

"Where are we?"

"What?"

"I said, Where are we?"

Nerunjanah answered with a word in Sanskrit.

"What?"

"In English, it's called a chapel."

"Oh. Well, if this is a chapel, then that little table up in front with the candle and little four-armed statue on it must be an altar."

"Right."

And with that, I exited, stage left, while Nerunjanah placed his pet rock on the altar and presumably accelerated the process of making a complete idiot of himself. It involved, he later explained, lots of bowing and genuflecting and offering up flowers and the like.

I asked him how he could just take an old stone and start worshipping it.

"Oh, that's not just any old stone, Baruch. Once, when Kushner was out walking, he walked over a high mountain, which he thought to be very beautiful. Kushner so loved the mountain that it became a part of him and became holy. The stone you saw me venerating comes from that mountain. I wouldn't tell this to just anyone, Baruch, but I'm sure that *you* understand."

Boy, did I understand! I saw him find the stone. I saw him paint it. I saw him glue bunny ears on it. And I almost saw him worship it. I mean, these guys were bananas! I probably wouldn't tell it to anyone either, I was thinking. Anyone I knew would think I was making it up.

But everything I had so far seen at the Grandville Ashram was *nothing* compared to what Nerunjanah did after lunch, with the Cow Purification Ritual. Do ask — I assure you, you DON'T want to know.

SPENDING the day with my very own spiritual guide had been a real education. Of course, I still couldn't see the attraction of genuflecting to arts and crafts projects and grossing out on prairie patties, but the experience had been an eye opener.

That evening, I got on the horn to Eugene, and although it took him a few seconds to remember who I was, he seemed quite receptive to my suggestion. As I had imagined, he didn't flinch at the expenditure involved. He liked the idea of conditioning the bail-out on Bruce's agreement to go along with the bar mitzvah. That way the money would not only enable Bruce to think things through, but help him to come to the correct conclusion as well. He said he'd speak to Stanley and get back to me. I asked Eugene to work fast, since I didn't want to stay in this cuckoo clock any longer than I had to.

I certainly didn't expect Eugene to call me back for at least twenty-four hours, and I resigned myself to another day of watching my spiritual guide worship sticks, stones, cows, lizards, flies, mosquitoes, and so forth. But an hour later, one of the local yokels called me to the phone.

It was Eugene and Stanley on a conference call — Eugene was doing the talking. He sounded really buoyant, but he said that he and Stanley also had a condition: "That you be the one to teach Keith and Stuart their bar mitzvah."

"Why me?"

"First of all, we don't know anyone in Grandville who can handle it. Second, I doubt that anybody in Grandville would be *willing* to. And third, if you can get Bruce to agree, then you deserve to."

What 'deserve,' I thought. What's the big honor of being marooned in Grandville for the three months or so it would take to prepare Bruce's boys? "I just can't do it, Mr. Feldman."

"Then the deal's off. Call me Gene."

I swallowed hard. "Please believe me, Mr. Feldman, Eugene, nobody wants this to happen more than I do. But I can't just take three months out of my life and move to Grandville."

"My brother Stan and I are each going to take a hundred thousand dollars out of our money."

"Hey, that's great, but I've got a job I have to get back to in Providence."

"Listen, Baruch. You know that all Jews are responsible for each other."

"Of course I do, Mr. Feldman, but right now, that's not the point."

"Call me Gene. What is the point?"

"The point is that there are plenty of people in the state of Florida, and I'm sure in the city of Grandville, who could do a great job with those boys."

"Name one."

"Well," I *fumfited*, "I can't give you any names just now, but let me get back to Providence and make a few phone calls. I'll give you a whole list of names."

"We want *you*. Bruce knows you and trusts you."

"Please, Mr. Feldman, Gene, maybe *you* can afford to drop everything and take a three-month vacation, but *I* can't. And even if I could, who says my job would be waiting for me when I got back?"

"Well now, if money's the problem, Baruch, just name your price."

"I didn't mean to make it sound like the problem is money, but..."

"Look, Baruch," he cut me off, "you picked up the ball, and now you've got to run with it. If you don't handle this bar mitzvah, no one will. My brother Stan and I will pay the rent for an apartment in Grandville; I don't want you living on that farm with all the loonies. We'll pay you the salary you're making now on your job in Providence — what do you do?"

"I work at a candy company's retail outlet."

"Okay, no problem. I'm sure we can manage it. And, of course, we'll pay you for the bar mitzvah lessons and any expenses you incur. If you want, I'll even call your boss and persuade him to hold your job for you."

Boy, these guys meant business!

"Well, Baruch, what do you say? Are you responsible enough to care for your fellow Jews? Are you prepared to deny these boys what might be their one and only chance to return to the fold? Will you just stand idly by as they transgress one of Judaism's three cardinal sins?"

I wished the cardiologist brother and not the lawyer was doing the talking. How could anybody argue with this guy?

"Okay," I said. What else could I say? "But I also have some conditions."

"Shoot."

"First, *you* have to break the whole thing to Bruce. If he says he has someone else to do the bar mitzvah, we don't argue. I pack up my things and go home."

"You got it. What's second?"

"I can't do anything until I talk to my Rabbi. I only go through with this if he tells me it's okay, and all of us do this bar mitzvah *exactly* as *he* says."

"Baruch, you drive a hard bargain." I knew that Eugene was enjoying his victory.

"Okay, Mr. Feldman..."

"Gene."

"Gene. Now you get on the phone to Bruce. Twist his arm like you just twisted mine. Tell him if he wants the bail-out, he's got to clear it with the leadership right away. And don't tell your Mom and Dad anything until a week or two before the bar mitzvah. I don't want to disappoint them if it falls through."

"You're going to make them a *real* bar mitzvah, right, Baruch?"

"Like they say in the jingle, Mr. Feldman, 'the real thing.'"

"What about Keith and Stuart? You think they'll go along with it?"

"I have reason to believe that they just might, Mr. Feldman."

"Gene."

"Gene."

V

AFTER MY conference call with Eugene and Stanley, things moved pretty fast. Next morning they spoke to Bruce, and I spoke to my Rabbi, the one who helped me become religious. Eugene knew that one of the cardinal rules of salesmanship is that when your customer is interested, you always press for a quick decision. How exactly he did it, I'll never know, but he got Bruce to agree to give a final answer within twenty-four hours. Given the stakes, it will come as no surprise that the answer turned out to be yes.

I spoke to my Rabbi at length. He wanted to think the whole thing through, but he also understood that any significant delay might result in any one of the three Feldman brothers backing out. When he called back in the evening, my Rabbi said he would support my involvement in the project only if a number of non-negotiable conditions were met.

Uh-oh, I thought. We had a pretty delicate situation

here, and a slew of new conditions might just be more than anybody could handle.

The first condition my Rabbi laid down was that for obvious reasons the bar mitzvah could not be held on the Ashram and not on Shabbos. The second was that Keith and Stuart be taught to put on *tefillin*. The third condition was that each of the boys was to write and deliver a *devar Torah* that had substance and — as my Rabbi put it — "comes from his heart." The fourth condition was that both boys, and if possible both parents, immerse in a *mikveh* a day or two before the bar mitzvah.

We were doing fine, I thought, since conditions one through four were likely to get the green light, especially with that "if possible" clause in number four. But I sensed that the clincher was yet to come.

I was right.

The fifth and last condition was that the Feldmans of Grandville, Florida — all four of them together and each one individually — observe Shabbos for the entire period leading up to the bar mitzvah.

Knowing Janardhana and Bhakti, I figured that big number five had about as good a chance of being accepted as one of their G.I. Joe Action Figures had of wishing me a *gut yontif*.

That same night, when Eugene Feldman called to tell me that he'd "closed" with Bruce and that he and Stanley would be calling their brokers in the morning, I told him that I had gotten my Rabbi's provisional go-ahead and spelled out his conditions. As I'd expected, Eugene responded to each one with a breezy "No problem," until I hit the last one. Then he went silent on me.

After a few hour-long seconds, Eugene asked, "Baruch, do you know what kind of lawyer I am?"

"No sir, Mr. Feldman, but I suspect you're a good one."

"Cut the 'sir' business and call me Gene."

"Sorry, Gene."

"Okay. I'm a *corporate* lawyer, Baruch. That means I'm involved in a lot of negotiations for my clients, that every day, my clients and I are cutting new deals. I *am* pretty good at what I do, Baruch, or I wouldn't have that hundred thou to put up for the bar mitzvah. Do you know what the key to my success is?"

"No, sir."

"Don't call me sir."

"Sorry."

"I'm successful because I'm a good negotiator. And as a good negotiator, I can smell a deal-breaker a mile away. Your Rabbi's number five is one heck of a deal-breaker."

"But..."

"Tell me, Baruch. How many Jews in this country — and I'm talking about regular Jews, now, not the kind that think that bowing to a bunch of Betsy Wetsies represents the wave of the future — how many Jews in this country could you get to keep Shabbos just by telling them they ought to?"

"Give me two hundred thousand dollars to throw around, and I'll let you know."

"Not bad for an amateur, Baruch. But the two

hundred buys us a bar mitzvah, not a conversion. I already closed with Bruce, and I can't reopen the negotiation. Reopening negotiations is not only bad luck; reopening negotiations is the supreme deal-breaker."

"The way I see it, Mr. Feldman, Bruce has two hundred thousand good reasons to accept just about any conditions we impose, and all things considered, these five are more or less lightweights.

"The bottom line, Mr. Feldman, is that I don't make a move without my Rabbi. He says: no Shabbos, no Baruch; that means the ball is in your court. Either you sell Bruce on number five, or you find another Baruch."

A few more hour-long seconds ticked by, during which I had plenty of time to think about getting back to my job at the candy store, chess games in the park, and other gloriously dull aspects of my pre-Ashram existence, which was looking better all the time.

"Okay, Baruch, I know when I'm licked. I'll handle Bruce, but you get to talk to Keith and Stuart."

"Me?! I thought their parents were going to do that."

"Bruce wants *you* to talk to them. He says that they're not very communicative and that you really drew them out, there at the Ashram Shabbos afternoon."

"Drew them out? Well, I guess if you can believe that statues eat breakfast, you can believe that I drew them out. I got Keith to stop chewing his gum for a few minutes, that's all."

"I'm sure you're being way too modest. So, you'll talk to them?"

Did I have a choice? "Okay." I said. "I'll talk to them."

"Right. Now that we've got that settled, where are we going to make it?"

That's it: confuse the enemy, I thought. "Make what?" I asked.

"The bar mitzvah. Where are we going to make the bar mitzvah?"

I'm busy racking my brains how I'm going to break the news to the boys, and he's already up to where we're going to have the bar mitzvah. "Uh, Gene, maybe you could handle that aspect. All I know is that it can't be out here on the funny farm."

"So you said, and I agree. But you see I've got a problem: Stan doesn't want Dad travelling anymore. So Grandville is out."

"You both live in Hartford, right?"

"Right."

"And your folks?"

"After Stan and I settled in Hartford, we sold the old house in Brooklyn and set Mom and Dad up here in their own place."

"So if you're all in Hartford, why not have it there?"

"Well you see, I've got a problem with that. It's the people in my shul. They're all pretty straight, see? And nobody knows who or what my brother is. I'm not saying they wouldn't let me have the bar mitzvah here. In fact, I'm pretty sure they would. It's just that I wouldn't really like to make waves if I don't have to. These congregants, well, a number of them, are my clients.

Once the word gets around about my connection to the Kushners... I'm sure you get the picture. So, if you have any ideas..."

As a matter of fact, I did. "Uh, Gene, do you think that Stan would let your father travel to Providence?"

"Rhode Island?"

"Yeah, Providence, Rhode Island."

"That's under an hour from here. I'll ask him what he thinks."

"If your father can get to Providence without endangering his health, I think I have just the place."

No sooner had I hung up with Eugene, than the phone rang again. It was my Rabbi, with condition number six, which made big number five pale into insignificance, and me along with it.

I hyperventilated for a while, and then redialed Eugene's number.

"Hello, Mr. Feldman?"

"Gene."

"Sorry. I know we just hung up, but uh, there's something real important we sort of forgot..."

"I know, Baruch, but don't worry — Stan and I have got it covered."

"Uh, Gene? Are we talking about the same thing?"

"Yes, Baruch, and like I said, Stan and I will handle the whole deal. Remember, Stan's a doctor."

"But he's a cardiologist!"

"No problem. This is minor surgery. Don't say a word to anyone. Stan will be ready to fly back to Grandville as soon as you say the word, and he has a great relationship with Keith and Stuart."

Whew! I sighed with profound relief, not to mention gratitude. There was *no way* that good ol' Baruch would have been able to handle the problem of a kosher bris for these two adolescents!

THE PAST four days of my life had contained more action than the preceding twenty-four *years*. Here's a quick rundown: I had landed (so to speak) in gorgeous Grandville on Thursday. I had spent Friday and Shabbos on an Ashram and been given my own "spiritual guide" to the Kingdom of Kushner. By Sunday, I'd inherited a whole family that was relying on me to restore *shalom bayis* and maybe lead its stray members back to Judaism. I had gotten two virtual strangers to put down a hundred thousand smackers each and committed myself to persuading Keith and Stuart, a.k.a. Kushner and Suraj, to have a bar mitzvah. I was about to give up my job, without knowing if I would ever get it back, and take up residence in Grandville (though everything I owned was still in Providence) for the foreseeable future.

It was eleven-thirty at night when I finally got off the phone with Eugene Feldman and started walking back to the guest house, understandably feeling just a little bit dizzy.

The next day, after Bruce finished his morning ceremonies, I left the Ashram, hoping never to see the place again. Bruce ran me into town, put me up in one of the bedrooms of his house for the time being, and went off to work.

Before he left, Bruce had slipped me an envelope, telling me that Eugene wanted me to have it. It contained four fifty-dollar bills and an American Express "gold card." "Gene said you might need to pick up some clothes and household items. We'll work out the rest of the financial arrangements after supper. Bhakti will help you look for a place of your own this morning, and with a little luck, you can be sleeping in your own bed tonight."

Beth had already circled some classified ads, and by ten-thirty, she and I were visiting the first apartment. Since I didn't find her apathy-shading-into-mild-hostility any more scintillating than I had on Shabbos afternoon at the Ashram, and since the first apartment we saw seemed clean, serviceable, and within walking distance of their place, I took it. Beth wrote out a check, and by one o'clock, I was finishing my Bubbie's leftovers in my own furnished apartment, and making notes to myself on what I wanted to do with the boys, hoping that the pace of things might begin to slow down a bit.

The next day was Tuesday, and I knew the boys couldn't call until after school. I slept late, took my time davening, bought some groceries and pots and pans, and dawdled over breakfast. Before I could finish eating, though, I heard a knock at the door. It was Keith and Stuart.

I gave them my usual, "Hey, guys," let them in, and led them over to the table where my Cheerios were rapidly going soggy. "You guys hungry?"

"Nah," Keith answered.

It was quiet for a minute; then finally Stuart said, "Talk to us some more."

"About what?"

"About being Jewish," Keith answered.

"Oh."

Monday night, as Bruce had asked, I'd walked over to his place to set up financial arrangements. When I got there, he gave me his patented two-handed handshake, told me for the umpteenth time how *glad* he was to see me, and led me into the family room. Beth, meanwhile, had left the room only to return with Keith and Stuart, who were looking as bored as ever. "Kushner, Suraj," she cooed, "Baruch is here to talk to you about something very important." And with that, Bruce and Beth disappeared like a couple of rabbits into a magician's top hat.

Me? I thought that tonight we were going to talk about finances.

"Uh, how you guys been?" Silence.

"Say, uh, you guys remember how you asked me what a bar mitzvah is?"

More silence. I could hear the house settling.

"Yeah, well, I thought you'd like to know," I continued, "that *every* Jewish boy becomes bar mitzvah when he turns thirteen — whether he knows it or not, whether he wants to or not."

"So what," Keith sneered. "We're not Jewish."

"Who told you that?"

"We've never been to Hebrew school," Keith answered hotly. "Never been to Sunday school. Never had a bar mitzvah or even been inside a synagogue. Our grandparents are Jewish, but we're Harry Kushners."

"I see. Well, that's cool. Anyway, I've got to be going. Uh, maybe you have a piece of paper here?"

Stuart left and returned with a sheet of notebook paper, and I began writing out my name, address, and phone number. "Like I said, I've got to be going, but since your grandparents are Jewish, I thought you'd like to know that we Jews have something called *Halachah*. It means Jewish Law. The word 'Halachah' comes from the verb 'to walk' or 'to go.' It's the Jewish *way*, the way we *go* through life."

"So what?" Keith challenged.

"So, according to the Halachah, if your mother was born Jewish, you're automatically Jewish too."

Both boys were staring hard at me now. I handed Keith the sheet with my particulars, took two steps towards the door, and then turned back. "You know how your mother said I wanted to talk to you about something important?"

"Yeah," they both answered.

"Well, that was what I wanted to tell you."

So here they were, finally, in my kitchen wanting to talk about "being Jewish."

"What's the name of that Jewish Law you told us

about?" Keith asked.

"Halachah?"

"Right. Halachah. Is what you told us the only thing that Halachah says?"

"No way! Halachah says lots of things," I was still trying to get them to pump me for information. "Halachah says that if you find lost property, you have to return it to its owner. Halachah says that you're not allowed to light a fire on Shabbos. Halachah says that you're not allowed to give false testimony and that you have to eat matzah on Passover. Halachah is Jewish Law, and it relates to just about everything, see?"

"But what does it say about being Jewish?" Stuart was speaking, but Keith wasn't stopping him.

"It says a lot about that too. But what I told you last night — that according to Halachah, if your mother was born Jewish, you're Jewish too — actually means two things. The first is: once a Jew, always a Jew. If you're born Jewish, even if you convert to every other religion under the sun six times over, you're still Jewish.

"The second thing it means is: anyone born to a Jewish mother is Jewish, and stays Jewish, no matter what he *or his mother* does."

"So you mean that even though we never went to synagogue or Hebrew school or got bar mitzvahed we're Jewish?" Stuart asked wide-eyed.

"Of course that's what he means, doofus." Keith whomped his brother on the head.

"Halachah also says you shouldn't say things to people that you wouldn't like them to say to you."

"What of it?" Keith wasn't giving any ground, at least not yet.

I shrugged. "Just thought you might like to know. Tell me Keith, how do you feel about what I told you?"

"About being Jewish?"

"Yeah."

"I dunno."

"And you Stuart?"

"I think it's neat!"

I let that sit for a while and then asked, "Aren't you guys supposed to be in school?"

"Maybe," Keith answered.

"Uh-huh. Are you sure you don't want anything to eat?"

"Nah." That was Keith.

"Nah." That was Stuart.

"Yeah, well, my cereal's getting all soggy here. You mind if I eat while we talk?"

"Nah."

"Nah."

"Coffee?" I asked.

"Yeah, I'll have some," Keith answered. Stuart was still thinking.

I made three cups of instant coffee and put them on the table. I sat there finishing my breakfast while the two boys drank. Finally, Keith spoke without being spoken to. "I thought you said you were going back to Providence."

"Your father didn't tell you why I stayed?"

"You joining the Ashram?"

"What do *you* think?"

"I think you said you were going back to Providence and now you've got your own place here in Grandville."

"What would you say if I told you that I stayed because your father wants me to make you boys a bar mitzvah?"

"I'd say you escaped from the loony bin."

"There's a phone over there. Why don't you ask your old man?"

"There's no way my parents are gonna let us have a bar mitzvah!"

"But Baruch," Stuart interrupted, "you never did tell us what a bar mitzvah is."

"You're right, Stuart. I owe you guys an explanation. Look, it's simple. Like I told you the other day, bar means son and mitzvah means commandment, so the words bar mitzvah mean son of a commandment. But what it really means is that you have to keep the commandments. Halachah is a set of commandments, and the commandments are written in a book called the Torah. Ever hear of it?"

"Nah."

"Nah."

"Ever hear of Moses?"

"Maybe," Keith wasn't allowing himself to look too interested.

"God told Moses how he wanted Jews to live, see? And Moses wrote it all down in this book I just mentioned — the Torah. The commandments tell us how God wants us to live. There are six hundred and thirteen of 'em."

Stuart let out a low whistle.

"Knock it off, Stu," Keith said belligerently. "This guy's lying. Everybody knows there are only *ten* commandments."

"I don't lie, Keith," I said indignantly. "The ten you're talking about are the ten 'big ones,' the really basic ones, like the commandments to believe in God and keep Shabbos and not murder anyone. But the Halachah is made up of *all* the commandments in the Torah, including the ten 'big ones.' I would bet you two already keep some of them, without even knowing it!"

"Yeah? Like what?" Keith was still fighting it.

"Ever murder anyone?"

Stuart giggled.

"I didn't think so. Well, there you go — that's one commandment you've both been obeying for years. But we Jews are supposed to keep *all* the commandments."

"So what's that got to do with a bar mitzvah?" Keith was getting impatient, but I knew it meant he was interested.

"Well, the Halachah says that when a boy reaches the age of thirteen, he becomes a *bar mitzvah* and that means that at thirteen he has to start keeping the commandments. Before that, he's not old enough to accept such a big responsibility. It's sort of like being old enough to vote. And just like voting is a responsibility and also a privilege, so is being a bar mitzvah."

"I don't get it," Keith shrugged.

"Well, on the responsibilities side, for instance, it means you have to keep kosher."

"What's kosher?"

"Kosher means what you're allowed to eat, but let me get back to that later."

"And what kind of privileges?"

"One of the privileges is that you can be counted for a *minyan*. When Jews pray in the synagogue, they need to have at least ten men present. That's called a minyan. In a big corporation, or an organization, if there isn't a certain minimum number of people present, no decisions can be taken and no important stuff can be discussed. In a synagogue, no minyan, no service. Once a Jewish boy is thirteen, he can be counted as part of the ten."

"You mean even *I* could be part of a minyan?"

"Right, Keith. How old's Stuart?"

"He's twelve-and-a-half."

"Okay, there you have it. You're over thirteen, you're already a bar mitzvah, so you *could* be counted for a minyan. Stuart's under thirteen, so he *can't*. As soon as he has his next birthday, though, he'll be a bar mitzvah, and he'll also be able to be counted."

"There's something I don't understand," Keith said.

"First you tell us that bar mitzvah means you have to keep the commandments and that I became a bar mitzvah automatically on my thirteenth birthday. Then you tell us that our father wants you to *make* us a bar mitzvah. So, how can you *make* us a bar mitzvah if the whole thing is automatic? And, if I'm already over thirteen, isn't it, like, too late?"

I couldn't believe it — a whole *paragraph* had actually come out of his mouth! "Good questions, Keith. You're right. Becoming a bar mitzvah is automatic, whether you celebrate it or not. But like I told you at the Ashram, people are in the habit of using the words bar mitzvah to refer not only to the boy and his new obligations, but also to the celebration marking the occasion. What your father wants is for me to help you two prepare for your bar mitzvah service and arrange the celebration in a synagogue.

"As far as it being too late, well, it's *never* too late. If someone who's about sixteen, for instance, someone who never knew about the commandments before, found out about them and decided that he wanted to start keeping them, and started learning all he could about being Jewish, I'd say that's a pretty big reason to celebrate. That hypothetical sixteen-year-old — you know what hypothetical means?"

"Yeah, my American history teacher is always saying it."

"Good. Anyway, that hypothetical sixteen-year-old could learn how to read the Torah, and be called up in the synagogue to recite a portion of it out loud. Maybe he could even say a few words afterwards, you know, make a little speech, telling everyone about how it feels to be really involved with Judaism for the first time. If that were to happen to some hypothetical sixteen-year-old, I'd bet his grandparents, and uncles, and maybe even his parents might be happy enough to come down to the synagogue and celebrate. They might just be happy enough to buy him a pair of *tefillin* and some books about Judaism and stuff."

"What's *tefillin*?"

"You'll find out. Let me go on.

"Now if that hypothetical sixteen-year-old had a hypothetical brother who was just about thirteen, and they *both* had an *aliyah* — that is, they were *both* called up to read from the Torah — on the same morning and *both* said a few words from their hearts, it would be like a *double* celebration. Are you starting to get my drift?"

Keith put his head down on his arms for a minute, the way kids do when they want to sleep in study hall, and when he looked up again, his eyes were all red. He stared at me a second and then said in a hoarse whisper, "And you think *my* folks are gonna go for all that?"

I walked across the room, picked up the receiver of the telephone, and held it out in Keith's direction. "You boys don't really know me yet," I said quietly, "but when you do, you'll find out that there are some things I don't joke about."

I had no doubt at that moment that — as Eugene Feldman would say — Keith, Stuart, and I had closed. But I was wrong. Apparently the subject of Jewishness and his relationship with his parents, grandparents, and uncles was so sensitive to Keith, so fraught with emotion, that he couldn't handle everything I was telling him all at once. Instead of taking the phone to call his father and verify what I was saying, or simply asking, "When do we start?", he jumped up and ran out of the apartment, slamming the door behind him.

Stuart stared at the closed door for a minute, then slowly got to his feet.

"See ya, Stuart," I said.

"See ya, Baruch," he answered as he walked out.

Me? I cleared the table and placed one call to my Rabbi and another to Stanley Feldman.

Y OU GUYS ready to start?"
"Yeah."
"Yeah."
"Good."

After the session in my kitchen, I'd called my Rabbi and asked him to purchase *tefillin*, *siddurim* and *chumashim* with English translation, some basic texts on Judaism, and some yarmulkas, and to send them to me by one of those overnight express services. I dictated the number on the credit card Eugene had left for me and said that everything was to be charged to that account.

The stuff arrived early the next day, as did Stan, who stopped by to say that the boys would be fine by Thursday and that he had to catch the next flight back to Hartford.

But when, by noon on Thursday, I hadn't heard anything from Bruce or his boys, I began to get a little nervous. About four-thirty in the afternoon, though, there was a knock at my door. Keith and Stuart were standing there, fidgeting and waiting to be asked in.

After getting settled around my kitchen table, they

produced one old yarmulka and one *machzor* for Yom Kippur, telling me that their father had said they should bring them. How Bruce had come by these two bits of exotica and why he'd bothered saving them were beyond me.

"Now, listen, guys, first we're going to learn some real basic things. We're going to learn about how Judaism got started — about Abraham, Isaac, Jacob, Moses, the Exodus from Egypt, and Mount Sinai. Ever hear of those things?"

"Sure."

"Sure."

I wasn't so sure.

I told them that we would then learn about the commandments — not all of them, of course — and then I would show them how to read from the Torah. I explained that to read from the Torah, they'd have to learn to read Hebrew and the special musical notes. I told them that the whole process would take about three months and that it would be up to them to work hard and practice every day.

"Now, are you both sure you wanna go through with this?"

"Yeah."

"Yeah."

Were there ever two Jewish kids more motivated to learn? Keith and Stuart were convinced that their parents were crazy. As Grandpa Sam had said, they had never invited a friend over to the house, because they were too embarrassed. They hated having to smear

Playdoh on their noses and wear those dumb sheets, and they craved "normal" food. They were wild about their uncles and grandparents and harbored secret fantasies that their father's relatives might one day adopt them. Deep down, of course, they knew that their parents would never give them up. Keith was old enough to think about leaving home after high school, though, and he hoped that one of his uncles might take him in and finance his college education. Uncle Stan had hinted as much during a recent visit.

Both boys saw in Judaism their ticket to normality, and they felt that anything good enough for Grandpa Sam and Grandma Esther was good enough for them. Their parents had been so zealous about keeping contacts with the rest of the family to a minimum, though, that the boys' knowledge of Judaism had remained shockingly meager. All this came out in very small bits and pieces over the period that I taught them. But right now I was so astonished by their interest in the *mitzvos* we were discussing, that I could focus on nothing else.

After I gave a rough outline of kashrus, Keith asked me, "Can *I* keep kosher?"

"You mean you already want to keep kosher?"

"Maybe. What do I have to do?"

"Well, come to think of it, you may almost be keeping kosher *now*."

"What do you mean by that?"

"Before I answer that, can we make a deal?"

"Whaddaya want?" Keith was again suspicious.

"The deal is simple. You don't lie to me, and I don't lie to you. If I ask you a question, and you don't want to answer it, you just say, 'I'd rather not answer,' but if you answer, you have to tell the truth."

"And the same goes for you?"

"Right. Same goes for me."

"You're on."

"What about you, Stuart?"

"Sure."

"Okay. Now look, Keith. All HKs are veggies, right?"

"Right."

"Are you a veggie?"

"Sure. That's all my mom ever serves."

"That much I know. But don't you ever cheat? There's a fast-food place not far from your house. You wanna tell me you never stop in for a burger and fries with your friends from school?"

Keith hesitated.

"Tell me the truth, and in a minute you'll see why I'm asking."

"Yeah, sure, sometimes I do. So what?"

"Okay. Now, remember that I told you that just about the only things that are unkosher come from the animal kingdom?"

"Yeah."

"That only meat, fish and fowl, or dairy products mixed with meat or fowl can be unkosher, that fruits and vegetables are all kosher?"

"Sure."

"Well, don't you see? If the only thing your mom serves is fruits and vegetables, all you have to do is stop eating out, and you're keeping kosher!"

"Wow!"

It was the same with *tefillin*, only much greater. This time it was Stuart who wanted to know if *"we* have to put on *tefillin*." I told him that I didn't know what he meant by *have* to. "Putting on *tefillin* is one of the commandments," I told him. "I put on *tefillin* every weekday morning and so do your grandfather and your uncles. How to put on *tefillin* is certainly one of the things I'm going to teach you, and since the bar mitzvah will be on a weekday, we'll *all* be wearing *tefillin* that morning."

"But we don't *have* any *tefillin*," he whined.

"Right," I said with a smile.

Both boys looked at me funny as I got up and went into the next room.

Knowing my Rabbi, he had probably purchased the best *tefillin* available, along with beautifully embroidered velvet pouches — one navy blue and the other wine-red. Since by this time, the boys actually had Hebrew names (thanks to Stan and condition number six), the velvet pouches were inscribed respectively *Kalman* and *Shmuel*, in ornate gold Hebrew script.

Keith's and Stuart's eyes went wide as I returned

and gently placed the pouches on the table in front of them. "Wow," they said softly in chorus.

"Compliments of Uncles Gene and Stan," I said. "This one's yours, Keith." I showed him how the letters spelled out his new name.

"Hey, mine must say Shmuel," Stuart exclaimed. The kid was a quick study.

Keith picked up his pouch gingerly. "Don't be afraid of it," I said.

Stuart picked his up, and I watched with enormous pleasure as both boys caressed the soft velvet pouches and touched the contents with a tenderness I didn't know either of them possessed. The room was dead silent and charged with more emotion than I could possibly put on paper. They were simply entranced and I wasn't about to break the spell.

I let the boys examine their treasures — that's really the only way I can describe how they handled the *tefillin* — and then I explained the rudiments. I showed them how to distinguish between the *shel yad* and *shel rosh*; I helped them put them on properly and had them repeat the blessings after me.

I have to tell you, the three of us were kind of misty-eyed by this time, but we for sure weren't going to make a big thing out of it. I said they could take their *tefillin* off and we would continue with our first lesson.

"Can't I keep mine on just a little longer?" Stuart begged.

"Sure you can, Stuart," I answered, my eyes filling up. "How do they feel?" I asked Keith.

"Good," he said, his voice a little choked. He cleared his throat. "They feel good. I think I'll keep mine on a while too, if that's okay."

"Sure," I said, seizing the moment. "Now, I want you both to put them on every weekday morning until the bar mitzvah."

It was Keith who answered, "No problem, Baruch."

VI

OR THE BAR MITZVAH, I chose *parashas Balak*, and I showed Keith and Stuart how it had to do with trying to resist God's plan for things. I explained about Bil'am, the gentile prophet who had been sent to curse the Jews but ended up blessing the nation, declaring that the Jews are a separate and special people.

I reminded the boys that they would each have to say a few words after the Torah reading. Neither wanted to sit down and write a speech, and I really had to twist their arms to get them to do it. When they asked me to help, I said I was willing to comment on the finished product, help them polish it and all, but that the speech had to be theirs alone.

We got into a routine. Every weekday afternoon the boys came for their lesson. At home, they put on their *tefillin* every morning and said *Shema* and *Shemoneh Esreh*. Nights, they were expected to devote at least half an hour to practicing Hebrew, and half an hour to rehearsing their Torah readings.

Shabbos...well, Shabbos remained a problem.

What I really wanted was for the boys to spend every Shabbos, or at least the meals, with me, and as it turned out, that was just fine with Bruce and Beth. After all, it kept *me* out of their house. I did spend two or three *Shabbosim* with the Feldmans at the beginning, instructing Beth in candle-lighting procedure, teaching Bruce how to make Kiddush, explaining about washing for bread and reciting *Hamotzi*. Bruce, of course, had to discontinue his Saturday afternoon Ashram activities, and Beth had to forgo a particularly cherished Friday night radio program. (It hadn't occurred to me until the matter came up, but apparently no self-respecting HK would dream of having a TV in his house.) Except for the Indian-*avodah zarah* decor, things *looked* pretty normal.

The truth is, Bruce and Beth really resented this part of the deal. They followed all my instructions, sure. But like I said, Bruce had two hundred thousand good reasons to do that, and I'm sure he figured out some way to get Beth to go along with him. Still, they had this hostility about the whole thing, and instead of it easing up as the weeks passed, it just got worse and worse.

There was a lesson in that, and for me it was kind of humbling. I remembered how great I had felt when I experienced my first Shabbos; I expected — naively, I guess — it would be the same for Bruce and Beth. I had had a really fantastic teacher and guide to Judaism, while all the Feldmans had was old Baruch. Kind of puts things in perspective, you know?

And there was another thing here. They say every man has his price, but I would like to believe that no amount of money could get me to want to desecrate Shabbos. Maybe, by the same token, no amount of money could get the Feldmans to *want* to keep Shabbos. Oh, yeah, they were keeping it, but *wanting to* had to come from inside them.

Finally, I took matters into my own hands and invited the boys to spend Shabbos at my apartment. Their parents agreed with so much enthusiasm that it was almost embarrassing. I could only hope that Bruce and Beth would continue observing Shabbos, even without my being there as a watchdog. Not that I ever behaved like a watchdog — really! But I think that was how they viewed me. Maybe, with me out of the way, they might be able to accept things more easily. Besides, I figured, I would have a lot more opportunity to develop my relationship with the boys over my *own* Shabbos table, on my own turf.

I consulted with my Rabbi and he agreed that there was no way to enforce the Feldmans' private Sabbath-observance, but he said I had to be adamant about their behavior in my presence or in public. Actually, they were still keeping a lot more than anyone ever would have expected, and that entitled them to some credit.

That first Shabbos, the boys and I paid a social call on their parents on Saturday afternoon. That was my way of reassuring Bruce and Beth that I was not trying to ease them out of things and also of reminding them that we both had to keep our ends of the bargain. The next week I invited Bruce and Beth for Friday night, and while they did come and were extremely polite about the whole thing, it was clear that they still were not warming up to Shabbos, so I didn't bother having them over much after that.

The Feldmans were noncomittal about the boys' staying with me — I suppose they didn't feel threatened by it — so that became part of the routine, as did my Saturday afternoon social call. I figured that Bruce and Beth might be cheating a little, but I never caught them at it — at least not until I came over on a Friday night instead of a Saturday.

❦

Don't ask me why I did it, because I really don't know. The Friday night meal with the boys had been particularly pleasant. We'd talked about everything from the NBA to Mt. Sinai, the boys were eating up everything I had to tell them with a big spoon (as we say in the Midwest), and I was feeling mellow as all get-out. I was also feeling good about the boys, finally at ease about my decision to stay in Grandville, and charitable towards Bruce and Beth. Maybe I was getting a little self-satisfied. But whatever the case may have been, I felt like really seeing if we couldn't share a little Shabbos spirit with the senior Feldmans. "Hey, whaddaya guys say about popping over to your folks?"

Stuart, by this time, would have agreed enthusiastically if I'd said, "How about a little stroll to the North Pole?" but Keith was more sober about the idea of dropping in on his parents unexpectedly. No matter, I thought; he's sixteen-and-a-half years old — he puts everything down.

I knew I'd made a mistake when we got about five or six steps away from the Feldmans' front door, and I could hear voices that sounded distinctly electronic. I remembered Beth's complaint about missing her favorite radio program on Friday nights. But it was too late to turn back.

After knocking for a while, I heard footsteps and then Bruce's voice from the other side of the door: "Who is it?"

"Good Shabbos," I greeted him as heartily as I could, the same greeting *he* had extended to *me* back on the Ashram.

"Uh, just a minute, Baruch," Bruce answered. Then I heard more footsteps, and the electronic-sounding voices clicked off. A moment later the door opened to reveal Bruce, smooth and smiling, with his hand extended to return my Sabbatical salutation.

I didn't really understand why my Rabbi had insisted on the Shabbos condition — old number five — and I certainly wasn't too keen about enforcing Sabbath observance under duress. But one thing was clear: I had to take a stand so that Keith and Stuart would see that when it comes to something as important as Shabbos, we don't make compromises.

Blow the whistle? I wondered. If I do, that's *it*. The whole thing's off. What'll that do to the boys? But what if I don't? Bruce and Beth know that I know. What's worse — the *boys* know that I know. I let this go by and what'll the Feldmans do next? Maybe they'll start pulling all kinds of other shtick. I've got to be firm here. For the boys' sake.

"Look, Bruce," I said, pointing at the radio, "I'm not going to mince words. I heard you had that on when we came to the door, and I know you turned it off before you let us in. The two of you made an agreement, and now you've violated it. For all I know, you've been violating it all along. As far as I'm concerned, the deal's off. I'll call your brothers tomorrow night and tell them that they're going to have to find another Baruch." The boys, of course, didn't understand everything that was going on, but they were sharp enough to get the bottom line.

"Baruch," Bruce oozed, "I haven't the faintest idea what you're talking about."

"Yes you do," I said calmly.

"As Harry Kushner is my witness, I do not know what on earth you are talking about."

"Like the man said, Bruce, 'Have it your way.'"

"No, Baruch," Bruce growled with more muscle in his voice than I had ever heard before. "Have it *your* way!"

"Believe me, Bruce," I answered, turning to the door. "That is exactly what I intend to do."

I guess you might say I stormed out.

❦

Did I feel bad about the confrontation? You bet I didn't! The tension between the elder Feldmans and me had been building all along. To be honest, it was a relief to have had it out with them and gotten things out in the open.

But I felt terrible for the boys.

I knew that they would suffer much more than either their parents or I would. I was convinced that Bruce would cave in, but the boys had no way of knowing that, and I was certain that they were going to have a rotten Shabbos — what was left of it. I felt it was important, though, that they see me take a stand on principle.

I was going to phone Eugene Sunday morning to put him in the picture, figuring he'd probably get brother Brucey on the horn and read him the Riot Act. But before I could call him, he called me. The boys, it seemed, had already reached him late Saturday night. They hadn't known the extent of his and Stan's role in the bar mitzvah, but as soon as they'd heard me mention their uncles, they knew whom to talk to. They were desperate.

Over the phone, Eugene pulled out his old "deal-breaker" line again and delivered the grandaddy of all I-toldya-soes. Then, after letting me squirm for a while, he informed me that Bruce and Beth had agreed to stop cheating.

I was skeptical, until Gene related the whole conversation. He said that the boys had spent all of Shabbos begging their parents to relent and let them have their bar mitzvah. Late Saturday afternoon, Bruce had left the house in a huff and driven out to the Ashram to resume delivering his weekly sermon. By the time he'd returned, the boys were already speaking to their uncle. "I asked them to put their father on," Eugene told me, "and Bruce and I came to a meeting of minds, or at least of bank accounts. I agreed that Bruce should let his boys believe he gave in only because he didn't want to disappoint them," Eugene concluded, "but between you and me, Baruch, my big brother knows he's in so deep that it would take a steam shovel to get him out. He just needed a gentle reminder."

After that, Shabbos was no longer an issue. I felt that Bruce and Beth were finally cooperating. I realized it was only for the money, but I'd already lost whatever illusions I'd had on that score anyway.

Before we knew it, it was time for our encounter with Providence.

BRUCE AND his boys went out and bought new suits for the occasion, and Beth purchased an appropriate dress. To my surprise, she also invited her folks to come in from St. Louis and was quite insistent about her father being given some honor at the bar mitzvah. I added his name to my list of *aliyah*s.

Stan Feldman confirmed that his father had never felt better and that the trip to Providence for his grandsons' bar mitzvah could only do him a world of good.

So that everyone would feel relaxed for the bar mitzvah and no one would be coming in at the last minute, we thought it would be nice if we could all spend Shabbos together in Providence. Itch Karlinsky was more than happy to make his million-room house available to the entire Feldman clan, Beth's parents, and me.

The Shabbos was incredible, fantastic — and amazingly free of tension. Sam Feldman, who was still in the dark about the financial arrangements, was very proud of his grandsons and gushing with gratitude for Bruce's having agreed to make them a bar mitzvah.

Also, I sensed a subtle change in Bruce and Beth. It wasn't anything I could put my finger on, but it almost seemed as though they were just the tiniest bit excited about the whole thing, now that it was really happening. That didn't make much sense to me, but who could plumb the mind of a Harry Kushner? I chalked it up to the fact that the end was in sight, and they knew they would soon be able to get back to full-time palsy-walsy with their Patty PlayPals. Certainly, they were not getting into being Jewish, but maybe — just maybe — they were getting into being the *baalei simchah*.

An unexpected dividend of the Shabbos at Itch's was a kind of reconciliation between the brothers Feldman. Bruce, Eugene, and Stan found themselves together in the kitchen on Saturday night. One thing led to another, and before long they were doing a full-blown rehash of their childhood. I think they sat up until well past two in the morning; every ten minutes or so, the whole house rocked with their raucous laughter.

Sam and Esther Feldman were, of course, radiant, and my friend Itch, who was at his charming and charismatic best, took them and Beth's folks under his wing, treating all four like visiting royalty. Itch, by the way, had the meals catered and insisted that we were all his guests. He wouldn't hear of anyone but himself picking up the tab for the food.

Itch had a barbecue planned for Monday afternoon (with plenty of salads and fruit and nuts for Bruce and Beth), but Sunday everyone sort of did his own thing.

Early Monday morning, I took the boys to my old apartment for their final bar mitzvah lesson. I wanted to make sure they knew their readings and calm them down if they felt nervous. Stuart read the first *aliyah*, and then Keith read. Both knew their parts perfectly.

"Your grandparents are really going to *kvell* tomorrow."

"What's *kvell*?" Stuart asked.

"It means they're going to get a lot of *nachas*."

"What's *nachas*?"

"*Nachas* is something like a good warm feeling in your heart. It's the feeling you get when your kids or your grandchildren do something really special, like take their first step or something."

Take their first step, I thought; not a bad analogy. Was it a coincidence that I had given that as my example of *nachas*? Is there any such thing as coincidence? From Grandville to Providence, from Harry Kushner to Torah, Keith and Stuart had come far indeed. Their first step was a giant-step. How many more steps might they be willing to take?

I looked at the two shining faces. "How you guys feeling?"

"Okay."

"Okay."

"Not nervous?"

"A little."

"A little."

"Okay. If you're just a little nervous, that's natural. Don't worry, you'll both do fine.

I have to admit that looking at the two of them, I *kvell*ed a little too. All right, a *lot*. There was no trace of the *Kushner* and *Suraj* I had met on the lawn at the Ashram. These were different boys altogether, and they were *great*.

"Keith," I said, "you know, I looked over Stuart's speech last week. Would you like me to look over yours?"

"No thanks, Baruch. It'll be okay."

"Sure?"

"Yeah, I'm sure."

I was a little uneasy. Keith still had a lot of pent-up resentment in him towards his folks, and giving him a chance to say any old thing he wanted to in front of his entire family was not without its dangers. I wanted to give him a little talk about "Love thy neighbor as thyself," but then thought better of it. What's done is done, I figured. I'd had three months to try and give these boys a way of looking at things; if I hadn't managed in all that time, I wasn't going to manage now.

"Tell me guys, are you glad you went through with this?"

"Sure," Stuart said, but Keith looked at me hard and, for the first time since I'd known him, said something bordering on the profound.

"Look, Baruch, *glad*'s not the word for this. *Glad* doesn't come close. It's a lot deeper and a lot more complicated than *glad*."

"Keith," I said, "you might not believe this, but that's exactly what I was hoping you'd say.

"All right, you guys — we're outta here. Today you are... *fountain pens!*"

"What?"

"What?"

"Never mind. Let's go."

THE GRODNO SHUL was holding its own very nicely on Shabbos, but it still did not have a daily minyan for *Shacharis*. We had no problem pulling one together for the bar mitzvah, though. Itch said he didn't want us to drown in the place, so we invited all the members of the original Ad Hoc Committee (minus Jimmy) to come down and help us to fill up the big, empty structure. The plan was to have the bar mitzvah and light refreshments there and to go back to Itch's for the family-only barbecue afterward.

Mitzvah goreres mitzvah, I thought as I stepped into the old place, "One mitzvah tows another in its trail." It was still a beautiful shul, and who knows? — maybe it was our efforts to save it that had led to the Feldman boys' bar mitzvah.

I had coordinated things with Itch in advance. The bar mitzvah was called for nine o'clock in the morning, and Itch went ahead and davened at an earlier minyan so he could announce pages and explain what was going on during the actual service. I was the *baal tefillah*.

I had Stan read out certain sections in English, to help those who didn't feel at home with the prayers to keep oriented and feel involved. I also decided to ask Stan to read the final prayer, the *Aleinu*, in English, as a nice closing touch to the services. Later on, I wondered whether *that* was a coincidence.

Everything went smoothly from the beginning. By now, the boys felt completely at home in their *tefillin*, and I could see that Sam Feldman was bursting with pride. We davened slowly, and I felt particularly good when we got to *Shemoneh Esreh*. After months of practice, the boys really knew how to say it. As a result, they felt at ease with it, and out of the corner of my eye, I could see how their lips were moving and how they were beating their chests and doing their bows. I knew that everyone in the family must have marveled to see Keith and Stuart standing there and davening as though they'd been doing it all their lives.

Itch gave Sam the honor of opening the ark. I took the Torah from him and made a circuit through the old Grodno shul. I saw Bruce hesitate a moment, then lay his hand gently on the Torah. He seemed distracted.

Stuart was called up and proceeded to recite the blessings and read his portion flawlessly. Next came his maternal grandfather, and I could see the pride in Stuart's eyes as he showed Mr. Klein the place. The third *aliyah* was Keith's — another flawless reading.

Eugene had *hagbahah*, and as he lifted the *sefer Torah*, he shot me a look of real appreciation. I could tell that he'd been deeply moved by the boys' davening and reading.

On an impulse, I asked Stan to read the English translation of the last *Yehi Ratzon*. "All of the House of Israel are our brothers," he recited, "be they in distress or captivity, be they on land or at sea. May God have mercy on them and grant them relief..." But he couldn't go any further. It took him three tries to get out the words, "...bringing them from darkness to light." Once he got through that passage, he was okay, though. He concluded: "...from servitude to liberty, speedily and very soon; and let us say, Amen." I glanced over at Bruce — the only man in the shul not wearing *tefillin*. He was looking a little pale.

Sam drew the curtain open, and I passed the Torah to him. He replaced it in the *aron kodesh* and drew the curtain back. Then everyone sat down. I stood up at the reader's table and introduced the boys, reminding those present that the Talmud tells us that it is more meritorious to keep the commandments because one is obligated, than to do so when there is no obligation. "We live in a time when people are trying to escape obligations," I said, "but today, we are here to celebrate the bar mitzvah of two young men who, unlike so many other members of their generation, come seeking them." Then I called on Stuart.

Stuart stepped up to the reader's table. He reached into his inside jacket pocket, pulled out a piece of notebook paper, unfolded it, and read stiffly: "Mommy and Daddy, Grandpa Sam and Grandma Esther, Grandpa Jack and Grandma Evelyn, Uncle Gene and Uncle Stan, and Baruch and Rabbi Karlinsky. In this week's Torah portion we read about Bil'am. Bil'am was a very smart man and a prophet who could talk to God, but he tried to go against what God told him to do. No matter how hard he tried, though, he could not go against God's plan. We are all here today because that is what God wants. God gave us the commandments to tell us how He wants us to act, and all of us Jews are meant to obey the six hundred and thirteen commandments, because that's God's plan. Thank you all for coming here to my bar mitzvah today."

Stuart paused for a minute and then continued, not reading from his paper: "And I would especially like to thank Baruch, not only for doing what he did and making all this happen, but for being my... my friend."

Now *that* was what I call *nachas*!

Stuart started to refold his speech, when everyone began applauding. He dropped his head modestly and walked back to where his grandfather was and sat down on Sam Feldman's right side. I shot a glance over at Bruce and saw that he was staring at his younger son with a strange look in his eyes. Sam, meanwhile, ran his fingers over Stuart's head, put both arms around the boy's shoulders, and gave him a loud kiss on the cheek.

Next it was time to introduce Keith, and I was still feeling a little uneasy about what he might say.

I hadn't really noticed before what an imposing figure the older Feldman boy cut, and it wasn't just the yarmulka and the new suit. He stood about five-nine or -ten, with broad shoulders and good, even features. His eyes were big and penetrating, and he held himself straight and tall. He walked up to the reader's table and turned to face his listeners as though he owned the place, but to my surprise, he did not reach into his pocket to take out a speech. Instead he swept us with those big eyes of his. His gaze lingered for a moment on his father. Uh-oh, here it comes, I thought, but then he continued panning the front row until at last his eyes came to rest on Sam Feldman.

"Grandpa," he said, "when we were studying for our

bar mitzvah, Baruch taught us that God gave the commandments to Moses, who taught them to the entire Jewish people. After the adults learned the commandments, they taught them to their children, and when their children became adults, they taught them to *their* children in turn. In every generation, Torah has been passed from father to son in an unbroken chain — a chain that leads from Mount Sinai to the present generation.

"We've been through a lot, Grandpa, you up here in the North, and us down there in Florida. You were sad, Grandpa, and angry, because you thought the chain was going to be broken." Here his voice dropped, "But it's not, Grandpa, I promise. I promise!" his voice rose. "I promise you," he thundered, "the chain will not be broken!"

With more presence than I imagined anybody could command in such a situation, Keith walked back to where his grandfather was and sat down on Sam Feldman's left. Sam put his arm around his grandson's waist, and Keith sat there looking straight ahead at the *aron kodesh*.

THE ONLY sound in the place was Esther Feldman's sobbing. I'd planned to address the boys when they finished, the way I've seen rabbis do at other bar mitzvahs, but after what I'd just seen and heard, there was nothing left to say. I jumped to my feet just a little too fast and in a little-too-loud voice read off the first verse of *Ashrei*. Itch took the cue and immediately announced the page, and the service was back in progress. Sam Feldman sat flanked by his two grandsons.

Then we hit *Aleinu*. Everyone, myself included, was still a bit shell-shocked from Keith's speech. I forgot that I had asked Stan to read *Aleinu* in English at the conclusion of the service, but Stan remembered, and he began reading. When he got to the second paragraph, he suddenly slowed down and his voice took on a new tone and emphasis:

"We hope, therefore, *Lord our God*, soon to behold *Your* majestic glory, when the abominations shall be removed from the earth, and *false gods* exterminated..."

I looked over at Bruce and saw that he was turning pale again. I was hoping he wouldn't make a scene.

"...when the world shall be perfected under the reign of the *Almighty*," Stan continued, "and all mankind will call upon *Your* Name, and all the wicked of the earth will be turned to *You*. May all the inhabitants of the world realize and know that to *You* every knee must bend, every tongue must vow allegiance..."

This was getting awfully heavy, but old Stan just kept going.

"May they bend the knee and prostrate themselves before *You*, *Lord our God*, and give honor to *Your* glorious Name; may they all accept the yoke of *Your* kingdom, and have *You* reign over them speedily, forever and ever..."

Bruce's head was bowed now. His hand came up as I watched, and he pressed his thumb and index finger over his closed eyes while his brother Stanley continued on mercilessly to the end of the prayer.

"...For the kingdom is *Yours*, and to all eternity *You* will reign in glory, as is written in *Your* Torah: 'The

Lord shall be King, forever and ever.' And it is said: 'The *Lord* shall be King over all the earth; on that day the *Lord* shall be *One*, and *His Name One*."

Nobody moved or said anything. I realized that everyone was looking at Bruce, and I was afraid that the entire bar mitzvah, the entire effort to save two young Jewish souls and at the same time restore some semblance of *shalom bayis* to the Feldman family, was about to blow up in our faces.

As Number One Harry Kushner in Grandville, Florida, and Number Two or Three in North America, Bruce Feldman had been the personification of poise, self-possession, and smoothness; as father of the two bar mitzvah boys, Bruce looked more nonplussed, uncool, and discombobulated than I ever could have imagined him. His hands had a slight tremor, his face was the color of a freshly dug up cadaver, and perspiration shone on his forehead and upper lip. His eyes, though, were by no means glazed or apathetic. His eyes, which were riveted to Keith, were on fire! He really looked like a man possessed.

He turned around to face the crowd. He cleared his throat — all the while staring at Keith. He reached into his pocket and took out a piece of paper — all the while staring at Stuart. (Uh-oh, I thought. Was old Bruce gonna make a *speech*?! This definitely was not in the script!) He began to unfold the piece of paper, but crumpled it instead — all the while staring at his sons.

Then he spoke. "Three people got together to make this bar mitzvah: my brothers Eugene and Stanley, and a surprisingly wise young man who I once thought was nothing more than a slightly freaky freeloader. The young man's name is Baruch, which means blessed, and blessed indeed he is.

"Eugene, Stanley, Baruch, and I are the only ones who know why I agreed to go through with this bar mitzvah and talk Beth into it, and I am ashamed to admit to them that the reason they know about was the *only* reason I agreed. Sure, I wanted to make Mom and Dad happy, but never would I have dreamed of going this far.

"But something happened to me over these past few days. Oh, it's not as though the experience brought back any memories. By the time Eugene was bar mitzvahed and the family was beginning to become observant, I was already away at college and dabbling in drugs, counter-culture, and Harry Kushner.

"What *has* happened is that I've become confused. I... I'm... *really* confused. It's not the first time. Last time I was confused like this, I latched on to someone who said he could help me, and he showed me a way which brought me out of my confusion, a way which I believed had all the answers. I knew my family wouldn't understand, but I didn't care. It worked for me, and that's all that mattered. That was twenty years ago.

"And where's it gotten me? The way I found twenty years ago gave me some answers, but it also raised an awful lot of questions. That way was supposed to lead me to peace and harmony, but it has brought turbulence instead. It caused me to become estranged from my parents, and estranged from my children. By a stroke of good fortune I'm not estranged from my brothers, or at least *they* never abandoned *me*. They were there for me when I needed them."

He faltered then. For a minute, he didn't know what to say, but then he continued. "Eugene, Stanley, and Baruch got me tc agree to this in order to try and bring our family back together, but I think they accomplished much more than that. I know they gave me something money can't buy. They gave me confusion.

"Confusion can sometimes be a bad thing. This time, I think, it's a healthy confusion. For three months, we've had Shabbos in our house. At first its presence was entirely against our will, and we resented its invasion of our lives. Later on... I don't know. Maybe later on, keeping Shabbos *wasn't* against our will — at least not entirely. Now that the bar mitzvah is over, I find myself wondering whether we'll ever have Shabbos again. If we were to vote on it, I know how my boys would vote. But me, I don't know yet. I'm still confused.

"What *I* do, though, doesn't so much matter any more; my boys are already 'sons of the commandments,' and I want to tell them that never, *never*, have I been as proud of them as I am today. And I also want to say that Keith, whose wisdom goes beyond his years, is right. My boys are already 'sons of the commandments,' and that's why no matter what their father's mistakes may have been, the chain won't be broken.

"And you know, Dad," he said, turning to a silently weeping Sam Feldman, "that's the *most* important thing. The chain won't be broken."

Bruce took a few steps in his father's direction and extended his right hand. His father took it and pulled Bruce's whole body to his own and pressed Bruce's head into his own shoulder. I could see Bruce's bent form heave as he indulged himself in what I imagined was the best cry he'd had in many, many years.

In fact, there wasn't a dry eye in the old Grodno Shul when Eugene grabbed Stan and the two boys and pushed them over to Sam and Bruce. Somehow, all the Feldman males managed to work their way into one giant tear-filled bear hug, and the six of them stood there bawling like little children for I don't know how long.

Me? I cried too. I *always* cry at bar mitzvahs.

Heard from: "Baruch"

Glossary

The following glossary provides a partial explanation of some of the foreign words and phrases used in this book. The spellings, tenses, and definitions reflect the way the term is used in *Give Peace a Stance*. Often, there are alternate spellings and meanings. Foreign words and phrases translated in the text are not included in this section.

ABBA — father.
AH CHUTZPAH — (Yid.) "What audacity!"
AH SHANDEH — (Yid.) "For shame!"
AISHES CHAYIL — a valorous woman.
ALEINU — the prayer at the conclusion of the prayer
  services.
ALIYAH — lit., ascent; immigration to Israel.
ARON KODESH — the holy ark.
ATTAH NORMALI? — (sl.) "Are you crazy?"
AVEIRAH — a transgression.
AVODAH ZARAH — idol worship.
AVRAHAM AVINU — our father Abraham.

BAAL TEFILLAH — the member of the congregation
  who leads the worshippers in prayer.
BAAL TESHUVAH — a penitent; a Jew from an
  assimilated background who has returned to

observant Judaism.

BACHUR(IM) — unmarried yeshiva student(s).

BAT MITZVAH — a Jewish girl who reaches the age of twelve, whereupon she becomes halachically responsible for her actions and is obligated to fulfill the mitzvos as an adult; the celebration of this occasion.

BEDIKAS CHAMETZ — the search for leaven conducted on the night before Pesach.

BEIN HA-SHEMASHOS — twilight.

BEIS MIDRASH — a house of study; a synagogue.

BEIS DIN — a court of Jewish Law.

BEKKASHEH — (Yid.) a long frock coat worn by men, often reserved for festive occasions.

BEN — son.

BIKKUR CHOLIM — visiting the sick.

BIZAYON — disgrace.

BOYCHIK — (Yid.,sl.) kiddo.

BUBBIE — (Yid.) grandmother.

CHAD GADYA — (Aram.) lit., one goat; a traditional song at the completion of the Seder.

CHAS VE'SHALOM — "Heaven forbid!"

CHASAN — a bridegroom.

CHASSID(IM) — follower(s) of the teaching of the Baal Shem Tov.

CHASSUNAH — a wedding.

CHAZZAN — a cantor.

CHEDER — (Yid.) a religious elementary school for boys.

CHOLENT — (Yid.) a hot stew traditionally eaten for lunch on Shabbos.

CHUMASH — [one of] the Five Books of Moses.

CHUPPAH — a wedding canopy; a wedding ceremony.

CHUTZPAH — gall.

DAS HEILEGE LAND — (Ger.) the Holy Land.

DAVEN — (Yid.) pray.

DER GROISSE — (Yid.) the big one.

DERASHAH — a discourse.

DIN TORAH — lit., Torah law; a dispute judged by a rabbinical court in accordance with the HALACHAH.

DREI NAZISHE GOITES IN MEIN HOIZ — (Yid.) "three Nazi women in my house..."

ELUL — the month of the Hebrew calendar preceding Rosh Hashanah, corresponding to August/September.

ERETZ YISRAEL — the Land of Israel.

FRAULEIN — (Ger.) an unmarried woman.

FRIMME VEIBLACH MIT TICHLACH — (Yid.) "religious women with head coverings..."

FREILICH — (Yid.) happy.

FRUM — (Yid.) religious.

GABBAI — a secretary of a synagogue.

GADOL (GEDOLIM) — great Torah sage(s) and leader(s).

GAN EDEN — lit., the Garden of Eden; Paradise.

GEMARA — the commentary on the Mishnah which together comprise the Talmud; a volume of the Talmud.

GEZEIRAH — a Divine edict.

GLATT — (Yid.) extra-strict Kashruth.

GUTT IN HIMMEL — (Yid.) "God in Heaven!"

HAGBAHAH — the lifting up of the Torah after the completion of its reading.

HA-MOTZI — lit., He who brings forth; the blessing recited before eating bread.

HALACHAH — Jewish Law.

HASHEM — God.
HASHGACHAH — Kashruth supervision.
HATZOLOH — a volunteer corps of emergency
　　medical technicians.
HECHSHER — Rabbinic certification of Kashruth.
HINENI HE'ANI MI-MAAS — the cantor's prayer
　　which precedes the afternoon service on
　　Yom Kippur.
HEH — the fifth letter of the Hebrew alphabet.

KADDISH — the mourner's prayer.
KADESH — the first rite of the Seder.
KALLAH — a bride.
KAPPOTEH — (Yid.) a festive long coat;
　　see BEKKASHEH.
KEL MALEI — lit., God Who is full of [mercy];
　　prayer to commemorate the deceased which
　　begins with these words.
KIDDUSHIN — the tractate of the Talmud which
　　deals with betrothal, marriage, etc.
KIPPAH — a yarmulka.
KISHKEH — (Yid.) stuffed derma.
KNEIDLACH — (Yid.) dumplings.
KUGEL — (Yid.) a baked potato or noodle pudding.
KVELL — (Yid.) to beam with pride.

LANDSLEIT — (Yid.) one who hails from the same
　　village or country.
LASHON HARA — malicious gossip; slander.
LECHAIM — "To life!"; a toast.
LITVAK — (Yid.) a Lithuanian.

MAARIV — the evening prayer service.
MACHER — (Yid.) a wheeler-dealer.
MADREGAH — a level.
MATZAH — unleavened bread.

MATZAH BRAI — fried MATZAH with eggs.

MAZEL TOV — "Congratulations!"

MENTSH — (Yid.) a decent human being.

MESADDER KIDDUSHIN — the one who officiates at a wedding.

MESHUGAAS — (Yid.) craziness.

MESHUGENER — (Yid.) crazy.

MIDDOS — good character traits.

MINCHAH — the afternoon prayer service.

MINYAN(IM) — quorum(s) of ten adult males required for public prayer.

MISHPOCHEH — (Yid.) a relative.

MITZVAH — a commandment from the Torah.

MOHEL — a ritual circumcisor.

NACHAS — pleasure.

NARISHKEIT — (Yid.) foolishness.

NEIN — (Ger.) no.

NIGGUN — tune.

NIRTZAH — the concluding section of the Seder.

NU, NU — (Yid.) "Oh well."

OIB DU GAIST, KIM — (Yid.) "If you're going, come!"

ONEG SHABBOS — lit., delight of the Shabbos; an informal get-together on Friday night in honor of the Sabbath at which refreshments are served.

OY — (Yid.) "Alas!"

PESAK — a halachic decision.

PEYOS — side curls.

POSEK — a halachic decisor.

RAV — Rabbi.

REFUAH SHELEIMAH — "A complete recovery!"

REBBE(IM) — (Yid.) rabbi(s) and teacher(s); chassidic leader(s).

REBBETZIN — (Yid.) the wife of a rabbi.

ROSH HASHANAH — the Jewish New Year.

SCHWESTER — (Ger.) a sister; a nun.

SEFARIM — (pl.) sacred books.

SEDER — the order of the Pesach night ceremony recalling the Exodus from Egypt and the liberation from bondage; a learning session.

SEMICHAH — rabbinic ordination.

SEUDAH SHELISHIS — the third Sabbath meal.

SHABBAT SHALOM — lit., Sabbath of peace; a Shabbos greeting.

SHACHARIS — the morning prayer service.

SHADCHAN — a matchmaker.

SHADCHANTE — (Yid.) (fem.) a matchmaker.

SHALOM — peace.

SHALOM ALEICHEM — lit., "Peace be upon you"; a greeting.

SHALOM BAYIS — domestic tranquillity.

SHELEIMUS — completeness.

SHELIACH TZIBBUR — a representative of the congregation; the BAAL TEFILLAH.

SHIDDUCH — a marital match.

SHIUR(IM) — Torah lesson(s).

SHOICHET — (Yid.) a ritual slaughterer.

SHTIBEL — (Yid.) a small, cozy synagogue.

SHTENDER — (Yid.) lecturn.

SHTICKEL — (Yid.) slightly.

SHTREIMEL — (Yid.) a fur-trimmed chassidic festive hat.

SHUL — (Yid.) a synagogue.

SHVARTZ — (Yid.) black.

SIDDUR — a prayer book.

SIMCHAH — a joyous occasion.

TAKKEH — (Yid.) veritably.

TALMID CHACHAM — a Torah scholar.
TALMUD TORAH — an afternoon Hebrew school.
TEHILLIM — [the Book of] Psalms.
TISCH — (Yid.) lit., table; a chassidic meal presided
    over by a REBBE.
TREIFA — non-kosher.
TZIDKUS — righteousness.
TZITZIS — a four-cornered fringed garment worn by
    males.

VAV — the sixth letter of the Hebrew alphabet.
VERTL — (Yid.) a brief Torah insight.
VEY — (Yid.) "Alas!"
VEY IZ MIR — (Yid.) "Woe is me!"

YAH SADDAM! — (colloq.) "Down with Saddam!"
YERUSHALAYIM — Jerusalem.
YERUSHALMI — a Jerusalemite.
YIDDISHE KOP — (Yid.) a clever Jewish mind.
YINGELACH — (Yid.) little boys.
YISGADEL V'YISKADESH — lit., exalted and
    sanctified; the first words of the KADDISH.

Z"L — of blessed memory.
ZOCHAH — (fem.) privileged.
ZOLLEN OISGERISSEN VEHREN — (Yid.) "May
    they be ripped apart!"; a Yiddish curse.

The Sound of Soul

In a dozen different titles **Hanoch Teller** has delighted the nglo-Jewish reader with inspiring tales of ordinary people ho do extraordinary things. With a cast of fascinating characters and modern spiritual heroes and heroines, these true, contemporary stories touch the soul of readers everywhere and strike a responsive chord in their heart. Joy and drama, laughter and pathos combine to create a new genre of Jewish literature: "soul stories."

Each one of Teller's cherished tales of Jewish souls from all across the globe, skillfully written with powerful, image-evoking prose, conveys the timeless precepts of Judaism to young and old alike.

Now, in response to requests from countless educators, commuters, housewives, students, and program directors, these masterpieces have been reproduced on audio cassettes, fully dramatized with musical accompaniment and vivid sound effects.

The **Sound of Soul** volumes I & II provide over two hours of listening enjoyment for the entire family. The most heart-warming, enlightening, hilarious and poignant of Teller's tales have been transformed into an audio classic. Each cassette also contains new enchanting stories not featured in any of Hanoch Teller's books.

These high-quality tapes are not available in book stores. Please direct all orders and inquiries to:

Israel Media Group
c/o New York City Publishing Company
37 West 37th Street, Seventh Floor
New York, New York 10018.